ON

2nd Ed

LEADERSHIP

what's broken in our society and how we fix it

PETE BOWEN

Dedicated to My Ladies

Angie, Mallory, Katie and Bailey

ABOUT THE AUTHOR

Pete Bowen has been practicing and teaching leadership for more than 30 years. An expert on ethics, leadership and culture, Bowen has been a guest on national television and radio shows including the O'Reilly Factor, Discovery Channel and Fox News Channel.

Bowen served 14 years as the CEO/President of Servite High School, a leadership and college prep school in Anaheim, California. At Servite, Bowen introduced student leadership and formation programs that served as a model for developing the next generation of leaders.

Bowen taught leadership, military history and ethics at Duke University where he was a visiting assistant professor and the officer-in-charge for the Department of Naval Science. He also taught at the University of North Carolina (Chapel Hill) and North Carolina State University.

Since 1998, Bowen has served as an instructor teaching leadership in the Command College course for law enforcement executives for California's Commission on Peace Officer Standards & Training. He has received the Outstanding Instructor Award twice.

Bowen was an AV-8B Harrier pilot in the United States Marine Corps where he served 11 years on active duty and retired from the Marine Corps Reserves after 24 years of total service.

Bowen served as the initial ethics officer for the Los Angeles Unified School District where he was responsible for creating the first ethics program for a public education agency. He established leadership and ethics training, public accountability programs, and programs that increased the ethics, efficiency and effectiveness of the district.

Bowen received his M.A. from Duke University and his B.A. from the University of Notre Dame, concentrating his interdisciplinary studies at both schools on leadership, ethics, philosophy, intellectual history and culture.

ACKNOWLEDGEMENTS

On Leadership is the result of a life-long learning process that was influenced by many people.

In many ways, this book is based on the transformative work of Alasdair MacIntyre on ethics and rationality in his books *After Virtue* and *Three Rival Versions of Moral Enquiry*. Contemporary leadership studies is a mess because there is little clarity or unity in our society on understanding human nature, human goals/purpose, community or life. MacIntyre's work on different rationalities (tradition, encyclopedia and genealogy) provided the key to untangling these conflicting understandings and organizing them into consistent views of life—what I call the Wisdom, Modern and Postmodern Paradigms. Once identified, those paradigms promptly revealed their correlating (and, between them, conflicting) understandings of leadership.

Much love to my daughters Mallory, Katie and Bailey, my father Denny, mother Morganne, brother Matt, and all those in my family who patiently put up with so much while providing critical insights.

I am deeply indebted to Dr. Stanley Hauerwas at Duke University for introducing MacIntyre and supervising my graduate thesis. And to the Duke MALS program for all I learned there.

Big thanks to the faculty, staff, students, parents, alumni and Servite Secular community at Servite High School especially Jim Carter, Mike Brennan, Larry Toner, Chris Weir, Rob Hoertz, Steve Beaird, Mark McElrath, Sue Hamrock, and the Servite Order especially Fr. Ed Penonzek, Fr. John Fontana, and Fr. Jerry Horan.

The list of those who impacted this effort is too long to fully recount, but includes Sr. Johnellen Turner OP, Hugh Hewitt, Tom "Vito" Carnesi, Matt Cunningham, Darren Aitken, the ND '86 email group, Jim & Cinci Foley, Peter Ganahl, Dr. Dave Lutz, Bette & Wylie Aitken, Hal Kwalwasser, Don Davis, Bob Harrison, Mark Divine, John McEntee, Jeff Moore, Matt Gentry, Jim Joffe and Ron Hodges.

Thanks to the Program of Liberal Studies at Notre Dame where this journey began taking shape.

And finally, thanks to all those with whom I served in the Marine Corps and learned about life, death and camaraderie.

CONTENTS

INTRODUCTION

America. The history of our nation is one of success and prosperity. It is a history of innovation, creativity, entrepreneurship, struggle and achievement despite overwhelming odds. It is a history of people from many lands and cultures finding community not primarily in tribe or blood, but through shared commitment to the timeless concepts upon which our nation was founded. Our nation is not so much about where or in what class you were born as it is about what you understand about life.

Our history is a story of leadership. Great leaders like Washington, Jefferson, Lincoln, Roosevelt and Reagan established our nation and guided us through difficult times. Business leaders like JP Morgan, Rockefeller, Ford, Gates, Walton and many others helped establish America as the most prosperous nation in history. The list of writers, religious leaders, civil rights advocates, scientists, engineers, doctors, jurists and so many others who have helped lead the continued growth of our nation is very long and distinguished.

As we reflect on the *Greatest Generation*—those Americans who grew up in the Great Depression, led us to victory in World War II and built our nation into a superpower—we can see that our success wasn't the result of a few "leaders" at the top giving orders to those below. Our success came from the hundreds of millions of Americans who demonstrated good leadership every day in every aspect of their lives. It was Rosie the Riveter, the women of our nation, who joined the workforce to replace men fighting overseas. It was the mental and physical toughness born from the suffering of the Great Depression and fighting in World War II. It was a generation of parents doing their best to raise good children despite hardship. Our greatness was the result of leadership in all dimensions from family to schools to work. Most of all, our greatness was the result of good people leading good lives.

Today, we possess unprecedented scientific and technological power. At the same time, we face tremendous challenges that range from our economy and unemployment to the environment, nuclear proliferation and terrorism. Like other critical times in our nation's history, we need good leaders to help us navigate the difficult challenges we face, and ensure that we use our vast power wisely and responsibly.

Unfortunately, at this critical time, we have lost trust in our leaders. Polls show that the American people aren't happy with the way things are, that we've lost confidence in our leaders, and that we think our nation is headed in the wrong direction. Few believe that our morality is good and a large majority thinks that our morality is getting worse.

At a time when national unity is more important than ever, our society feels like it is being torn apart by competing special interests. The timeless ideals that bound us together as Americans are being attacked and undermined. Our American nation, bound for so long by a common understanding of life, is being divided into ever smaller fragments by a new way of looking at life that emphasizes selfishness. Despite our unprecedented success and prosperity, more and more people are wondering whether our nation has already peaked and started to decline. We seem to be out of answers to how we can get our nation back on track.

With business heavily regulated and jobs headed overseas, our economy has become stagnant. For the first time in a long time, our children don't seem to have the opportunities their parents had.

But our decline is not inevitable.

By far, the greatest assets of our nation are our people and our way of understanding life. Our grandparents and great grandparents had a fraction of our wealth or education, and still somehow managed to build the greatest nation in the history of the world. Our ability to get our nation back on the right track isn't limited by a lack of resources, education, infrastructure or legal-political structures. We have all these things and much more in abundance.

What we need is good leadership in all dimensions and at all levels. Family leadership. Educational leadership. Business leadership. Cultural leadership. Moral leadership. Leadership in science, technology and engineering. Personal leadership. Political and government leadership.

If we can form the next generation of good leaders in all these areas that we can trust to do the right things for the right reasons in the right ways, then our future is bright.

Good leaders will use our vast power wisely and successfully to navigate the challenges we face. Good leaders will leverage American ingenuity, creativity and industriousness to prevail in global competition, and take our nation and world to the next level. Good leadership will provide our children and grandchildren with a bright future.

Unfortunately, as critically important as leadership is for our future, we have a very poor understanding of it. Leadership studies, as a discipline, is full of competing ideas and theories, but hasn't made any significant progress. We don't have a commonly accepted understanding of what leadership is or how it works. We have lots of descriptions of leaders but no recipe to make good leaders. We can't even agree on what it means to be a "good leader".

We stand ignorant of the very thing—leadership—that we need most.

To solve these problems, we must dive deep into the nature of leadership. We must understand why leadership studies, despite the billions of dollars spent, hasn't progressed as a discipline or provided us answers. We will learn that our understanding of leadership is a direct product of our understanding of life.

That will lead us to examine the three fundamental ways of understanding life: the *Wisdom*, *Modern* and *Postmodern* life paradigms. We will find that the confusion and lack of progress in leadership studies today is a result of Wisdom *Covenant Leadership*, Modern *contractual leadership* and Postmodern leadership trying to operate in the same space at the same time.

To break out of that confusion, we need to select one of the life paradigms and its leadership model. We will move forward with Wisdom *Covenant Leadership* because 1) it is True; 2) it provides us leaders of knowledge, character and wisdom; and 3) gives us the most effective, most efficient, and the highest performance leaders and teams possible. With that knowledge, we can derive a step-by-step process that can reliably produce the next generation of leaders that we can trust with our future.

Through this process we will understand that each of us is called to important leadership: leading our own lives, leading our families and leading others in our work.

We will see why and how our American education system, though full of good and well-intentioned people, is taking our nation the wrong direction. Our only way to new leadership is to find a better way of developing our children into the next generation of leaders we so deeply need.

We will realize that the old divisions of conservative vs. liberal and Republican vs. Democrat are obsolete, and that while the culture war is a real and decisive conflict, it has been grossly misunderstood.

Our new understanding of leadership will increase trust throughout our society, reducing the bitter infighting that has divided our nation, and enable us to unite and work together in very powerful ways that no other nation can match.

Finally, we will integrate your personal life and work life in some deep ways that will increase your leadership and performance at work, while making your professional and personal lives more meaningful and fulfilling.

There is no doubt that we face daunting challenges and that we need good leadership to successfully navigate them.

If we fail, our nation will continue in the same direction and our children will suffer.

If we succeed, the opportunities for our nation and children expand exponentially. Developing good leaders is the most important thing we can do to safeguard the future of our children and make any other aspect of our world better.

And so we stand at a crossroad, our own leadership tested. Will we continue down our current path with poor leadership, putting the future of our nation and children at risk? Or do we have what it takes to develop the next generation of good leaders that we can all trust to guide our nation into a bright future?

Success isn't a question of financial or educational resources; we have greater wealth and knowledge than our grandparents or any previous American generation. Our success is really a question of whether we can demonstrate the same character, creativity, toughness, commitment, courage, ingenuity and unity that characterized *The Greatest Generation*—or not.

This is our call to greatness. Your call to greatness. How will we respond?

This book charts the course. We must provide the willpower, commitment, courage and leadership to make it happen.

When our descendants record our generation's chapter in the history of our nation, will they tell the story of a generation that understood leadership, prepared the next generation of good leaders, and took America to greater heights?

Or will they say that our generation let our nation fragment and slide into decline because we lacked the knowledge, commitment, courage and toughness that previous generations demonstrated every day when they made America great?

Leadership Challenges

Let's start by framing the challenges we face.

We possess enormous scientific and technological power. We have walked on the moon and sent spacecraft almost 11 billion miles to the edge of the solar system. We have mapped the human genome and delved deeply into subatomic quantum reality. Computer technology and the Internet connect us around the world real-time, and enable us to perform incredible calculations and store huge amounts of information. We save tens of millions of lives each year with advanced medicine and pharmaceuticals. Engineering knowledge enables us to build cities providing transportation, electricity, food and water for hundreds of millions of people in our nation.

We also have the power to destroy our civilization with nuclear weapons. We can cripple our environment with pollution and the reckless pursuit of natural resources. We can bio-engineer organisms that can kill hundreds of millions of people in a pandemic. Computers and the Internet make it possible to invade your privacy, track your location real-time, and make us vulnerable to software viruses, network attacks, misinformation and identity theft. The enormous power we possess to do so much good for our nation and world can just as easily be used to destroy our nation and world.

The national and international challenges we face are staggering. On the global level, there are tough questions about the world economy, global competition, world government, nuclear proliferation, terrorism, the environment, climate change and so much more. On the national level, we face hard questions about our economy, unemployment, health care, pension plans, immigration, the size and role of government, rights, crime and education.

Technology has made our world a much smaller and more interconnected place. Political and economic news in one part of the world has a real-time impact on nations and markets around the world. Computer driven stock trading can create out of control market crashes.

In 1905—just over a hundred years ago—it took the Russian fleet nine months to sail around the world to engage the Japanese fleet in the decisive battle of the Russo-Japanese war. Today, nations can destroy other nations around the world in minutes.

While the political world is dominated by nation-states, our economic world is dominated by multi-national companies with clients, leadership and workers competing across nations and continents.

International business leaders make decisions every day about jobs, profits, consumer safety, pension and health plans, and the prices we pay at the store and gas pump that affect billions of people.

Leadership decisions made today have a much greater impact on more people with much greater speed than any time in history. With the ability to help, harm or even kill hundreds of millions of people with just a few decisions, it is more important than ever that we use our vast power wisely, carefully and responsibly.

And that brings us to *leadership*.

We depend on our leaders—government, business, and professional—to help us wield our enormous power and navigate our tough challenges well.

With poor leadership, sooner or later we will experience disaster. Poor leadership that fails to gain the trust of different groups in our nation will not develop the broad support required to solve long-term economic, unemployment, budget, health care or immigration issues.

Poor leadership that fails to gain the trust of other nations can take us into wars that cost us trillions of dollars, hundreds of thousands of lives and put us on the brink of nuclear war.

Poor economic or business leadership will squander millions of American jobs, cause economic and environmental catastrophe, and threaten the safety and retirements of hundreds of millions of Americans.

Given the power we possess and the challenges we face, poor leadership will inevitably take us deep into economic, political and environmental disaster, and down a road of national decline.

We need good leaders that we can all trust to make good decisions for the right reasons.

With good leadership, we can come together as a nation, use our power wisely and overcome our challenges. With good leadership we can navigate tough problems like unemployment, health care, immigration, nuclear proliferation, terrorism and climate change. With good leadership, our nation can take advantage of American innovation, creativity and teamwork to prevail in global competition.

With good leadership that we can all trust, the futures of our nation and children are promising, bright and hopeful.

OUR LEADERS HAVE PERFORMED POORLY

Unfortunately, all too often our business, government and other leaders have failed to use power wisely.

We don't have to look too far into the past to gather examples of poor business leadership causing economic disaster. Time after time, high-powered business leaders focused on making money have led us into the collapse of multi-national companies, and the loss of trillions of dollars and tens of millions of jobs.

In the late 1990's, leaders of the Enron Corporation, in conjunction with top accounting firm Arthur Andersen, used irregular accounting practices to hide enormous business losses while making Enron appear profitable. Enron executives used inside knowledge of their problems to sell their stock while telling others that the company was doing well. In 2000, the year before Enron declared bankruptcy, the company claimed revenues of over $100 billion, $65.5 billion in assets and 20,000 employees (Enron 2000). When Enron collapsed, tens of thousands of employees lost their jobs and billions of dollars in their retirement portfolios because they trusted the Enron leadership (Kedia 2006). The deceptive accounting practices of Arthur Andersen's Houston office working with Enron led to the collapse of the entire Andersen firm worldwide. The Enron debacle resulted in criminal indictments and decertification of the Andersen firm as a certified public accountant (Alexander, et al. 2002).

A symphony of bad leadership decisions led to the subprime mortgage crisis of 2007-2008. Government leaders and politicians relaxed lending regulations and encouraged Fannie Mae and Freddie Mac to purchase high-risk subprime loans from lenders. Leaders at Fannie Mae and Freddie Mac were applauded for the loans they enabled while serious risks were largely ignored (Holmes 1999). Mortgage brokers sold mortgages to unqualified applicants because the brokers could make big money on commissions without having to take responsibility for the bad loans they were making. Families took on mortgages that they couldn't pay hoping that housing prices would continue to rise so they could refinance their mortgage later. Banks created and sold risky mortgage and financial products that maximized their profits while hiding the increasing risk and dangers.

When it all collapsed in the subprime mortgage crisis and world-wide recession, bad leadership cost us $8.3 trillion (Altman 2009), 18% of our net worth (Bajaj 2009), and almost 8 million jobs (Isidore 2010). An entire generation of Americans saw their retirement plans evaporate, and their futures dramatically changed for the worse.

Enron and the subprime mortgage crisis are just two examples from a long list of large companies, employees and stockholders suffering from poor leadership.

In addition to these scandals, the constant and bitter fighting between the major political parties has caused Americans to lose confidence that our political leaders can govern our nation wisely.

Political rhetoric between the parties has become increasingly heated and nasty, making it appear that our leaders are much more interested in advancing their own political careers than in what is best for our nation. Important legislation becomes stalled as legislators take uncompromising and increasingly polarized positions. With little common ground for discussion, political leaders often resort to vilifying opponents, lowering trust in each other and trust with the public even more.

We have a real and deep leadership crisis in America. We depend on our leaders to wield vast power and we have lost trust in their leadership. As we go into the future facing even bigger challenges and wielding ever increasing power, how can we trust these leaders to guide us safely and well? What can we do to ensure that we have the good leaders we need for our future?

Before we can tackle those questions, we need to dig deeper into why we're in crisis. Why have we lost trust in our leadership?

WHY HAVE WE LOST TRUST IN OUR LEADERS?

The most obvious reason we've lost trust in our leaders is that their poor decision-making led us into a recession that cost us trillions of dollars and millions of jobs. Another is the apparent inability of our political leaders to work together across parties. There are few things that can cause as deep a loss of trust in leadership as monumental failure, or strident and bitter conflict.

But we need to go deeper than that. What is at the root of the poor decision-making? Why are people taking such strident, uncompromising positions? What is at the core of the underlying feeling that our morality is getting worse and our nation is headed in the wrong direction?

The short version is this: A *community* is defined by the things that the community members share, the things that they have in *common*, that bring them *unity*. When the things that define and unite the community break down, the community breaks down.

When the timeless concepts and basic morality that binds us together as Americans breaks down, our community—our nation—breaks down as well.

If we can identify the underlying breakdowns, we can address those problems and build trust. We can better ensure that our next generation of leaders will lead us into success instead of failure.

I think there are four main issues at play in the loss of trust in our leaders:

1. We don't trust that leaders will make decisions that are moral and ethical
2. We have lost the shared morality that unified our communities and our nation
3. The timeless concepts that have unified our nation and our understanding of life are being undermined, eroded and lost
4. Our leaders have failed to maintain unity in our communities and nation

We have lost trust in our leaders because we question whether they have the character to make moral decisions, placing what is right and good above their own ambition.

Looking deeper, we find that the morality we used to share as a community and nation has broken down. We have lost trust in our leaders because we cannot be sure that they share the same understanding of morality that we do.

And when we look even deeper, we find that the breakdown of morality in our society is really a symptom of a more fundamental problem. The timeless concepts that have been the foundation for our nation, our unity, and our understanding of life and morality, are being undermined, eroded and lost.

Finally, we are losing trust in our leaders because they have failed to maintain the foundation that has, to this point in our history, unified our communities and nation.

Leadership, trust and moral decisions

When it comes to leadership, trust and decision-making, there are two very important parts to any decision: *knowledge-skill* and *character*.

When we follow the guidance of any leader—whether it is our doctor in health matters, our politicians in governmental matters or our mechanic in auto matters—we place our trust in that person's knowledge and professional skills.

We make an act of faith in our doctor that he has the knowledge and professional skill to correctly diagnose and treat our illness.

We make an act of faith in our mechanic that he has the knowledge and professional skill to correctly diagnose and fix the problem with our car.

We make an act of faith in our accountant—we trust—that he has the knowledge and professional skill to lead us through the complexities of the tax code.

If we don't have faith in their professional skills and knowledge, we won't let them treat us, fix our car or handle our finances.

When we look at our top business and national leaders, it is apparent that they aren't lacking in knowledge, skills or education. Many of them have been educated at America's top schools and received the finest training. They are often the best of the best, the brightest of the brightest.

The book and movie about the collapse of Enron are titled *The Smartest Guys in the Room*. It takes well-educated and sophisticated people to develop the complex financial schemes that made Enron appear very profitable, and that set up the sub-prime mortgage crisis and the Great Recession.

Lack of knowledge, education, or professional skills is not the major reason we've lost trust in our leaders.

Character is the other, equally important part of trust in leadership. When we follow the guidance of a leader, we place our trust in that leader's character. We trust that our leader will put what is right and good for us and our community ahead of any personal, selfish ambitions or motives. We trust that our leader will have the character to stand up for what is right and good—even when he's in a tough situation and doing what is right might cost him everything but his integrity.

Our loss of trust in leadership comes from our loss of trust in the character and morality of our leaders. We no longer trust that our leaders are choosing what is right and good over their own ambition, or desire for money, power or prestige.

We lose trust when our political leaders choose their careers and powerful special interest groups over working together to make critical, tough decisions that benefit our nation.

We lose trust when business leaders choose to maximize short-term corporate profits and their own wallets over the good of their consumers, communities and employees.

We lose trust when a repair man charges us for extra parts or repairs that aren't needed.

We've lost trust in our leaders because we don't have confidence that they know or will do the right thing.

And we shouldn't be surprised.

We used to learn morality from our families, churches, schools and community. What our parents taught us at home about morality was continuously reinforced by others in our community.

Today, we see morality as something taught by parents with little or no reinforcement from the community. Even our churches take few moral stands because they fear alienating church members. The few morality or ethics programs in public schools are often embarrassingly weak and poorly executed. And when we think about the public schools, whose morality or ethics are they supposed to teach anyway?

Our leaders have tremendous, high-quality professional knowledge and skills—and we trust that knowledge and those skills—because we spend time as a community making sure that they are well educated and trained.

It's the opposite with morality. We have lost trust in the morality of our leaders because their character is poorly formed. That is because we—as a community—have spent little time and done a terrible job preparing them.

It gets worse.

As a community, we're not even sure what is moral anymore.

I have been leading seminars with executives on high performance leadership and ethics for almost 20 years. When people tell me that it is not a fact that the Holocaust or slavery was wrong, it becomes clear that that an increasing number of people in our nation no longer share the same fundamental understanding of morality.

What happened to the idea that there are moral facts like "The Holocaust was wrong"? How did we get to the point that many believe that whether the Holocaust was wrong or not is nothing more than personal opinion?

We have lost our shared morality

In our nation, we used to share a common sense of morality. Different religious or ethnic communities might have different ways to express that morality, but everyone generally agreed that there was true *right* and *wrong,* that you should treat people with respect, and that life was about becoming a *good person* who demonstrated characteristics like honesty, justice, courage and love.

Everyone understood that there were moral facts. People knew that it was a *fact*, not just an opinion, that lying, cheating, stealing and murder are wrong because these behaviors went against our religion and because these behaviors went against our nature as human beings. People knew it was a fact that slavery and the Holocaust were wrong. This understanding that there are moral facts is known as *objective morality*[1].

For example, in earlier times, everyone in society agreed that it was a fact that *cheating is wrong.* In addition, we all shared the same reasoning about *why it is a fact* that *cheating is wrong.* Because we had a shared understanding of what *cheating* is and *why cheating is wrong*, we could have rational, public, community discussions about it. Those public discussions continuously reaffirmed our shared understanding of cheating and why it is a fact cheating is wrong.

And because those discussions were continuous, they enabled us to hand down those shared understandings from generation to generation, maintaining general consistency.

---

[1] By *objective morality* we mean that there are universal moral facts. For instance, objective morality would say that it is a fact, and not just a matter of opinion, that integrity, honesty, justice and courage are right, and that cheating, murder, dishonesty and cruelty are wrong. For this book, we'll contrast objective morality (there are moral facts) with *moral subjectivism—* the idea that there are no moral facts, just personal moral opinions. Moral subjectivism would say that *cheating is wrong* is not a fact, and is nothing more than a statement of personal opinion.

We need to be careful and note that it wasn't the community agreement that made it a fact that cheating is wrong. Rather, it was an independent fact that cheating is wrong, and the community simply agreed on that fact and the basic rationale behind it.

This was a public morality understood and shared by everyone. We could all have confidence that we were raising a generation of kids, of future leaders, with similar understandings of basic morality and ethics. We could even feel comfortable correcting each other's children who cheated, because we all shared the same basic understanding of morality when it came to what was right and wrong, and why.

We could trust our leaders because we all knew that community members and leaders all shared the same basic understanding of morality.

Over time, for reasons we shall discuss more deeply in later chapters, we stopped talking publicly as a community about *why cheating is wrong*. When we stopped talking publicly about *why cheating is wrong*, we quit reaffirming the community accepted reasons *why cheating is wrong*.

Over time, due to lack of public discussion, we replaced the objective, community-shared reasons *why cheating is wrong* with our own personal reasons (opinions) why *cheating is wrong*.

When we stop talking as a community about *why cheating is wrong*, we even begin to replace our public, shared understanding of *what cheating is* with our own personal opinion of *what cheating is*.

The idea that there are community-shared moral facts was slowly undermined and replaced by the idea that morality is nothing more than a matter of personal opinion, or *values* (subjective morality).

In other words, you have your personal opinions about what cheating is and why it is wrong, and I have my personal opinions and reasons, and it is impossible to establish, as a fact, that one opinion or value is true and the other false.

That doesn't just apply to the reasoning about *why* cheating is wrong, but to whether cheating itself is wrong or not.

For example, you may value honesty over high test scores. Other people may value high test scores over honesty. In this new world of *values* where there are only opinions and no moral facts, honesty and cheating are morally equivalent. Cheating is no better or worse than honesty. They are just different opinions—different values. Among our next generation of leaders—Americans born between 1990-1995—47% agree that "morals are relative; there are not definite rights and wrongs for everybody." (Smith, et al. 2011)

Without continuous public discussion and affirmation, the same words begin to mean different things to different people. For instance, when older generations—let's say those born before 1965—use the term "wrong", as in "cheating is wrong", they usually mean that it is a fact that cheating is wrong.

When younger generations use the term "wrong", they generally mean nothing more than *it is their opinion* that cheating is wrong. It might not be wrong for everyone. Who are they to judge? To younger generations, the terms "right" and "wrong" often mean little more than "I like this" and "I don't like that."

We use the word *wrong* thinking that everyone else uses it the same way. In reality, older and younger generations may have very different, almost opposite, meanings for *wrong*.

When different people use the same terms but mean very different things, it lowers trust. Different meanings for the same word gives the appearance that the other side is lying to you.

When we switch from *moral reasoning publicly shared, discussed and accepted by all* to *a moral reasoning based on personal opinions,* we lose the ability to discuss or practice morality as a community. Morality goes from something that can be discussed and applied as a community, to something that is a matter for your private life. Morality goes from the public to the personal.

The common moral ground that formed the foundation of our community cracks and breaks. We become *morally fragmented.* We go from a society that was unified by and found strength in a shared understanding of objective morality, to an increasingly divided society with people holding millions of their own fragmented, subjective opinions about what is right and wrong.

The impact of this dramatic change in how people understand morality has been documented. Two-thirds (66%) of young people could not answer basic moral questions or even identify what a moral problem might be. Most have simply "not given much or any thought to many kinds of questions about morality…" They share no common moral framework (Smith, et al. 2011) (Brooks 2011).

The younger generation—those born around 1990—have little or no moral foundation or understanding.

The implications of this loss of a shared morality reach wide and deep.

Take public education, for example. It is impossible for our public education system to teach our children without also teaching them a moral view. Our public education system teaches morality directly when we tell children that it is wrong to lie, cheat, steal, bully or sexually assault someone. Our public education system teaches a moral view indirectly when it teaches kids how to think about, interpret and value history, literature, science and health.

If we have a public, shared understanding of morality, then there is no problem with the public education system teaching that shared morality in our schools.

But when we have moral fragmentation—a bunch of competing, irreconcilable personal moralities operating in our communities and nation—whose morality or value system is the government-run school system supposed to teach?

In a world of values, there is nothing objectively wrong with people who value high test scores and power (i.e. bullying) over honesty and compassion.

In a world of values, if public schools decide to enforce honesty and compassion over cheating and bullying, it isn't because those values are right or True, but because the public schools have arbitrarily selected those values and possess the raw power to force them on students and families.

When we had a shared, public morality, we shared, as a community, the same basic reasons for understanding why it is a fact that certain behaviors are right or wrong. The shared morality bound us together as a community and nation. We could have high trust in each other and our leaders because we all knew that we were saying and meaning the same things.

In contrast, when we stopped publicly discussing and reaffirming our shared morality, we traded our community-shared understanding of morality for personal values, or opinions why we like certain behaviors and dislike other behaviors. This moral fragmentation—this breakdown and loss of a public, shared morality—is devastating to trust in our leaders and each other because we can never be confident that people using the same words actually mean the same thing or share the same moral reasoning.

Erosion of the timeless concepts at the foundation of our nation

This moral fragmentation is a symptom of a deeper and broader fragmentation that is occurring within our society.

Our nation was founded upon and has been unified by a shared understanding of life that includes, at its very core, the existence of timeless and changeless concepts. These timeless concepts are ideas like:

- All people are created equal
- All people possess inalienable rights
- Human dignity
- Freedom to pursue Happiness
- Government of the people, by the people and for the people
- Meritocracy
- Natural law

These timeless concepts capture fundamental aspects of what it means to be human no matter what your race or ethnic background, no matter what religion you practice or time you live in. From the beginning of our nation, people have understood that there is an objective Truth and objective morality.

America has held a special place in history because it is the first nation founded explicitly upon these timeless ideals.

Throughout our history, people have rightfully challenged whether we are living up to our ideals or not.

There is little doubt that our nation has sometimes fallen far short of these ideals. Our nation imported, enslaved and oppressed African-Americans. Our nation repeatedly violated treaties with native Americans, depriving them of land and property. Our nation interned Japanese-Americans during World War II, depriving them of their freedom for ethnic reasons. There are many other instances when we did not live up to the timeless and changeless ideals upon which our nation was founded.

Historically, people have pointed out that our nation has fallen short of our timeless ideals to challenge us to reform, regroup and reengage those timeless ideals that have defined our nation.

Indeed, the fundamental acceptance of these timeless values is the very thing that has enabled our society to understand that institutions like slavery are fundamentally wrong and eliminate them.

But today, something very different is happening. Instead of challenging us to live up to our ideals, our founding ideals themselves are being challenged and questioned at the most fundamental levels. The challenges come from a completely different way of understanding life—a postmodern understanding—that rejects timeless, changeless ideals or the principles that flow from them. Over time, this new way of understanding life has chipped away at the timeless concepts, and eroded the understanding and principles upon which our nation was founded.

The danger of this cannot be overstated.

We'll go into much more depth about the dynamics and history of this conflict between these two different understandings of life in later chapters, but let's go through a summary here that captures the basics.

These two ways of understanding life—one that acknowledges timeless and changeless ideals and one that denies their existence—

are so different that they share little or no common ground for rational discussion. We will find later that they cannot co-exist or tolerate each other.

Imagine a person whose entire reality is understood in terms of football trying to have a conversation about *playing the game* with someone whose entire reality is understood in terms of golf.

Both football and golf are games. Both use balls. Both keep score. But that's where the similarities end.

Golf uses clubs and a small, white ball, and the object is to get the *lowest* score. Football uses an oblong ball, helmets and pads, and the object is to get the *highest* score. Golf plays on 18 fields of different shapes. Football is played on only one field of a constant shape. In golf, you can only advance the ball using the clubs. In football, you advance the ball by running or passing it.

The conversation between the two people from very different sports would make no sense to either because: 1) the fundamental goals of the two sports contradict each other; 2) the way you play each game is completely different; and 3) while they sometimes use the same terms—like *ball*—they mean very different things by those terms.

These two people from two very different sports have no common ground for rational discussion about *playing the game*.

You can either *play the game* in terms of golf or *play the game* in terms of football, but you can't *play the game* in terms of both at the same time. To the extent that you're playing the game in terms of football, trying to score the most points, you can't be playing the game in terms of golf, which is trying to score the fewest points. You can't try to score the most and the fewest points simultaneously, and be rationally coherent.

In much the same way, the common understanding of life, our nation, and morality that used to unite and bind us into a national community is being challenged by a contradictory understanding of life. They have no common ground for understanding life or our nation. The result is a breakdown or fragmentation of our society into different groups holding fundamentally different understandings of life, nation and morality.

When these opposing groups and understandings run into each other—especially in politics, society, morality or education—it is like combining matter and anti-matter. They become deeply and bitterly polarized against each other.

Imagine the football guy arguing passionately that playing the game is all about scoring the most points running, passing and kicking the ball, with the golf guy arguing just as hard that playing the game is all about scoring the fewest points using different clubs. With no common ground or understanding for rational discussion, the different sides are left making bitter personal attacks against each other.

Does this sound familiar?

The moral fragmentation we discussed earlier is a prime example of the conflict between the two different ways of understanding life.

Objective morality with moral facts flows from one understanding of life. Subjective morality with no moral facts, just values, flows from the opposing understanding of life.

One argues that we can know objective Truth. The other argues that there are only personal truths.

These opposing understandings of life have very little if anything in common. Nothing in common upon which we can build trust. No common ground for unity.

In fact, when a group of people no longer shares anything in common, they are no longer a community.

This fragmentation of our society into groups with nothing in common causes a devastating loss of trust in our leaders and each other at the most fundamental levels. It literally destroys community. We shall find that it is, quite literally, the greatest threat our communities and nation face.

Our leaders have failed to maintain unity

We know from experience and history that the more unified a team, community or nation is, the more that group will thrive and achieve success. Teams, communities and nations that are not unified—that are divided or fragmented—don't last long. Success depends on unity.

As Americans, we hunger for unity. The success and future of our communities and nation depend on unity. But unity can only be achieved when our people and communities trust each other because they share the same vision—the same understanding of life.

America has been the most successful nation in the history of the world. We have achieved this success by using a shared understanding of life to bring together and unite people from hundreds of different ethnicities and religious traditions.

So many times in world history, having different ethnicities or religions in a nation results in a nation divided and at conflict internally.

In America, united by a shared understanding of life, our diversity has been the wellspring of opportunity, creativity and freedom resulting in a nation thriving and full of success.

The biggest reason we have lost trust in our leaders is that our social, educational, political, spiritual, moral, business and family leaders have failed to teach and reinforce the common understanding of life and timeless ideals upon which our nation was founded. They have allowed our shared vision, our shared understanding of life, and the trust that flows from it to be undermined by a fundamentally divisive and incompatible understanding of life. This opposing view of life infiltrates, fragments, fractures and divides our communities and nation. We have lost trust in our leaders because they—the very people who are supposed to keep us unified in trust and vision—have allowed our communities and nation to become a house divided.

Our leaders' failure to maintain our unity and the resulting fragmentation of our nation sabotages our success. A house divided cannot perform well. The fragmentation has an enormous negative impact on our performance in our businesses, our communities and our nation. It degrades our ability to compete globally and threatens our future as an American nation. We cannot thrive, and in the long run may not even survive, as a house divided.

When we watch our leaders make decisions that put their own desires, power, career and/or wealth above the good of the community and nation, we lose trust in their character, morality and leadership.

When we lose the ability to teach and discuss morality in public because the shared understanding of an objective morality is replaced by the idea that morality is nothing more than a matter of personal opinion or values, we lose trust in our leaders and each other.

When we lose the shared understanding of life and the fundamental concepts that unite us as a nation are sabotaged, we shouldn't be surprised that our nation loses its shared vision and trust. We shouldn't be surprised that our nation fragments into competing and increasingly polarized groups fighting for power and their own agenda. And we can't help but feel that our nation is headed in the wrong direction.

When our leaders in all areas—society, education, politics, religion, morality, business and family—fail to keep us united in understanding and vision, we lose trust in their leadership.

And we come to the realization that not only do we need leaders we can trust to make good decisions, wield the enormous power that we possess wisely, and successfully navigate the tough challenges of our future. We need leaders who can also keep us united as nation with a shared understanding of life.

WE FIND OURSELVES AT A CRITICAL CROSSROAD

We have experienced time and again the awful cost of leaders making bad decisions. We have lost trust and confidence in key social institutions including our government, our schools, big business, media and our courts. We are losing the very things that define us as a nation and enable us to teach our children, through shared moral reasoning, that there are such things as *right* and *wrong*. As we become increasingly divided socially, politically and morally, we have lost confidence that our nation is headed the right direction.

We've lost trust in our leadership not because we've lost trust in their knowledge or skills, but because we've lost trust that they can exercise the tremendous power we possess with good character.

> Every significant issue in our society today requires good leadership to reach a good solution.
>
> Of all the things we can do to make our lives better, developing good leaders must be a the top of the list, for all other things we can do to make our world better depend first on good leadership.

When we combine enormous power and poor leadership, the risk of bad decisions and catastrophe skyrockets. Poor leadership is dangerous. It puts all of us, our future and our children at great risk.

We need good leaders that we can trust to make good decisions—for the right reasons and in the right ways—in complex 21st century situations. We need good leaders who can get the most out of our economy, and maximize our work and standard of living for the right reasons and in the right ways. We need good leaders who can ensure that our nation is well-defended and our children are safe. We need good leaders who can minimize man-made disasters by ensuring responsible interaction with our environment. We need good leaders in business who make good decisions that benefit companies, employees and society all together.

We need to be confident that our leaders are taking our nation in the right direction. We need leaders who can bring us together in a shared vision and understanding of life, and rebuild trust in our key social institutions like government, business, education and media.

Given the enormous power we possess and the challenges we face, leadership is the central, critical issue of our time. Every significant issue in our society today, from war to the environment, from law and rights to health care and education, requires good leadership for success.

Of all the things we can do to make our lives, our futures, and our nation and world better, developing good leaders must be at the top of the list, *for all other things that we can do to make our world better depend first on good leadership.*

Every significant challenge we face today can only be solved if we start with good leadership. We need good leadership and a shared understanding of life to get our priorities right. We need good leadership to analyze our challenges and find the right solutions for the right reasons. We need good leadership to implement those solutions. We need good leadership to unite our nation as we make tough decisions and take action. Without good leadership, we can't even get started.

But good leadership also provides us much more. Good leaders put together high-performance teams—whether it's in government, business, the military or non-profits—that routinely beat the competition and achieve great things.

Good leadership means that you can become a better leader too, increasing your professional success.

Good leadership produces better products and services with greater efficiency improving results while lowering costs—and that benefits all of us in every dimension of our lives.

Good leadership means keeping our nation at the forefront of global competition in the right ways.

We must make sure today that we are raising the next generation of leaders with the knowledge—and most important—the *character* and *wisdom* to lead our nation and world well. If we can systematically and deliberately form the next generation of leaders with wisdom, then we can put trust back in our leadership, and come together as a nation to address the challenges that confront us. The more we can systematically develop the next generation of leaders, the more confidence we can have that our nation is headed in the right direction, and that the future of our children is bright.

So what are we doing to systematically develop the next generation of good leaders we can trust? Almost nothing.

We have systematic and effective step-by-step processes to develop highly-skilled doctors, lawyers and accountants. We have systematic and effective programs to develop highly-skilled academics, auto mechanics and airplane pilots. With some precision, we can assess their level of expertise and performance against widely accepted standards in their professions. We can provide specific training programs that will predictably improve their professional performance.

In a wide variety of areas like medicine, law, finance and engineering, we can show real progress in professional performance over time just as we can show real progress in auto design, performance and safety over the last 100 years.

We can't say the same about leadership.

Corporations, governments and the military spend billions of dollars each year on leadership training, seminars and materials. So why haven't we developed a widely accepted, effective, step-by-step process to create great leaders? Why don't we have widely accepted standards for assessing leadership expertise and performance? Despite the vast resources spent, why can't we show real progress in leadership studies like we can show in automotive performance, design and safety? Why can't we systematically, reliably and effectively produce good leaders?

And that leads to the big question:

What must we do to systematically develop the next generation of leaders we can trust to use our power wisely, address the challenges we face, and rebuild unity, trust and confidence in our nation?

To answer that question, we must explore the nature of leadership. We must understand why leadership studies, despite the billions of dollars spent, hasn't really progressed as a discipline or provided us answers. We must come to an understanding of leadership that not only provides us leaders of knowledge, character and wisdom, but also gives us the most effective, most efficient and highest performance leaders and teams possible. Understanding these things, we can develop a step-by-step process that can reliably and effectively produce the next generation of leaders we need for our future.

Through this process we will see why and how our American education system, though full of good and well-intentioned people, is taking our nation in the wrong direction. Our only way to new leadership is to find a better way of developing our kids into the next generation of leaders.

We will see that the old divisions of conservative vs. liberal and Republican vs. Democrat are obsolete, and that while the culture war is a real and decisive conflict, it has been grossly misunderstood.

We will tie together work, purpose and performance in life in meaningful ways that will increase your professional performance at work, and make your work and personal family life much more fulfilling.

If we have the courage and fortitude to make the commitment to form the next generation of leaders, our nation and people will go through a deep and powerful rejuvenation.

Developing the next generation of good leaders is the most important thing we can do to safeguard the future of our children, and make any other aspect of our world better.

Right now, we have no plan. Instead of systematically developing good leaders, we're hoping that good leaders just randomly show up. Heck, we can't even agree what "good leadership" is or how to recognize a good leader if he or she does show up. We are rolling the dice with our future.

It is time to change course and make whatever commitment is necessary to systematically develop the good leaders we need for our future.

Leadership and Life

LEADERSHIP PERMEATES EVERYDAY LIFE

If we broadly and simply define leadership to be *one providing guidance to another*, we can see that leadership is deeply woven into every aspect of our lives. It impacts us from birth to death, 24 hours a day and seven days a week.

Just about every human interaction that involves *guidance or direction* involves leadership at one level and intensity or another.

Every day we are led by people in some areas of our life and, at the same time, lead others through areas of their life. At work, we follow the lead of those in positions senior to us and provide leadership to those in junior positions. At home, we follow the lead of our parents through the first 20 years of our lives, and then provide direction for our children and grandchildren for the last half of our lives.

> Leadership is one providing guidance to another

Church leaders provide guidance through difficult questions about life, death and faith. Doctors, attorneys and accountants lead us through the complicated mazes of health, law and taxes. Financial advisers help us with our investments and retirement.

We depend on the good leadership of teachers and administrators to make sure our children are well-educated. We depend on good leadership in the contractors who remodel our homes and the mechanics who keep our cars running well. We depend on the teammate at Trader Joe's to track great food choices for us; the Nordstrom's shopper to make us look good; and the kid from Geek Squad to lead us through computer installations.

Athletic coaches lead our children in the development of their ball skills, teamwork and character. As parents, we lead our children through the formative years of their lives so they can have the best foundation possible for success and happiness in life.

With some reflection, we can see that leadership is among the most basic of human relationships and a fundamental aspect of our lives as humans.

Leadership has been around since the beginning of humanity, occurring the first time that humans organized to accomplish some goal or the first time one human taught another. Leadership is pervasive to the human experience, transcending nations, cultures and history. Our lives—professional and personal—are full of relationships where we *trust the guidance* of others and others *trust the guidance that we provide.*

Without the ability to depend on these billions of leadership relationships going well each day, our society would quickly decline or collapse. People in nations around the world suffer every day because they can't depend on these leadership relationships due to problems like corruption, poor education and poverty. Poor government leadership causes loss of trust and confidence, leading to crippling economic inefficiencies and poor economic, social and cultural performance.

Sometimes the importance of good leadership is most clear and tangible when it fails.

Have you ever had a building contractor fail to complete the work in your house as you planned? Have you ever found out, after the fact, that the auto mechanic took advantage of you and charged you to fix things that weren't broken?

What happens to trust when you get ripped off?

Finally—and this is very important—we must understand that leadership is something that applies to every one of us. As American citizens, we lead our nation when we vote. As consumers, we lead our nation through the purchasing decisions we make. As family members, we help lead our children, siblings and even our parents at different times in our lives.

Whether business leader, janitor, ball player, teacher, parent or usher, we are all called to lead others on a regular basis.

Leadership is not something that is interesting to read about but doesn't really apply to our own lives.

Leadership is not the specialized activity of some other group of people called *leaders*.

No matter who we are or what we do, we are all leaders and followers, and leadership is woven seamlessly through every aspect of our lives. Of your life.

LEADERSHIP AND TRUST

Leadership and trust are fundamentally connected; in many ways two sides of the same coin. We cannot understand leadership and how to form the next generation of good leaders unless we first understand the connection between leadership and trust.

By its very nature, leadership involves relationship between the one providing guidance (the leader) and those receiving guidance (the followers). That relationship necessarily involves some level of trust between the leader and the followers that can range from *complete trust* to *no trust* at all.

The more trust that exists between leader and follower, the more willing and quickly the follower will act on guidance from the leader.

When trust is high, we can dramatically increase performance, effectiveness and efficiency. This is true in just about any team.

When followers trust their leader, they are more highly motivated, more creative, make deeper commitments to their leader and goals, and are more willing to take the initiative and take appropriate risks. A leader who trusts his team is much more willing to let followers make decisions on their own. That increases performance, effectiveness and efficiency, and frees up the leader's time to pursue more strategic issues.

The more deeply team members trust their leader and each other, the more effectively and efficiently the team will perform.

When trust in leadership is low, we lose performance, efficiency and effectiveness. The teammates are less motivated and less committed to goals and their leader. They are less likely to demonstrate initiative or creativity, and less likely to take risks. Less trusting of their leader, they are much more likely to second-guess leadership and hedge against leadership guidance that might prove wrong.

Imagine that I am your auto mechanic or your doctor and give you a diagnosis of what is wrong with your car or your body. If you trust my guidance, you can take immediate action to get the problem fixed quickly, effectively and at a minimum cost. If you do not trust my guidance, you are much more likely to seek a second opinion, spending money and time anxious about whether to follow my guidance or not. The lower trust costs extra money and time, lowering effectiveness and efficiency. Trust has a direct impact on performance and effectiveness.

We rarely think about how important trust is in our everyday lives.

Every time you use a light switch, you make an act of faith in the people who designed and installed the switch that you won't get electrocuted. Our trust is so deep that we don't even think about the risk.

Trust is a two-way street. The leader earns the trust of followers as they see him perform well in stressful and important situations. The followers earn the trust of the leader as the leader sees them perform well in stressful and important situations.

It is while observing people perform under pressure that we see their skills, character and commitment—what they are really made of—and develop trust. Seeing people perform under pressure answers the question "Can I trust and depend on this person when we have to perform together in a challenging situation?"

Compared with many other nations, America functions well because we still have an underlying, implicit sense of trust in our society.

We trust our legal system and courts. We trust our cultural and social systems. We trust that most other Americans are good people inclined to honesty and doing the right thing. We trust that the drivers heading the other way on the road really will stay on their side of the line while we pass, inches away, with 120 miles per hour of closure.

We have implicit trust in those who lead us in most aspects of our lives from the national level to our personal, daily relationships with others. While the polls show that there has been a big erosion in that trust, the foundation of implicit trust is still there.

Trust is the foundation of good leadership—especially the high-performance leadership we need for our future.

WISDOM, TRUST AND CHARACTER

Leadership, trust and team performance are all deeply connected. If we are going to create the next generation of good leaders, and maximize leadership and team performance, we need to dig even deeper to understand trust.

When we talk about trust, we are quick to recognize the importance of trust in the knowledge and skills of the leader, but we often tend to underestimate the importance of trust in the *character* of the leader as well.

For example, when you turn to your doctor for guidance in your health issues, you need to trust your doctor's medical knowledge and skills. Your doctor needs to be able to accurately diagnose any health problems and prescribe the appropriate treatments.

At the same time, you need to trust your doctor's *character*. You want to be sure that he is ordering tests and scheduling surgery with your best health in mind rather than his financial interests. You want to know that even if he is having a tough year, he's got the character to do the right thing for the right reasons. What he does and whether you can trust him depends on his character.

The problem at Enron wasn't that we lost trust in the knowledge or skills of the employees; Enron made a point of hiring the smartest and most highly skilled people possible. The problem was that we couldn't trust what Enron and those very intelligent, highly skilled people were doing with those skills. It was a character and wisdom problem.

This deep connection between trust and character is true of every leadership relationship. When your accountant is handling your taxes or your lawyer is handling your legal issues, you need to trust both their professional expertise and their capacity to know and do the right thing. You want to hire the general contractor with good character who won't take advantage of the fact that you're not a construction expert to overcharge you. You want an athletic coach for your kids who will emphasize integrity, sportsmanship and character development rather than a "win at all cost" mentality. The more your children admire your character, the more they will trust, listen and follow you.

Trust in both skills and character is very important. Compromise trust in one or the other and the leadership relationship and performance break down.

Now let's take it one more step to *wisdom*.

Wisdom is what you get when you combine good knowledge and skills with good character. Wisdom is *right knowledge* plus *right action*. Wisdom is understanding Truth and having the character to do the right thing with that knowledge.

By *knowledge*, we mean understanding of what is *true*. *Knowledge* includes understanding things like information, systems and practices, and the intellectual skills needed to accomplish goals. A teacher is knowledgeable about the subject she teaches and methods of instruction. A lawyer is knowledgeable about the law. A doctor is knowledgeable about the human body. A salesman is knowledgeable about making and closing deals. *Knowledge* has to do with the *intellect*.

Character refers to the person you are and the qualities—especially moral qualities—that you possess and demonstrate.

If you are a person of *good character,* then you consistently demonstrate virtues like honesty, justice, courage and integrity because those virtues are a fundamental part of who you are as a person.

Another way to think of it is that your character includes the very *characteristics* that make you who you are. A person of good character is a person who consistently demonstrates virtues, *right action*, in all aspects of her life. While knowledge is about the intellect, *right action* has to do with your *will*.

Wisdom is the key to good leadership. High performance leadership depends on trust, and trust depends on good knowledge/skills and good character—or wisdom. So when we talk about the deepest trust, and highest performance leadership and teams, we're really talking about *wise* leadership.

> **WISDOM**--*Knowledge of what is true or right coupled with just judgment as to action* (Random House 2010)
>
> ### KNOWLEDGE + CHARACTER = WISDOM

As we look to the future of our communities, nation and children, our success really depends on our ability to form the next generation of wise leaders. And since leadership permeates every aspect of our lives, relationships and society; since we are all leaders one way or another; that means that wisdom must be the focus of our own lives and the development of our children.

The State of Contemporary Leadership

If developing the next generation of leaders is so important for us, and the future of our families and nation, then we need to get it right. While leadership is pervasive in our lives and critical to our future, we know very little about it. We have a deep almost desperate need for good leaders in our society, but we don't know how to produce them.

Health care is very important for our society, so we've developed a very sophisticated system to develop highly effective doctors and nurses.

The legal system is very important for our society, so we've developed a very sophisticated system to develop highly effective lawyers.

If you want to become physically fit, you can hire a trainer. The trainer will design a specific, step-by-step exercise plan. On certain days you will do a certain number of sets of leg and core body exercises with a certain number of repetitions for each set. You will rest for a certain amount of time between sets of exercises. On other days you will do aerobic exercises—running or biking perhaps—for certain amounts of time and with certain levels of difficulty. The trainer will also give you a diet plan that will include the right kinds of foods in the right quantities at the right times to maximize your health benefits. The trainer will tell you to make sure that you get enough sleep. The trainer will push you hard to achieve goals and caution you against over-exercising.

We know enough about getting in good physical shape that the trainer can give you an extremely detailed, step-by-step plan that covers all these things in minute detail. And it works. If you follow the plan, you will predictably and reliably get into great physical shape.

If we can systematically develop the next generation of leaders like a trainer systematically gets people in good physical shape, then our future is bright. A systematic approach to leadership development means that we can plan, assess, adjust and quality control the development of our future leaders with assurance. We can be more confident that the leadership of future generations—our children—is headed in the right direction and less likely to go off track. That confidence and predictability in leadership will enable us to plan much further down the road, giving our organizations, community and society a much more powerful way to take advantage of future opportunities and avoid future problems.

If we can systematically develop good leaders, we can take advantage of the creativity, ingenuity and teamwork of our fellow Americans, and flourish in a globally competitive world.

If we can systematically and deliberately develop good leadership, then a leadership trainer can help you become a more successful professional by improving your leadership just like a physical trainer can help you get in better physical shape.

If we really don't understand leadership, then our development of future leaders will be haphazard rather than systematic. Our future will be uncertain and at risk.

The good leaders that we do have in our society often rise by chance rather than by deliberate cultivation. We get lucky. Even then, especially in politics, many of those described as good leaders by some are often considered genuinely poor leaders by others. Our assessment of whether a national leader is good or bad is often based much more on how that leader's political or cultural views match ours than on any actual skill in leadership.

If leadership is so important, you would think that we would have a good understanding of leadership and how to systematically develop good leaders. But we don't.

What we have is a wide variety of competing leadership theories, lots of descriptions of leadership, and leadership stories and anecdotes, but we don't have a common understanding of leadership that enables leadership studies to move forward and demonstrate real progress.

When good leaders surface, we don't have much way of knowing whether it was the result of a leadership program or because they were natural leaders from the start. Despite all the leadership institutes and centers that have been established, books written and the billions of dollars invested, our understanding of leadership is more unsettled than ever, and leadership studies are chaotic, confused and stuck in a rut. Evidence includes:

There's no movement forward in leadership studies

We can look at the study of chemistry and clearly see movement forward. We can show in a systematic manner how we progressed from a lesser knowledge of chemistry in the 1930's to a much deeper understanding—and practical application—of chemistry today. We can do the same with the study of astronomy, medicine and even psychiatry. In the automotive and aircraft industries, it is easy to show tremendous real progress in the design, safety, efficiency and technology of automobiles and aircraft over the last 50 years.

Despite all the institutes and centers and billions of dollars spent on the study of leadership, despite all the books on leadership you can find at the bookstore, we haven't moved forward in our understanding of leadership.

In his book *Leadership for the 21st Century*, Joseph Rost conducts a comprehensive review of literature on leadership published in the 20th century. He identifies all sorts of leadership theories that come and go through the different decades (Rost 1993). But none of that leadership work builds on earlier leadership work in a progressive manner which shows actual growth or real forward movement, in leadership studies.

Even when we have successful leadership institutions like the military academies in the United States, military leadership is often understood to be fundamentally different than business or non-profit leadership. Many military leaders can make a successful transition to leadership in other areas, but often their success is understood to be despite their military leadership training and not because of it.

Enormous amounts of money spent. Over 100 years and billions of hours dedicated. No real movement forward. We have a lot of leadership alchemy, but no leadership chemistry.

Lots of ideas that sound good in the seminar, but don't work in the real world

How many times have you listened to a motivational speaker or been to a leadership seminar where they share exciting techniques to help you become a better leader only to find that the ideas fall flat once you return to work? Why is that? Why do things that seem self-evidently true not work when they encounter the real world of your work place?

We can't identify *good* leadership

In the many leadership training sessions and seminars I have taught, there are often great arguments over what constitutes *good* leadership.

Some argue that *good leadership* is the same as *effective leadership.*

Others argue hard that good leadership must include moral goodness in the manner of leading or the goal of the leadership, or both.

If we can't agree on something as simple as *what is good leadership,* how will we move forward with leadership studies? Our inability to identify good leadership is a symptom of our poor understanding and conflicting views of leadership.

There are lots of descriptions of leadership but no good recipes

If I ask you to describe a great chocolate chip cookie, you might tell me that it includes wonderfully rich chocolate chips, it's soft and chewy, and has great taste and texture.

That description can help me identify whether a chocolate chip cookie will taste good or not, but it doesn't tell me how to *make* that great chocolate chip cookie. The description is not a recipe.

When I have a good recipe, I can adjust the ingredients and quantities, the way they are combined and the way they are baked to adjust different qualities of the cookie. The recipe allows me to bake outstanding chocolate chip cookies in a systematic, deliberate, step-by-step manner every time. No guessing or rolling the dice on the result. Whether it is cookies or leadership, the description is nice but, the recipe is 1000 times more important.

Go to the bookstore or go online and take a good look at the literature on leadership. You will notice that it is overwhelmingly *descriptive*. The books tend to describe:

- The life of a leader who has successfully navigated some difficult challenge like a war or 9/11
- The leadership of a successful organization (Describe what happened that worked)
- A list of characteristics or qualities of highly successful leaders
- A list of principles by which you can lead more effectively

A *description* of good leadership is not a *recipe* for making good leaders.

We have lots of descriptions of and stories about leadership, but we don't have the step-by-step recipe for developing leaders. Those descriptions are enlightening and inspiring, but they don't really get us what we need: the development of good leaders.

We don't understand or appreciate the fundamental importance of leadership

We talk about leadership in a wide variety of settings from national leadership to business leadership to a quarterback leading the offense down the field in a football game, but we almost never see the interrelated bigger picture.

We do not appreciate how deeply woven leadership is into our everyday life or how it permeates nearly every aspect of our human experience. We have allowed leadership to become fragmented by its different applications rather than understand it as part of a unified whole of human experience, an intimate part of our relationships with other humans whether those relationships are personal, professional, cultural or political.

We miss how deeply important leadership is to our future because we miss how deeply woven leadership is in every aspect of our lives.

Our education system is focused on the wrong thing

Our future depends on good leadership. More than anything else, our nation needs and our schools should be focused on developing good leaders in every aspect of our society. For everyone in our society is called to be a leader at some level or another, even if it is just voting or the capacity to lead his own life.

Good leadership requires *wisdom* which only flows from the combination of *right knowledge* and *right action*, or *character*. Our school system should be working with parents and the community to develop good leadership in all young people by developing their wisdom through the cultivation of good knowledge (academics) and good character formation.

Unfortunately, we are spending hundreds of billions of dollars on an education system that over-emphasizes half of the wisdom equation: intellectual knowledge, academics, grades and test scores.

But that is very dangerous. Enron and other debacles have shown us that the most dangerous result from a school system is not a high school dropout with a gun, but the highly educated, very smart graduate who lacks a well-formed character and conscience.

The graduate of a top university who is motivated by money and leading a Wall Street firm can do tens of billions of dollars of damage and ruin thousands of lives in ways that a high school dropout could never touch.

Many of the best leaders I know in business and the military were not top academic stars. Some of the smartest academics I know are very sharp, nice and accomplished, but aren't much as leaders. Good leadership is a function of knowledge and character, not good academic grades alone.

The most dangerous result from a school system is not a high school dropout with a gun, but the highly educated graduate who lacks a well-formed character and conscience.

Even when our schools do attempt to address character and ethics, it is almost always done as an academic, intellectual exercise in the classroom rather than as real character development on the athletic field or court, or performing arts stage.

It is through team-based activities—like athletics, performing arts and robotics competitions—that we learn to perform under pressure as part of a team. These team-based activities reveal our character, and test it and form it. When we participate in these team-based activities, we have a real responsibility to others to develop our own wisdom and trust.

But these team-based activities also tend to be the first to be eliminated when education funds are tight because these activities are "outside the classroom."

We want and need good leadership, but we spend hundreds of billions of dollars to develop *knowledge* alone—the most dangerous part of the wisdom equation. Then we wonder why we have smart and powerful leaders making bad decisions that cost us trillions of dollars, millions of jobs, and the loss of trust in our societal institutions.

We spend very little time or money on character development and wisdom, and then wonder why our leaders make bad decisions and we lose trust.

If we really understood the importance of leadership, our school system would be transformed to focus on forming wise and good leaders, rather than just academic achievers.

Defining Success

It's easy to say that we need to get past the chaos and confusion, and develop a good understanding of leadership, but what will that understanding look like? How will we know that we have achieved success? How will we know that we have the best understanding of leadership and not just another fad leadership theory?

We need a full, comprehensive and deep understanding of what leadership is, how it works, and the role it plays in our larger understanding of the world and life. A good understanding will account for how other theories of leadership fit within its understanding of leadership and life. A good understanding of leadership will enable us to:

- Have a common understanding of what leadership is and when it occurs
- Identify and understand the fundamental components of leadership
- Understand how leadership is developed and cultivated over time
- Create a step-by-step program that develops good leaders
- Show demonstrable progress, real movement forward, in leadership studies
- Identify *good*, *bad* and *effective* leadership
- Understand the relationship between leadership, character and life
- Build high-trust, high performance leadership relationships and teams

A full understanding of leadership will be a gift from our generation to our children and grandchildren. It is a gift that can, more than any other gift we can give, provide them the best hope for their future.

But a good general understanding of leadership must do more as well. It is possible to invent all sorts of leadership theories. We need to find the right and best leadership understanding out of the many possible theories.

Effectiveness

A good way to identify the best leadership understanding is by its *effectiveness*. Which understanding will provide us with the highest performance leadership? Which understanding will provide us with a systematic program that predictably and reliably develops great leaders?

We want an understanding that:

- Enables us to identify leadership gifts and potential in young people
- Provides us with a recipe for developing great leaders in a step-by-step manner
- Quantifies aspects of leadership so that leadership progress can be measured
- Enables us to adjust the leadership development program so we can maximize the development of each leader

We want an understanding that enables us to develop groups of people into high-performance teams with reliability. We want an understanding that will teach us the keys to maximize team performance and get maximum performance from each team member. We want an understanding that integrates continuous improvement in a natural, seamless manner. We want an understanding that shows us how to create a culture and tradition of excellence that sustains our team's high level of performance over extended periods of time—especially after we leave the team.

We want to know how to teach our subordinates, step-by-step, how to be great leaders themselves. The better leaders they become, the more they can contribute to the team and the more successful all of us will be.

Comprehensive, handling all types of leadership

The best understanding of leadership should also be *comprehensive*. It should be able to handle all leadership situations and types. No matter what the leadership context—business, military, public service, non-profit, church, community, youth sports, family, etc.—the best understanding should explain leadership in a common way and equally well across all contexts.

Accounts for other leadership theories

The best leadership understanding should have breadth, providing a 'big picture' understanding that accounts for other leadership theories. It should readily explain how other or less comprehensive leadership theories fit within its larger and better theoretical framework.

Integrates with your understanding of life

The best leadership understanding should be fully consistent with and seamlessly integrated into your big picture understanding of life. If not, you will be doing one thing with regards to leadership and something different and inconsistent in the rest of your life.

Seamlessly integrates ethics and morality

Some leadership theories focus on completing a task quickly, effectively and efficiently without discussion of any moral or ethical dimensions. Other leadership theories do the same, but add a caveat that the *means* of accomplishing the task and/or the *purpose* of the task must be good. In these theories, morality is a kind of awkward add-on to leadership.

In the best leadership understanding, ethics and morality aren't bolted on to the theory like after-factory accessories, but are a seamless, integral part of understanding leadership itself.

In the best leadership theory, good morality-ethics naturally enhances effectiveness and performance.

Highest performance people and teams

It's relatively easy to understand what we mean by *breadth* and *accounting for other leadership concepts*, but what do we mean by *effectiveness* and *highest performance* leadership?

We mean that we want the leadership understanding that helps us develop the most powerful people and teams possible.

If we're a business, athletics or the military, we want leadership that provides high performance teams that beat the competition or opponent. If we are a non-profit or in public service, we want the leadership understanding that gives us high performance teams that provide the best services with the greatest impact and efficiency, and at the lowest cost. In our schools, churches and families, it means leadership and high-performance teams that form good citizens, leaders, parents and children.

One way we can help identify the best leadership theory is by understanding how a theory handles extreme leadership challenges. The best leadership understanding will enable us to develop the people and teams we need to make the best decisions for our future, beat the competition, and/or survive in the most demanding situations we can devise. If the understanding can show us the way to success even in the extremes, then it will likely handle all other cases as well.

We're facing those extremely challenging leadership situations today in all sorts of areas.

Whether you're working in business, military, public service or non-profit, our markets and environments are fast-paced, constantly changing, high-stress, diverse, multicultural and ambiguous. These markets and environments are global and operate continuously: 24 hours a day, seven days a week, 365 days a year.

Your company may import goods from an overseas manufacturer in China and distribute goods around the world via the Internet. Commodities are bought and sold real-time across the globe. You no longer just compete against local or regional companies, but with companies on other continents. With tough global competition, product and service improvement must be continuous. As you purchase materials or sell products in different nations, you must be aware of local culture, law, customs and marketing attitudes. If you can't keep up, you will be out of business.

It doesn't get any easier in public service, non-profits or the military. Even remote American communities find themselves handling multicultural issues they never encountered before. Police must deal with international gangs and crimes that cross borders. Technology crimes require new policing skills, technologies and techniques. Non-profits frequently cross borders and cultures to help those in need. New technology means that non-profits can broaden their fundraising base, but also means they are in competition with many more non-profits for that larger donor base.

> To prevail, you need the highest performance teams possible: people and teams that you can trust to make good decisions in fast-paced, complex, and ambiguous situations with minimal supervision

Those serving in the military must be ready to serve anywhere in the world on very short notice. They must constantly prepare for all types of conflict from nuclear war to conventional combat to counter-terrorism operations. They must be ready to fight in every environment from the tropics to the arctic, and in every kind of terrain from the mountains to the plains. They must be ready to defend our nation against weapons systems that can reach around the world at any time with very little notice. They must anticipate threats from space, chemical and biological weapons, and the cyber world.

We live in a different world than previous generations. It's faster, and more sophisticated and complex. There is less room for error, and errors can carry much more risk and cause much more damage.

Sometimes there is so much information that it's difficult to sift through it all and make a decision. Sometimes events move so fast that you must make decisions before you have enough information.. Everyone has a cell phone camera and someone may well be recording what you are doing.

To prevail in these markets and environments, you need the highest performance teams possible. You need to have people and teams that you can trust to make good decisions in fast-paced, complex and ambiguous situations with minimal supervision.

You need *teams of people* because no one person has all the skills or the time necessary to be successful alone.

You need people and teams making *good* decisions. By *good* we mean that the decisions must be both effective and moral[2]. If a decision is not understood to be good and moral, the decision will lower trust and negatively impact performance.

When decisions are made at the lowest possible level, by people on the scene and intimate with the details of the situation, the decisions can be both responsive and customized for the situation.

The decisions are responsive because the decision-cycle is short. Your people can decide on the scene and implement it immediately rather than wait for information to travel up the chain of command, have a decision made, then have that decision travel back down the chain of command for implementation.

The decisions are custom-made because your people on the scene are in the best position to understand the nuances of the situation and craft an appropriate solution. When things must go up the chain of command for decisions, the situation can rapidly change before the decision returns, making whatever decision that returns less effective for an evolving situation.

Good, custom solutions provided quickly add at least two more very powerful performance advantages.

When your team is making decisions more quickly than other teams—when your decision-cycle is shorter than (or inside) your opponent's decision-cycle—then you can make more decisions in the same amount of time than your opponent. It's like a game of chess where you get to make two moves for every one move that your opponent makes. It's an enormous advantage.

---

[2] One could argue that dropping a requirement that decisions be *moral* provides higher performance potential because it allows the decision-maker to choose from a greater range of possible actions that includes actions that are moral and actions that are not. There are several problems with this argument, but the biggest problem is that immoral actions reduce team performance because they reduce trust.

The second advantage comes when you actually *trust* your people to make the decisions on their own. When your people can be trusted to make decisions on their own, it relieves you of that decision-making and enables you to spend more time focused on larger, more strategic issues.

> ### The more trust you have, the higher the performance.
>
> ### The less trust, the lower the performance

That brings us to the fundamental high-performance issue: *trust*.

The real key to having the most powerful people and teams possible is being able to trust your people to make good decisions on their own in these complex situations. If you actually trust them to make those decisions, all the advantages of responsiveness, custom-made solutions, shorter decision-cycles and extra time to be strategic come with it.

If you don't actually trust your people, then you won't push decision-making down to the lowest possible level and you won't let them make decisions on their own. Your decision cycle will be longer and your attention will be on the immediate situation rather than on strategic issues. You will lose performance on several levels. Your competitors who have high-trust teams will have a big advantage over you.

The more trust you have, the higher the performance. The less trust, the lower the performance.

Trust is the key.

To create the next generation of good leaders, we must get past the confusion of contemporary leadership studies and develop a good understanding of leadership. That understanding of leadership will provide us with the program we need to systematically and reliably form good leaders for our future. That understanding of leadership will also help America compete in the global economy, help you become a better and more successful leader, and help us integrate leadership, character, our families and our personal lives.

There are many possible understandings of leadership, so how can we identify the best understanding from among the alternates? The best understanding of leadership will:

- Be *most effective* by providing us with the
    - o Highest performance people and teams and the
    - o Best program for developing great leaders for our future
- Be *comprehensive* by handling leadership in all types of organizations and situations
- *Account for other leadership theories* by showing how they fit within the best understanding's larger theoretical framework and understanding of life
- Seamlessly integrate ethics and morality
- Integrate with your understanding of life

The Nature of Leadership

We've already discussed how leadership pervades our lives. Now we want to go deeper into the very substance of leadership. When we break it down, what is at the core, what is the essence, what is the fundamental nature, of leadership?

When you talk about the nature of leadership you must talk about:

- Leader and follower
- Goals
- Human nature
- The nature of human relationships/community

LEADER AND FOLLOWER

Leadership necessarily involves at least two, a leader and a follower, because leadership means *one providing guidance* to one or more others who receive that guidance.

Leadership is not simply going someplace or traveling to a destination with another. Leadership is not just companionship. Leadership means *guiding* that other to the destination or goal. A leader shows or tells the follower how to arrive at the destination or goal.

In most cases the leader and follower are two different people, but it is possible for the leader and follower to be the same person. Philosophers, for instance, may talk about an individual person's *intellect* leading that same person's *will*. Most of us have experienced occasions where our *intellect* knows that we should exercise, eat correctly and rest, and tries to lead our *will* to do that.

GOALS

Leadership necessarily means guidance towards something—a goal. The goal can be just about anything: intellectual knowledge, a geographic location, the accomplishment of a task, spiritual enlightenment, etc. There can be multiple goals and even multiple levels of goals. For example, someone might lead you to Orange County, California, (first level goal) where you want to see Anaheim Stadium and visit Disneyland (second level goals).

The goals of the leader and the goals of the follower do not have to be the same. This is especially true where there are multiple levels of goals. People often come together on a team for different reasons and with different levels of goals.

Goals are often tied up with the motivation of the leader to lead and the follower to follow, and the question: Why should a person follow the leader? What is the motivation?

HUMAN NATURE

If we discuss leadership as a human activity, then human nature must be a necessary part of that discussion. What is human nature? What motivates us? Why would we follow?

Is human nature fundamentally the same for all people across cultures and throughout history? Or can human nature itself be changed?

> Change your understanding of human nature and you change your understanding of leadership

Are there such things as fulfillment of human nature, meaning in life or Happiness? In what and how do we find meaning or fulfillment of our human nature? Do we all naturally seek meaning, fulfillment, Happiness?

NATURE OF HUMAN RELATIONSHIPS/COMMUNITY

By its very nature, leadership involves a relationship between leader and follower. What is the fundamental nature of human relationships? Are human beings fundamentally social beings? Are we fundamentally individual beings who only come together in specific conditions? Are relationships nothing more than the way people exert power over each other? What is love? Is love a transcendent relationship between people or is it nothing more than a product of a chemical reaction in the brain?

We can only understand leadership when we understand the nature of human relationships.

Our understanding of human nature is by far the most important factor in our understanding of leadership because the other factors of leadership—goals, motivations and relationships—all flow from our understanding of human nature. Human nature provides the starting point for understanding what these other factors are, and how they come together and interact in that activity we call leadership.

Change your understanding of human nature and you change your understanding of goals, motivations and relationships. Change your understanding of human nature and you change your understanding of leadership.

The Quagmire

Our understanding of leadership depends on how we understand each of these four factors of leadership and how they fit together in our understanding of life. Change your understanding of human nature or the nature of human relationships, and your entire understanding of leadership, how to become a leader and how to lead will change with it.

It goes deeper. Your understanding of life itself depends on your understanding of human nature, goals and the nature of human relationships. Different people with different understandings of these core aspects understand and experience life and reality differently.

Your understanding of these factors determines your understanding of leadership and your understanding, or paradigm, of life.

Let's start by being clear about what we mean by *paradigm*. A *paradigm* is:

A set of assumptions, concepts, values, and practices that constitutes a way of viewing reality for the community that shares them... (Houghton Mifflin 2000)

A *life paradigm* is the whole way that you understand life, what life is and how all the parts of life fit together.

The basics of this are not new. In *The Structure of Scientific Revolutions*, Thomas Kuhn developed the idea of different and often irreconcilable paradigms developing throughout the history of science. Many of the great revolutions and developments in science involved a radical change from an earlier paradigm, or understanding of science, to a very new paradigm.

Influenced by Kuhn, Alasdair MacIntyre, widely considered one of the most influential philosophers of our time, used a similar approach to explain how philosophy—and especially ethics—has entered a crisis or quagmire very similar to the one we face in leadership.

From 1981 through 1990, Alasdair MacIntyre published three books, *After Virtue*, *Whose Justice, Which Rationality?*, and *Three Rival*

Versions of Moral Enquiry. Analyzing changes in ethics and philosophy through history, MacIntyre showed several things:

- Your understanding of ethics depends on what he called your "rationality", or understanding of life
- Through history, very different and often irreconcilable understandings of philosophy and ethics developed
- We find ourselves in an ethical crisis/quagmire today (much like our leadership quagmire) because of these multiple, irreconcilable understandings of life (paradigms) competing in our society today

Basically, MacIntyre showed that by taking a historical view of philosophy and ethics, we can find the reasons for the crisis in ethics and philosophy that we face today. And by understanding the cause of the crisis, we can develop a solution.

In *Three Rival Versions of Moral Enquiry*, MacIntyre calls these three competing rationalities Tradition, Encyclopedia and Genealogy.

In this book, we take MacIntyre's cutting-edge, historical approach to philosophy and ethics, and apply it to our crisis with leadership studies. We'll expand the treatment of the rationalities from philosophy and ethics into broader understandings of life, and call them the *Wisdom, Modern* and *Postmodern* paradigms.

We have so many problems in leadership studies today because we have three different, competing and ultimately irreconcilable understandings of human nature, goals, and the nature of human relationships. Essentially, we have three competing and irreconcilable ways of understanding life. The confusion and chaos in leadership studies is the result of these three conflicting understandings— conflicting paradigms—of life competing at the same time in the same space. So long as we have the three paradigms competing in the same space, we will have chaos and confusion in leadership, and no forward progress.

Let's go back to our earlier sports analogy. This time, because we have three life paradigms involved, we'll add basketball to our previous discussion that included football and golf.

Each sport has its own self-contained *set of rules*, a *ball*, a concept of what it takes to *win*, a concept of *team*, and a way to *score points*. But their understanding of what the rules are, what a ball is, how you win and lose, what a team is and how you score are very different. Essentially, each sport is a different paradigm for athletic competition.

In football, you use a large oval ball, hit people as hard as you can to knock them on their tails, and move the ball forward by running with it or passing it. You can make one downfield pass per play. You try to score as many points as possible using 22 players with 11 on offense and 11 on defense. You score by running or passing the ball beyond the goal line, or by kicking the ball through goal posts at the end of the field.

In basketball, you use a large round ball and get ejected from the game for hitting people. You move the ball forward by dribbling it or passing it. You are not allowed to run with it. You pass the ball repeatedly during play. You win by scoring more points than the other team. The same five people play on offense as defense. Like football, basketball games have time limits. Unlike football, play is continuous through offense and defense. You score by tossing a ball through a hoop at the end of the court.

In golf, you use a small, dimpled ball and move that ball forward by hitting it with a club. You never touch other players and time is not generally kept. While passing the ball is fundamental to the game of football and basketball, throwing or passing the ball down the fairway will get you disqualified in golf. You don't win by scoring the most points but by scoring the fewest strokes. You can play as part of a team, but you usually play as an individual. While football and basketball use the same playing area over and over, golf is played on 18 different playing areas.

Now imagine walking into an area and seeing basketball, football and golf going on at the same time in the same space. It would be chaotic and crazy.

You see a guy wearing pads put a big orange ball on top of a tee and try to hit it with a 5 iron to a wide receiver down the fairway. You see a running back wearing trousers and a polo shirt try to dribble the football as he runs through a sand-trap towards the free throw line. You see someone in a basketball uniform trying to kick a golf ball off a football tee from behind the three-point line.

As you watch, you realize that the players and coaches see all of this as *one activity*, unaware that it is made up of three different sports entangled with each other in the same space. They are unable to differentiate between any of the sports. They only see one thing going on that involves helmets and clubs and orange balls and everything else.

What's going on?

It turns out that several generations ago, only one of the sports was played here. Over time, the other sports gradually started playing in the same space at the same time until the sports became entangled and eventually merged. The players and coaches don't know that history. All they see, all they have known, is this one merged activity.

The coaches and players complain that in all this activity, they can't make any athletic improvement or progress.

Everyone is using terms like *ball, team, score, rules* and *equipment* in different and confusing ways. They hear that the goal is to score the most points and other times they hear that the goal is to score the least.

One coach teaches how to dribble the small white dimpled ball as you go for a field goal and try to score the fewest points.

Another teaches how important stroke is as you use a putter on the oval leather ball to get the most points. A third teaches techniques for shooting free throws from a water hazard.

An official throws a yellow flag for entering a water hazard and gives the player an opportunity at the free throw line.

It is absurd.

What are some of the lessons we can learn from this?

Each sport makes sense within its own set of rules, but doesn't make sense when you combine it with rules from other sports.

While these sports often use the same terms, they often mean very different things by those terms, and share no common ground with the other sports. Each sport has a *ball*, but the ball in each sport couldn't be more different. Basketball and football use the same term—*field goal percentage*—but mean and measure very different things by it.

While each sport has its own ways of measuring *good*, *bad* and *effective*, there is no common, accepted standard across the sports by which we can measure these things. In football, the measures will be things like yards per carry, passing efficiency, 3rd down conversions, and field goal percentage and distance. In basketball, the measures include shooting percentage, free throw percentage, points, assists, rebounds and personal fouls. In golf, players have a handicap. It wouldn't make any sense to talk about handicap in football or basketball, or to talk about field goal percentage in golf.

Because the different sports have such different rules, terms and even ways of understanding *ball* and *scoring*, you will never have the common ground required for discussion between or merging the sports in any way that makes sense. The sports are *incommensurable*.

When you combine and confuse elements of the different sports, you don't get a good game, improved skills or higher performance in any of the sports. You get chaos, confusion and nonsense.

You won't get any better at golf hitting a basketball off a tee. You won't get any better at basketball by dribbling a football or dunking a golf ball. You will never understand basketball if you adopt golf's outlook on scoring.

With no common ground between the sports, it is impossible even to identify good performance and bad performance in the merged activity. So long as elements of the sports are entangled, it is impossible to improve or make progress.

The only way to have progress or improvement is *within* one of the sports paradigms. To improve we must identify which sport is going to be played and pursue improvement within that sport.

The aspiring basketball player must clearly understand what the *ball*, *objective*, *rules* and *scoring* of basketball are without being confused by the ball, objective, rules and scoring of golf or football. Only when the basketball player understands that he doesn't bring a five iron on the court or wear a helmet and pads at the free throw line, will he be able to focus on improving his basketball game.

Making improvement or progress requires identifying the sport to be played and eliminating the influences of the other sports. The sports cannot coexist or tolerate each other in the same space at the same time.

Finally, as Americans, we are often tempted by the "buffet mentality." Pick and choose the stuff you like most from each sport and then combine them into something new and better.

It should be obvious that this buffet approach will end in failure. Because they share no common ground, there is simply no way to integrate these three different sports into an activity that makes sense and is simultaneously consistent with any of the sports. You can't try to maximize your score (basketball and football) while at the same time trying to minimize your score (golf). It is ridiculous.

It might be helpful to think of this last point another way. Imagine a steam engine, a gasoline engine and a jet engine.

The steam engine heats water to create steam that goes through turbines to provide power. The gas engine sparks a fuel-air mixture in a piston that moves the piston up and down to crank a driveshaft providing power. The jet engine ignites a fuel-air mixture creating tremendous pressure that is directed out a nozzle as thrust.

All of them are engines. All of them provide power. All of them are designed using fundamentally different approaches.

If you try mixing and matching parts of the different engines, you don't get a more powerful engine, you get something that doesn't work at all. The same is true about the sports and the life paradigms.

That is why leadership studies is stuck in a quagmire. Different life paradigms have very different understandings of leadership. So long as we have conflicting paradigms operating in our society and lives, we'll have conflicting understandings of leadership. There will be no progress in our leadership, lives or society until we select one life paradigm and eliminate the others.

A couple of issues make our situation even more challenging.

First, we are painfully aware of the political conflicts between liberals and conservatives, and between Democrats and Republicans. There is a tremendous tendency and temptation to try to understand life in these terms. We need to be clear that the conflicts between conservatives and liberals, and Democrats and Republicans, <u>are not the same</u> as the conflicts between the paradigms. There are liberals and conservatives, Democrats and Republicans, across each of these conflicting paradigms.

This book will make the most sense if you simply drop thinking in terms of conservative-liberal, Democrat-Republican while reading it.

Trying to figure out which party corresponds to which paradigm is like trying to figure out which golf club is best to kick a field goal.

We must be careful that our habit of dividing things into conservative-liberal and Democrat-Republican is not confused with and does not divert our attention from the more fundamental and important conflicts between these three competing paradigms.

> Conflicts between conservatives and liberals, and Democrats and Republicans, <u>are not the same</u> as the conflicts between the rival paradigms

Second, there are often paradigm inconsistencies within a writer, speaker or seminar. It is common for a leadership writer or speaker to say something from the perspective of one paradigm and then, a few minutes later, say something from the perspective of a different paradigm without even realizing it. Using our sports analogy, we're back to a football coach talking about how to dribble the ball through a sand trap during a running play. Leadership writers and speakers often unintentionally and unknowingly do similar things.

Third, our sports analogy, like all analogies, has a limit. Contrary to what golfers might think, among the three sports that we have been discussing, none of them is more right or true when compared to the rest. They are simply different games and different means of exercise and competition.

The life paradigms are different from the sports in that one of the life paradigms is true and provides the most powerful understanding of leadership, while the other paradigms are flawed and provide less powerful understandings of leadership. While there is no correct sport, there is a correct life paradigm.

To develop the next generation of leaders, we must figure out which of the competing paradigms is correct and right, and provides the most powerful, highest-performance people and teams. When we know which paradigm is right, we can derive an understanding of leadership and a step-by-step recipe for making great leaders for our future.

It can be challenging to learn a new game or paradigm, but it is very important to understand each paradigm in as much depth as possible.

The better we understand the correct paradigm, the better our leadership development program will be.

Even though they are incorrect, we need to understand the other paradigms so we can understand their influences in our society and life, and minimize their negative impact. We need to understand how others have been confused or misled by the other paradigms so we can best lead them.

If it sounds a bit vague right now, be patient. It will make a lot more sense as we understand the conflicting paradigms in our society and how they interact. Let's look at these different paradigms so we can identify which paradigm provides the best understanding of leadership, the best leadership performance and is right.

The Paradigms

There are three basic ways of understanding life: the *Wisdom Paradigm*, the *Modern Paradigm*, and the *Postmodern Paradigm*.

These paradigms arise out of a historical context and have a story behind them. To understand these paradigms, we must tell that story, that history, and learn how they are interconnected and flow from one to the other.

Presentation of this history is challenging. We need to present enough detail that the context and story are accurately recounted without going into so much detail that we get lost in a sea of minutiae and philosophical jargon.

Let's put the challenge in geographical terms. It is true to say that the Mississippi River flows south. The Mississippi flows from Minnesota south to the Gulf of Mexico. At the same time, that broad statement misses a more nuanced truth that the Mississippi River, when you examine a map closely, also flows east, west and even north.

For the purposes of our discussion on leadership, we're going to talk about the flow of intellectual history at the same level that we would if we said the Mississippi River flows south.

Experts can point out that there are lots of different points, counterpoints and exceptions in the way we discuss the history of these paradigms just as experts can point out that the Mississippi flows in every direction if you look at it on a small enough scale.

On the micro level these experts are right. And just as it is valuable to study the Mississippi in detail to appreciate its incredible nuances, so it is valuable to study intellectual history in detail so you can better appreciate the intellectual currents, counter-currents and eddies of the last two millennia. If you find this stuff interesting, I encourage you to explore it in depth.

But the fact that the Mississippi River, when considered in detail, flows in all sorts of directions doesn't change the most important fact that, on the grand scale, the Mississippi flows south. And the fact that there are all sorts of different currents and counter-currents in intellectual history doesn't change the big picture flow of thought that we are going to discuss.

Keep your eyes on the big picture flow as we consider the three competing, conflicting and ultimately incommensurable life paradigms.

The Wisdom Paradigm

The Wisdom Paradigm is based on the idea that we, as human beings, all have the same *human nature* and have the same *purpose* in life—to pursue fulfillment of our human nature and achieve *Happiness*.

According to the Wisdom Paradigm, no matter what culture or time period, human nature has remained and will continue to remain the same throughout history.

> **WISDOM PARADIGM**
>
> All people throughout time and across cultures have the same human nature and therefore the same purpose in life: to seek Happiness

That's why we all understand things like fear, courage, joy, anxiety, love, and so many other experiences the same way no matter our culture, ethnicity or era. The fact that we have the same human nature, the same concerns about life and death, and community, is what unites us as one humanity across cultures and time.

While our DNA is what makes us *homo sapiens*, it is our shared human nature that makes us all *human*.

We read English Shakespeare today because, 400 years after his death, what he said about love, betrayal, humor and ambition remains deeply insightful and very relevant to us.

We read the Jewish *Psalms* in the Bible because King David's trials, tribulations and joys still provide profound insight and guidance to us living in a completely different culture and time. When facing difficult times, don't many of us turn to Psalm 23? We gain comfort reading that though we walk in the valley of the shadow of darkness, we fear no evil because God is at our side. More than 3000 years after they were written, the Psalms remain deeply powerful for us today because we have the same human nature.

We read the *Analects by Confucius* from a distant culture, China, and a distant time, 500BC, because they contain great insight into human nature that have direct application today. "The Master said, "If the people be led by laws, and uniformity sought to be given them by punishments, they will try to avoid the punishment, but have no sense of shame. If they be led by virtue, and uniformity sought to be given them by the rules of propriety, they will have the sense of shame, and moreover will become good (Confucius 2011)."

Even when we go all the way back to the most ancient written story we have—the *Epic of Gilgamesh*—an ancient Sumerian epic at least 4000 years old, our timeless human nature enables us to understand and relate to Gilgamesh's experience of brotherhood, love, meaning and mortality.

While times change, environments change and technology changes, human nature has not.

The Wisdom Paradigm understands that it is a fundamental part of our human nature that we seek fulfillment in life. Because all people have the same human nature, we all have the same fulfillment in life.

Christians call that fulfillment *salvation*. Others may refer to the fulfillment as *nirvana* or *moksha*. Some refer to human nature being fulfilled as *flourishing*. Aristotle taught that humans seek fulfillment that he called *Happiness*.

While there are important differences between each of these formulations of fulfillment or Happiness, they all share fundamental attributes:

- Meaning and purpose in life
- Joy
- Freedom
- Total contentment
- No more pain or suffering
- The sacred
- Participation in something deeply profound and transcendent.

For the purposes of this text, we'll bring all these formulations of fulfillment (salvation, nirvana, etc.) together under the term *Happiness*.

Because we all have the same human nature, we say that we all have the same *purpose* in life: to become good and achieve fulfillment of our human nature—Happiness.

We all pursue the same human fulfillment in life but, because we all have different qualities, talents and interests, we pursue the same fulfillment through different means. Some will do so through art. Others through medicine, business, a trade, parenting, coaching or ministry.

As humans, throughout time and across cultures, we are united by our common human nature and have the same purpose in life—to pursue fulfillment, Happiness. So how do we pursue that fulfillment or Happiness?

OUR PURPOSE IS FULFILLMENT/HAPPINESS

It will be easier to understand how we pursue fulfillment if we use a parallel with which most of us are very familiar.

All human beings across cultures and throughout human history have the same physical nature. The commonality is written in our genes and DNA. When we talk about being in *good physical shape* or *good health*, we are really saying that we have fulfilled our physical nature as human beings. *Good* means that our weight, heart rate, blood pressure, etc. are all where they should be given our physical nature as humans.

We all know that it is important to be in good physical shape. We all know that it is a fact that that if we are in good physical shape that there are lots of benefits:

- We have the best chance to live a long life
- We have the best chance to avoid disease, and recover from illness
- Our work performance is enhanced
- We have more energy
- We have the best chance to gain the attention of a spouse and have children

Good or *healthy* means that you are acting in a way that benefits and fulfills your physical human nature. *Bad* or *unhealthy* means that you are acting in a way that impedes fulfillment of your physical human nature.

It is important to remember that *good*, *healthy*, *bad* and *unhealthy* are statements of <u>fact</u>, not just opinion, when it comes to physical fitness. For example, it is a fact that if an adult's blood pressure averages 110/65 to 140/90, they have a healthy/good blood pressure, and if their blood pressure is dramatically higher or lower, they have an unhealthy/bad blood pressure.

We all know that it's a <u>fact</u> that practicing *healthy* behaviors like exercise, good diet and rest will get us into good physical shape. These are physical *virtues* because it is *by virtue of*, or through these behaviors, that we get in good physical shape and fulfill our human physical nature.

We also know that it's a <u>fact</u> that practicing *unhealthy* behaviors like excessive eating or drinking, smoking, drug use, failure to exercise or lack of sleep will prevent us from achieving our physical potential. These behaviors are *vices* because it is a fact that they degrade our physical fitness. They prevent us from getting into our best physical shape and fulfilling our physical nature as humans.

Just as our physical nature as humans has remained the same across cultures and time, so our human nature has remained the same across cultures and time. Again, that is why writings from thousands of years ago are deeply relevant today.

Just as it is a fact that there are benefits to the fulfillment of our physical nature, so it is a fact that there are benefits to fulfillment of our human nature: Happiness.

Just as it is a fact that there are certain behaviors that help us fulfill our physical nature as humans, so it is a fact that there are certain behaviors which help us fulfill our human nature and achieve Happiness.

Now let's switch from your physical body to the corresponding part of your human nature—your *character*. A *good person* is one who develops and possesses good character. A *bad person* is one who develops and possesses poor character.

It is a fact that if you are a *good person* there are lots of benefits. A good person has the best chance to resist temptation and avoid the terrible problems that are associated with behaviors—vices—like addiction, substance abuse, greed, lust, gambling abuse, gluttony, etc.

If you are a good person, when life is good you will possess deeper insight that enables you to better appreciate your blessings. When life is tough, you will possess the character that gives you the best chance to weather the storm.

If you are good, you will treat your spouse in the special way he or she deserves. You will raise your children in a way that gives them the best chance to achieve fulfillment/Happiness in their lives. You will gain the deepest insights into *meaning* in life. Most important, as a good person, you have the best chance to achieve fulfillment or Happiness in your own life.

The benefits of being a good person are real and factual.

So how do you become good and achieve Happiness?

Just as it is a fact that practicing certain behaviors like exercise, good diet and rest enable you to fulfill your physical nature, so it is a fact that practicing certain behaviors—the *virtues*—will enable you to fulfill your human nature. If you practice virtues like love, selflessness, honesty, justice, courage, wisdom, etc. until they become habits and a seamless, fundamental part of your character—of who you are as a person—then you will become a good person and have the best chance to achieve Happiness.

Fully integrating the virtues into your very self brings fulfillment and Happiness.

Some virtues, like temperance, enable us to avoid temptation, harmful excess and addiction.

Virtues like love, selflessness and justice enable us to enter into deeper and more fulfilling relationships with others as individuals, families and communities.

Virtues like courage and honesty give us the strength to do the right things even when the challenges are difficult.

And when we integrate right knowledge and good character we develop the virtue of wisdom that enables us to lead others with trust and confidence.

The key concept in the Wisdom Paradigm is that we all have the same human nature and therefore the same purpose in life: to become good, fulfill our human nature and achieve Happiness. We achieve goodness and Happiness by practicing the virtues until they become a fundamental part of who we are.

OUR UNDERSTANDING OF LIFE IS BUILT ON THE FOUNDATION OF PURPOSE AND REASON

Imagine that we're a community of people living in New York City and our purpose is to pursue Happiness by traveling to San Diego, California. Imagine that it is a long expedition that will take many generations of people within our community to complete.

When we know what our purpose/destination is, we can use reason to figure out how to achieve our purpose and get to our destination.

Importance of Purpose

Everything in life is focused on our purpose—to become good

New York

If our purpose is to travel from New York to San Diego
It is a fact that the right direction is SW
It is a fact that west is a wrong direction

Virtues help us travel the right direction (fact)
Vices take us in a wrong direction (fact)

San Diego (Purpose/Destination is the key)

Reason tells us that if we want to travel from New York to San Diego, we must travel southwest.

It is a fact that if we travel southwest from New York, we are headed the *right* direction to get to our destination. It is also a fact that if we travel any other direction, southeast for instance, we will be headed the *wrong* direction.

In the same way, the Wisdom Paradigm is built on the foundation of purpose and reason. Your purpose is to become good, fulfill your human nature and achieve Happiness. Reason tells you how to achieve your purpose: practice the virtues until they become a fundamental part of your individual character, of who you are as person.

For many (i.e. Christians), *purpose and reason* can be restated as *faith and reason*. Faith tells the Christian what his purpose or destination is (salvation) and reason helps the Christian move towards that destination.

Purpose and reason are very effective when working together. Purpose provides a destination, a goal, for reason. Reason tells us how to achieve the purpose; how to get to the destination.

Separate from each other, purpose and reason lose their effectiveness. Purpose without reason is an unattainable goal. You know that you have a destination, but you don't have any way to get there.

Reason is a very powerful tool, but without purpose, without a destination, reason can and eventually will literally lead you anywhere. Even very bad places.

YOUR LIFE

Your life, then, is the unique story of how you pursue Happiness using your unique gifts and talents in the context of your community, culture and time period.

While we all have the same purpose in life, we all take different paths—according to our talents and interests—to achieve Happiness. Some will pursue Happiness using their talents as physicians, business people or as public servants. Others will pursue Happiness through service as teachers, artists, ministers or parents.

In physical fitness, it doesn't matter what exercise you do to get in good physical shape so long as the exercise gets your heart rate elevated for an extended period, and provides resistance that builds your muscles and strengthens your bones.

> The more frequently and intensely you practice the virtues, the more deeply ingrained and integrated they become in your character, the more the virtues become who you are at your core

The same is true when it comes to developing your character. It doesn't matter what your work is or what you do so long as your work and activity gives you the opportunity to practice and strengthen your virtues (i.e. love, honesty, justice, courage, wisdom, etc.).

You become what you do. You become what you practice. An athlete practices a sport until it becomes second-nature and he doesn't have to think about it. A musician plays a musical piece over and over until it is mastered, and his own interpretation of the piece is revealed. Baseball infielders practice double-plays until it becomes totally habituated, natural, automatic.

The same is true with the virtues. The more frequently and intensely you practice the virtues, the more deeply ingrained and integrated they become in your character. The more you practice honesty, the more it becomes part of you, and the more likely you will be honest even in very difficult situations.

Life is really your opportunity to practice the virtues in everything you do—work, play, family life, religion/spiritual—to make those virtues a fundamental part of who you are so you can become good and achieve Happiness.

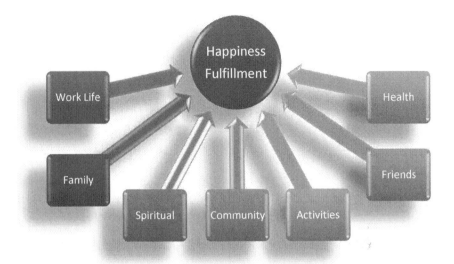

It is very important to remember that in the Wisdom Paradigm, *everything you do in life*—everything—either helps you achieve goodness or moves you away from goodness. That means that everything you do in life should be focused on helping you achieve your purpose, and finding fulfillment and Happiness. Everything includes your work, your family, your church, your neighborhood, your interests and 'outside' activities—*everything*. Even your thoughts. Everything you do or think in life should be focused on helping you become good.

In a time when we are used to keeping our public life separate from our private life, our work life separate from our personal life, the Wisdom Paradigm is different because it integrates all aspects of our life to focus on achieving our purpose: Happiness.

WE ARE ALL SOCIAL BEINGS

The Wisdom Paradigm understands that all people are fundamentally social beings.

Being human means *relationship* is a fundamental part of our human experience. From the very beginning, we are born into a family relationship. We seek relationship with others throughout our lives. We naturally want to share the good things in our lives with others and need the support of others when times are difficult. Our deepest joys include friendship, marriage and family. One of our deepest fears is being left alone. Solitary confinement in prison is considered by many to be cruel punishment, even torture, because it deprives us of something so deeply a part of our nature: relationship with others.

Our desire to love and be loved is fundamental to our human nature.

We cannot truly understand a person unless we also understand his social relationships. What was his family life like? In what ethnic group did he grow up and how has that influenced his life? Is he part of a religion or church? Who are his friends? Does he belong to sports teams or clubs, or participate in social activities?

To understand who a person truly is, we need the answers to these questions because we are so deeply impacted, shaped and formed by the communities in which we grow.

THE PURPOSE OF ALL COMMUNITIES IS TO BECOME GOOD

The Wisdom Paradigm understands that *the purpose of all communities is to become good* and help us—as individuals—become good.

By community we mean any group of people organized for just about any reason including teams, families, companies, organizations, churches, neighborhoods, athletic teams, community service groups, schools, etc.

By *good*, we mean that a community should possess the same characteristics, qualities and virtues—love, honesty, justice, courage, wisdom, etc.—that a good person possesses.

The purpose of all communities is goodness because goodness brings the community the same benefits it would bring any person. Love, selflessness, honesty, justice and wisdom all help communities develop tighter, more beneficial relationships and help improve community performance whether it is a company, athletic team, non-profit, church, etc. Vices like selfishness, unfairness, dishonesty and imprudence tear communities apart and destroy community performance.

A community or team achieves its purpose (*of becoming good*) by practicing the virtues in pursuit of its *mission*. So a sports team becomes good by practicing honesty, justice and courage by trying to win games. A family becomes good by practicing the virtues as they try to raise good children. A company, a non-profit, the military or a church all become good while practicing the virtues as they provide a product for profit; provide a beneficial service for the community; defend the nation; or help people develop a deeper relationship with God.

A community or team also becomes good by cultivating the virtues within the team members. The more the team members are good, the more good the team will possess and demonstrate.

Practicing, habituating and fully integrating the virtues not only makes a community good, but also increases the performance of the community. The more a basketball team practices and integrates virtues like discipline, selflessness, justice, courage and determination, the better of a team they become, the better their performance, and the more likely they are to accomplish their mission: winning games.

The *purpose* of all communities and teams is the same—to become good—while the way each community or team becomes good— through their *mission*—often differs.

COVENANT RELATIONSHIP: GOOD OF THE INDIVIDUAL & TEAM ARE THE SAME

In the Wisdom Paradigm, the good of the community (or team) and the good of the individual person are the same.

Any community/team is only as good as the people who make up that team. Just as a chain is only as good as its weakest link and a team is only as good as its weakest member, the better the community/team members are, the better the team will be.

If a community/team wants to maximize performance and goodness, then it needs to invest in the development of its members. The more the team invests in each of its members—in their skills, teamwork, character (goodness) and leadership—the better the team will be.

On the flip side, if you want to become a good person, you need some activity in which to practice the virtues like honesty, justice, wisdom, courage, etc. The best way to do that is to become part of a community or team where you can practice those virtues as part of the team accomplishing its mission.

The more effort you put into the team and its mission, the more you will grow in your skills, teamwork, character and leadership. It is almost always better to practice the virtues as part of a team than it is to practice them on your own because teammates will push you harder than you will push yourself. And because some virtues—like love and justice—require relationship, they and can only be developed as part of a community or team.

So, the good of the team and the good of the individual are the same. The more the team invests in each member, the better the team gets. The more the individual invests in the team, the better the individual gets.

Covenant Relationship

High-Trust - High Stability
Bonds under Pressure

Individual

Team

The Good of the individual and the Good of the team are the same

The more the individual commits to the team, the better the individual gets

The more the team commits to the individual, the better the team gets

If you've been part of a special sports or work team, or been part of the US military, you have probably experienced this type of relationship where everyone is close, trust is high and the commitment to each other is very deep. No one is in it for the money. Everyone is in it for each other and honor. You put your life on the line for a teammate.

We call this a *covenant relationship*. Because it involves deeply committed relationships, it is high-trust and very stable. The more you put a *covenant team* under pressure, the tighter and more committed their relationships become.

It is important to note that the Wisdom Paradigm understands **all** relationships should be practiced as covenant relationships, not just those that have to do with your work, family or athletic teams.

For instance, whenever you do a business deal with another company, or sign a contract with a client or supplier, you should do so as part of a covenant relationship with them. In a covenant relationship, the good of your partner or client is your good as well. This will create a high-trust, stable bond and relationship with them. The high trust relationship itself has lots of value because it increases performance and efficiency, and reduces risk.

If you try to establish a relationship with another in a manner that does not intentionally pursue the actual good of both, then you undermine your own development of the virtues, your own honor and your own pursuit of Happiness. It will also lead to less trusting, less stable and less productive relationships with others. Lower trust relationships are less efficient, riskier and lower value.

THERE IS AN OBJECTIVE MORALITY

In the Wisdom Paradigm, morality is objectively or factually true. That means there is a right and wrong that are not dependent on personal opinion or a particular culture, but are facts that are true for all people throughout history. It is not just a matter of opinion, but a fact that honesty, justice, courage and the other virtues are right and true.

As we said earlier, according to the Wisdom Paradigm, it is a fact that all human nature is the same and all people have the same purpose in life: to become good, find fulfillment and achieve Happiness.

It is also a fact that practicing certain kinds of behaviors—the *virtues* like love, honesty, justice and wisdom—will help us achieve our purpose of becoming good and achieving Happiness.

So how do we know that being honest is objectively right and true?

Just as we know that it is a fact that proper exercise and diet will get us in good physical shape, so we know for a fact that if we practice honesty, it will help us become good and achieve Happiness. In the same way, we also know for a fact that if we practice dishonesty or engage in vices like drug abuse, it will prevent us from becoming good and achieving Happiness.

The same is true for the rest of the virtues: it is a fact that practicing love, wisdom, integrity, courage and justice will help us become good too.

Let's go back to that metaphor about traveling from New York to San Diego. It is easy to understand that all our movements (or actions) are either going to get us closer to our destination or take us further from it. All movement that takes us closer to our destination is objectively good and right, and all movement (or action) that takes us away from our destination is objectively bad and wrong. Simple enough.

Real life offers us a wide variety of potential actions. Not all those choices that take us closer to our destination will take us the right direction for the same distance or at the same speed. Those actions that take us further and faster towards our destination are more moral than those actions that don't take us as far or as fast.

> Wisdom morality and ethics are focused on the kind of person you become by what you do. Wisdom morality is focused on *character*. Actions are important insofar as they help you become good.

The more moral action that takes us further and faster towards our destination is sometimes more difficult to act on than the alternatives. Doing the right thing can have negative consequences, and involve pain and suffering. You should choose the right thing anyway because it will help you become good and achieve Happiness faster and more effectively.

In the Wisdom Paradigm, morality is focused on the kind of person you become by what you practice. Morality is not some arbitrary imposition "from above" or from a bunch of unhappy old guys disconnected from the realities of life. Rather, morality is simply a road map written in your human nature for your benefit to help you become good and achieve Happiness.

TRUTH AND BEAUTY

In the Wisdom Paradigm there is an objective Truth and an objective Beauty, though there may be disagreements on the specifics of their nature and how we experience them.

The pursuit and discovery of the Truth about life is a fundamental part of our search for Happiness. We seek to understand the Truth about who we are, the nature of cosmos, where we fit in our community, and where we fit in the cosmos. The fundamental search for meaning in our lives is a search for the Truth.

As with everything else in the Wisdom Paradigm, knowledge is pursued not for its own sake, but because it helps us become good by better understanding the Truth. In the Wisdom Paradigm, therefore, we pursue a certain type of knowledge—*wisdom*—which is knowledge of what is true or right coupled with good character. Wisdom is knowledge applied to life and the pursuit of Happiness.

Therefore, the highest degree, the PhD, is the Doctor of Philosophy: one who teaches (Latin *docere*) the love (Greek *philo*) of wisdom (Greek *sophia*).

What is the book of wisdom? Scripture, of course. For Scripture combines our purpose—the pursuit of Happiness (i.e. salvation)—with the type of knowledge and wisdom we need to achieve Happiness. It combines the *what* (knowledge) and the *how* (right action—character) with the *why* (Happiness).

In the Wisdom Paradigm, the process to prepare young people to become adults is known as *formation*, and is focused on developing wisdom.

In formation, academic/intellectual/mental development is very important. Children and adolescents must be taught how to think correctly and critically.

But just as important, formation also focuses on character development. Young people must not only be taught what is true (intellect), but how to use that knowledge to do what is right (character). It is just as important for the youth to be part of athletic and performing arts groups where they develop character while performing as part of a team under pressure, as it is for youth to focus in the classroom.

> The Wisdom Paradigm pursues a certain kind of knowledge--*wisdom*--which *is right knowledge* plus *character*.
> **What is the book of all wisdom?** *Scripture.*

While there are different understandings of the nature of Beauty, there is widespread acceptance in the Wisdom Paradigm that Beauty is an objective quality that works or objects possess in greater and lesser degrees. Many understand Beauty to be a quality in a work or in nature that captures or conveys a glimpse of the divine or transcendent.

MOTIVATION IN LIFE

In the Wisdom Paradigm, what is our motivation in life? Happiness.

You do want Happiness in life, don't you?

Remember that in the wisdom understanding of the world, everything in our lives is either helping us become good or not. We are either practicing the virtues as we live our daily lives, and progressing towards Happiness, or not.

So the primary motivation in life is the desire for fulfillment—the pursuit of Happiness.

This makes sense when we are talking about what motivates us in our personal life. What about our work or public life? Are we motivated by something different there?

No. In the Wisdom Paradigm there is no distinction between personal life and work life. Everything in life—including work—is an opportunity to practice the virtues, become good and achieve Happiness.

When you are primarily motivated by something other than Happiness, you cannot become good. Other motivations, other desires—whether it is money, power, sex, drugs, etc.—can never be fully satisfied. They will never fulfill you. You will always want more, and more will never be enough. As you pursue more of that desire in your search for fulfillment, you risk addiction. Goodness and Happiness will be elusive.

Today, while we pretend that money is the prime motivator for people at work, studies have repeatedly shown that work place satisfaction and fulfillment are ranked higher than compensation, and that meaning, creativity and self-direction (not compensation) drive performance (Pink 2010).

In the Wisdom Paradigm, what really motivates people to action is their desire for fulfillment—Happiness.

MEASURING SUCCESS IN LIFE

So how do we measure *success* in the Wisdom Paradigm? The most obvious way is by whether a person is good and has achieved Happiness or not.

> Honor is the respect a person is owed for the kind of person he is; for the character he demonstrates.
>
> His goodness is worthy of being *honored*.

You can also measure progress on the path towards Happiness in terms of whether a person possesses the virtues and to what degree. Does she possess honesty, justice, wisdom, love and courage? How much does she possess each of these virtues? Does she possess integrity, the virtue that binds the others together and ensures there are no cracks in character?

The real measure of progress? *Honor.* It is a word that has lost its meaning in our contemporary society, but in the Wisdom Paradigm it goes to the very core of what is meaningful.

Honor is the respect a person is owed for the kind of person that they are. It is the respect a person is owed for the character they possess. It is the respect a person is owed for their goodness.

WORK

Fisher, smith, shoemaker, miller, weaver, mason, carpenter… What are these?

In earlier times, if your name was Smith, you were probably the black*smith* in town. If your name was Weaver, it was probably because your family wove fabric. Miller was the man who milled the grain into flour. You can probably figure out Fisher, Shoemaker, Mason and Carpenter on your own.

Smith was not a *job*, not something that you did just for money, but more of a *vocation*[3], a calling, a fundamental part of who you were. Smith was part of your identity. As the smith, the product of your work represented you personally. As the weaver, the quality and finish of your fabric reflected you directly. Your work contained, expressed and embodied you. Your work was you and you were your work.

Today, most of us think of work as having a job so we can earn money, make a living, and eventually retire to go do those things we find really fulfilling. We don't think of work and fulfillment as going hand in hand. We're often told that we're not supposed to find our work fulfilling. It's a job.

On the other hand, we hear stories about and applaud people who give up the big paying job so they can pursue work that they find

---

[3] By *vocation* we mean the work, occupation, career or profession that one feels particularly called to by the nature of their gifts and talents. It can, but does not necessarily mean, a calling to a religious vocation or to a career in the trades.

fulfilling. It gets our attention because we find it unusual and admirable.

Today we divide everything into our professional-work life and our personal-private life, but in the Wisdom Paradigm, everything in life is focused on becoming good and achieving Happiness. Work is one of the best opportunities to practice, habituate and internalize all sorts of virtues. Any work, no matter how grimy, nasty or subordinate, is honorable, good and has dignity if it provides an opportunity for a person to practice the virtues.

Better to be the lowliest worker in the nastiest job who practices honesty, integrity and justice in his work than to be a billionaire CEO who has made it to the top through greed and the exploitation of others. The first may well find Happiness in life while the latter will never be satisfied.

WHAT ARE RULES FOR?

Rules provide us guidance that helps us get better at things faster than if we had to figure them out on our own.

By *rules* we mean much more than simply the laws governing the play of a sport. We also mean the principles, best practices and standards of play that guide one towards success in any sport or activity. Every baseball player, for instance, knows that you never swing at a 3-0 pitch. Every track sprinter knows that you run all the way through the tape.

Let's say you want to learn how to play cricket. You could walk out on the field with a willow and a bail, and try to figure out on your own what is going on with the creases, wickets, bowling and the googly. While this is an option, it is probably going to be a long time before you have a clue what is going on in a match, and even longer before you can play yourself.

A much better option is to find a cricket expert, a coach, and ask him to teach you the game. He will certainly teach you the Laws of Cricket (as the official rules are known), but he will go beyond that. He will show you how to be a striker, how to play as a fielder and how to bowl. He will show you how to hold the bail, make your run up and use your wrist in your bowling delivery. He will teach you the techniques and strategies, and show you how to practice to become the best cricket player you can be in the shortest amount of time. He will teach you the rules of thumb you need to be good at cricket.

The same is true of just about any activity you want to learn. If you want to play piano, you find a good piano instructor who will teach you the rules of playing good piano. You will learn and practice the scales, then play works ranging from simple to complex. In basketball, the coach will teach you how to dribble and shoot the ball, and how to play defense. He will also teach you other rules of thumb of the game—like not making long, cross-court passes.

We all know that the best way to learn anything is to find an expert, a master of that activity, who can show us the rules we need to understand and practice to be good at that activity. If we follow, internalize and sufficiently practice those rules, we might become masters of that activity ourselves.

A master of an activity is one who intuitively understands all aspects of the activity and how they fit together. A master can feel the flow of the activity and can see where things are headed, how things are unfolding, long before others.

Take Michael Jordan on the basketball court or Wayne Gretzky on the ice. Both were accomplished masters of their respective sports. When playing, they intuitively knew where all the other players were, how they were flowing together (or not), and therefore intuitively felt the flow and direction of the game. Each could feel exactly when opportunities were opening or closing. They could feel to a split second when the ball or puck had to be passed or shot. They knew what was going to happen in the game before anyone else did.

In the military, they call this knowledge of how things are flowing and where they are headed *situational awareness* or *SA*. The more situational awareness a person has, the greater their advantage in their activity whether it's an athletic contest, business, public safety or their family. Situational awareness comes from fully internalizing the rules through experience. The more one practices, the more one develops situational awareness and progresses towards becoming a master of that activity. Later, we will refer to this knowledge as *vision*.

In the Wisdom Paradigm, rules are really the wisdom of the masters expressed in a simplified way to help us become good as quickly as possible at whatever it is we are doing. Good at baseball. Good at serving the poor. Good at raising a family. Good in the work place. Good at cricket.

And perhaps, with enough commitment, practice and perseverance, good at life.

FREEDOM

Freedom has several important meanings in the Wisdom Paradigm.

First, wisdom is a core element in our pursuit of the Truth and the Good. The cultivation of wisdom requires the freedom to make and learn from mistakes.

Second, freedom in the Wisdom Paradigm means freedom from the vices and addictions that can so easily own us and destroy our lives. The more you practice the virtues, the less likely you are to be caught up in life-destroying addictions like drug use, alcoholism, gambling or sex addiction. Freedom from the chains of addiction. Freedom from temptations like greed, power, lust, etc.

Third, we all possess different qualities, talents and interests. Some people have talents and interests that make them good physicians. Others possess talents and interests to be business people, serve their nation in the military or public safety, or be artists, parents, coaches, ministers or practice a trade.

A key part of achieving fulfillment in life is the opportunity—the freedom—to maximize one's talents by pursuing one's interests to the greatest extent possible. This is where fulfillment and Happiness are maximized, and the greatest discoveries and insights into life occur. In earlier times, people were often very limited by class structure, ethnicity or education in the kinds of work they could pursue, and the talents they could develop and demonstrate. It is important that people have the freedom to develop their talents and pursue their interests.

Finally, Happiness is only possible and meaningful if it is the result of our own free choice to become good. That means you must be free to choose goodness and Happiness.

LEADERSHIP

Just like any other leadership approach, leadership in the Wisdom Paradigm involves one providing direction to another (our definition of leadership) focused on accomplishing some goal or mission. But the way the Wisdom Paradigm understands human nature, human relationships and goals brings a lot more to the table.

The key element to remember in the Wisdom Paradigm is that everything is bound together by our common purpose in life: to become good and achieve Happiness. That means all action—whether in private life or public life—by the leader and the follower is ultimately focused on becoming good. So leader and follower are not just united by their focus on the immediate goal or mission, but are also united by their ultimate goal in life, Happiness.

In conventional leadership, the leader is generally responsible for achieving goals and accomplishing the mission within financial, legal and (hopefully) ethical parameters. The follower really functions as little more than a means to achieving the goal or mission.

With the Wisdom Paradigm's covenant relationship, the leader has a deeper relationship with and responsibility to the follower in several ways.

First, the leader can never treat the follower as merely a means to accomplish a goal or mission. When a leader treats a follower as merely a means to an end, the leader treats the follower as a *thing*, which objectifies and dehumanizes the follower. Treating people that way prevents the leader from becoming good.

A leader must always be focused on the long-term goodness of the follower. The leader must always be concerned with what is best for the follower. When a leader focuses on the goodness of the follower, the leader practices the virtue of love and that helps the leader become good.

A leader who is focused on the goodness of the follower is genuinely interested in the holistic (professional and personal) formation of the follower for the follower's sake, not simply for the leader's sake or improved team performance. That means that on the professional level, the leader must invest in the skill, character, teamwork and leadership development of the follower. This will improve the follower's performance and team performance, and help the follower develop professionally for his future whether that future is with the leader or not.

In return, the follower has the responsibility of wholeheartedly pursuing the opportunity the leader offers in all its dimensions.

Remember that this understanding of leadership is as fundamental and true in business as it is in non-profits, churches, your family or even while coaching your daughter's soccer team.

In the Wisdom Paradigm, leadership is not just about working with others to achieve a goal, but about the deeper and more important opportunity to use that work to become good and help lead another to become good. This leads to deeper, higher-trust and more committed relationships, which leads to higher performance teams and better outcomes.

Indeed, in the Wisdom Paradigm, leadership and life really are the same thing. For our lives are the stories of how we each lead ourselves and lead others to goodness and fulfillment.

WRAP UP

No matter what time or culture, the Wisdom Paradigm argues that all people have the same human nature and therefore the same fulfillment and purpose in life: *Happiness.*

Reason tells us that it is objectively true that certain behaviors called the *virtues* help us become good and achieve Happiness while other behaviors, the *vices*, prevent us from achieving goodness and Happiness. Virtues include love, honesty, justice, courage, wisdom and integrity while vices include behaviors that can lead to addiction and other problems like greed, gluttony, lust, substance abuse and sloth.

Our lives are our own unique stories about how we use our gifts and talents to practice virtue and overcome vice to become good in our pursuit of Happiness.

Since our purpose in life is to achieve Happiness, everything in our lives including work, family, church, athletics and hobbies should focus on helping us become good by practicing the virtues until they are a fundamental part of our character, of who we are as individuals.

Virtue can only be developed through activity. We participate in community—on teams—because they are opportunities for us to more deeply develop virtue. The more we practice the virtues in team activity, the better people we become. This applies in every community or team context—every relationship—including families and our work.

Since a community or team is only as good as the individual members, a team can only become better by making its members better. The more a team invests in developing the virtues, skills, teamwork and leadership of its members, the better the members become and the better the team becomes.

That means that the purpose of the individual and the purpose of the team or community are the same: to become *good*. We call this a *covenant relationship*. By their very nature, covenant relationships are very stable, very strong and high trust. When you put a covenant relationship under pressure, it does not break, but gets stronger. The stability and deep trust means that covenant teams are high performance and powerful teams.

In the Wisdom Paradigm, we seek Truth through wisdom, the combination of right knowledge and good character.

If you want to get good at something as quickly as possible, it makes sense to listen to the wisdom, expressed as *rules*, of those who have already mastered that activity, whether its business, music, athletics, your family or religion. They are the best and fastest guide to success. To ignore or dismiss the rules is unwise.

Finally, in the Wisdom Paradigm, life and leadership are really the same. If life is about becoming good and achieving Happiness, then life is necessarily the story of you leading yourself and those around you towards that goal of Happiness.

For the last few thousand years, the fundamental concepts of the Wisdom Paradigm have been fundamental qualities of most of the world's great religions, philosophies and cultures. This is certainly true of Western civilization, the Judeo-Christian religions and most of the classical Greek philosophy upon which Western civilization is grounded.

I am not arguing that Western civilization ever historically contained or successfully embodied all these ideas at the same time. Far from it. Some communities lived aspects of the Wisdom Paradigm while also inheriting or accepting characteristics that were inconsistent with the paradigm. A motivated intellectual historian could probably develop a long list of communities who embraced ideas inconsistent with some of the properties of the Wisdom Paradigm.

Nevertheless, the important point is that despite inconsistencies and counter examples, the idea that, as humans, we all have the same human nature and purpose in life (Happiness); the idea that certain kinds of behaviors lead us towards goodness and Happiness while other behaviors lead us away; and the idea that we are fundamentally social beings, are all concepts from a way of looking at life (Wisdom Paradigm) that has been the dominant understanding of life for the last several thousand years.

The Modern Paradigm

In the 16th and 17th centuries, Europe was besieged by a series of wars, many of them stemming from religious differences. These wars devastated large parts of France and Germany, and led to the deaths of millions of people. The wars took a terrible toll on Europe, impoverishing millions more and bringing governments to the point of bankruptcy. In many areas anarchy reigned as rival armies marched back and forth, plundering the countryside. Civil wars broke out in many states as people took advantage of religious differences and rulers with empty treasuries to seek power themselves.

The suffering throughout Europe was enormous and long-lasting in a way that is difficult for us to understand today. People and nations became exhausted by the suffering that seemed to be systemic and unending. Philosophers began to search for a new way to understand life that could get them out of the terrible religious, political and civil conflicts of the 16th and 17th centuries.

THE MODERN PARADIGM IS BUILT ON THE FOUNDATION OF REASON

The Wisdom Paradigm is based on a foundation of *purpose* and *reason*. As we said before, our purpose is our destination in life and reason tells us how to get there.

Ever since Europe had become Christian, *faith* had taken the role of *purpose*. So for European Christian civilizations, the equation was essentially *faith/purpose* and *reason*. Faith provided the destination (salvation) and reason helped people understand what was needed to achieve salvation.

With that in mind, the answer to ending the suffering of the religious conflicts for many of the European philosophers was obvious enough: we need to drop that thing, *faith*, which seemed to be at the root of the conflict and reconstruct our understanding of life on *reason* alone.

It seems to make sense. Reason is a very powerful tool. All rational people possess it. Arguments from reason seem to be available for objective examination and discussion. Why not use reason, this powerful and promising instrument, as a tool to build a new understanding of life that could be accepted and discussed by all rational people?

Reason is a tool and a tool is only good if it has material to work on. What material or data would give people the greatest certainty in their search for knowledge? The philosophers of the Modern Paradigm generally focused on *sense experience* and quantifiable evidence in an approach known as *empiricism*. They focused on things they could touch and measure.

And so many of the philosophers of the 16th, 17th and 18th centuries introduced us to the Age of Reason and the Age of the Enlightenment. Collectively, they helped reconstruct our understanding of life, moving us from a Wisdom Paradigm based on faith/purpose and reason to a Modern Paradigm largely focused on reason and quantifiable sense experience (empiricism).

The hope was that the reliance on reason would give all rational people a common, objective way to understand life and get society away from an understanding of life based on conflicting religions. In other words, we'll stop basing our understanding of life on something about which we violently disagree (religion) and base it on something on which we all agree (reason).

THE REJECTION OF PURPOSE

The Modern Paradigm rejected the concept of purpose so central to the Wisdom Paradigm not just because of its tie into faith and the religious wars, but also because of what philosophers call the *is-ought* problem or the *problem of induction*.

Basically, philosophers like David Hume argued that logic does not allow us to reason from specific instances (the *is*) to more general principles or conclusions (the *ought*). In other words, just because we have seen the sun come up every morning (the specific instances or *is*) doesn't necessarily mean that the sun will come up every morning in the future (the general principle or *ought*).

To make that connection between the sun rising in the past and the sun rising in the future, we must assume that the future will be the same as the past. We must say that because the sun has come up every day in the past (the fact or *is*), we can establish a general principal that the sun ought to come up tomorrow. But that conclusion is based on an assumption, not a logical necessity.

Another way to understand this is that reason (or science) can tell us the *how* and the *what* (the *is*) about things, but cannot logically tell us the *why* (the *ought*) of things. For example, science can tell us *how* photosynthesis works and *what* is going on, but can't tell us the *purpose* or *why* of photosynthesis.

In the Modern Paradigm, just because we know human nature (the *is*), we cannot logically induce that people therefore have a purpose (the *ought*)—to become good and achieve Happiness. Without going into more detail into the philosophical arguments, the point is that modern philosophers like Hume used reason to reject the idea of purpose.

If we go back to our earlier metaphor where we are in New York and our purpose is to get to San Diego, then the Modern Paradigm eliminates the purpose, the destination. Just because all previous generations have travelled southwest towards San Diego doesn't mean that we can induce that it's our purpose as humans to travel southwest to San Diego.

The rejection of purpose for historical as well as philosophical reasons has far-ranging implications. When purpose is eliminated, everything within the Wisdom Paradigm that depended on purpose—like morality—must be rethought and re-justified.

Almost as important, the elimination of purpose means that purpose (becoming good and achieving Happiness) no longer serves as the central, unifying element that ties our understanding of life together.

THE SPLIT: PUBLIC LIFE AND PRIVATE LIFE

In the Wisdom Paradigm, the idea of purpose unifies all aspects of our lives—work/public life and personal/private life—into a focus on becoming good.

With the rejection of purpose, we lose the unifying focus of purpose in life. With the new emphasis on reason and the quantifiable (empiricism), life in the Modern Paradigm gets split into what reason can more easily discuss—the *public*, quantifiable side of life—and what reason has difficulty discussing—the *private*, difficult-to-quantify side of life.

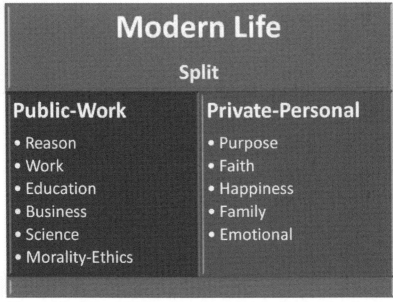

Modern Life

Split

Public-Work	Private-Personal
• Reason	• Purpose
• Work	• Faith
• Education	• Happiness
• Business	• Family
• Science	• Emotional
• Morality-Ethics	

The public side of life based on reason is understood to be more objective—that is the whole point of relying on reason. The Modern Paradigm depends on reason to guide us to objective Truth. The private/personal side of life and the things in that category, like faith and feelings, are understood to be subjective—a matter of personal opinion.

This is the familiar split where some things are part of your *public* or work life, and other things are part of your *private* or personal life. Science and business are quantifiable, so they belong on the public side of life. Purpose, religion, Happiness, emotions, feelings and fulfillment are difficult to quantify or grasp with pure reason, so they belong on the private side of life.

At first, morality was on the public side of life. But over time, as morality became more difficult to justify with reason alone, it appeared to become more subjective. Morality became more a matter of opinion than fact and moved from the public side of life to the private side. Today, many consider morality to be a personal issue, not something that is appropriate for public discussion.

HUMAN NATURE

In the Wisdom Paradigm, understanding human nature is essential to understanding the nature of life, our purpose and fulfillment. It is the starting point for understanding everything that follows. Understanding human nature was critical to understanding purpose, goodness, fulfillment and Happiness. It goes to the very meaning of life.

In the Modern Paradigm, with purpose eliminated from pubic discussion, understanding human nature is not so important.

On the public side of life, we can study human nature from a scientific perspective—psychology and psychiatry. A scientific understanding of how the mind works in individuals and how minds work in groups is valuable in a wide variety of areas including developmental, educational, industrial and social psychologies.

On the private side of life, questions about human nature and purpose are usually tackled in terms of one's religion.

We can imagine a person suffering deeply from a question about the meaning of life. In the Wisdom Paradigm, the answer to the question "What is the meaning of life?" is obvious: to achieve Happiness.

The modern rejection of purpose has a problem, however. Remember that science, on the public side of life, can tell us the *how* and the *what* about things, but—due to the rejection of purpose— cannot tell us about the *why* of things. The *why*, or purpose, of things is reserved for consideration in our private life. And so the Modern Paradigm cannot tell us about the *why* of life.

And so, with the Modern Paradigm's separation of life into the public and private, fundamental and important questions about the meaning of life almost inevitably receive two hard-to-reconcile answers: one from the public life's psychologist with the other, using a very different conceptual framework, from a minister.

By rejecting the concept of *purpose*, at least as it relates to the public side of life, the Modern Paradigm is deeply compromised in its ability to answer the deepest and most meaningful questions about life.

THE CONTRACTUAL NATURE OF HUMAN RELATIONSHIPS

Because we are all obviously involved in a myriad of relationships ranging from our families and churches to our neighborhoods and nations, the Modern Paradigm must account for human relationships and how we come together as community.

In the Modern Paradigm, humans are often understood to be free individuals without fundamental, pre-existing relationships with others. Individuals, existing in a *state of nature* with lots of freedom, but little security, come together and form communities by agreeing to a *social contract*. The individual gives up some freedom to the community, but receives more security in return. The Modern Paradigm understands all relationships from family to business as essentially contractual relationships.

The understanding of *contractual relationship* in the Modern Paradigm is very different than the understanding of *covenant relationship* in the Wisdom Paradigm.

Remember that in the Wisdom Paradigm, people are understood to be fundamentally social beings. The more that the individual commits and gives to the team, the better the individual becomes. The more that the team invests in the development of the individual, the better the team becomes. Because the good of the team and the good of the individual are the same, the covenant relationship is high trust and very stable. When you put the covenant relationship under pressure, the bonds and relationship between teammates become stronger.

In contrast, the modern contractual relationship is not expressed in what is *good* for the individual or the team, but rather in terms of what is in the *self-interest* of the individual or team. The change in terms from *good* to *self-interest* between the Wisdom and Modern Paradigms is deliberate and meaningful.

Let's take the work relationship between an employee and a company. The self-interest of the employee is to get as much money from the company for as little work as possible. In contrast, it is in the interest of the company to get as much work from the employee for as little money as possible.

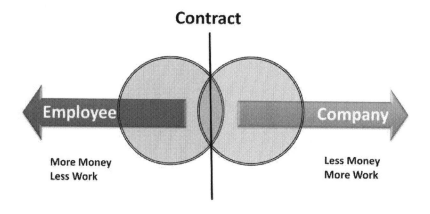

Modern Contractual Relationship

Low Trust – Unstable – Shatters Under Pressure

Contract

Employee — More Money / Less Work

Company — Less Money / More Work

The interests of the company and the employee are not the same, but are defined in direct opposition to each other. What is good for one is bad for the other. Nevertheless, employees need work and companies need employees, so they negotiate and eventually sign a contract. The contract is the only thing holding together opposing interests.

Because the interests of the employee and company are, by definition, in conflict with each other, the modern contractual relationship is inherently low trust, unstable and shatters when you put it under pressure.

When the company is short on cash, it lays off employees. When an employee feels like the company isn't paying him enough, he leaves for higher-paying work elsewhere.

In the contractual relationship, you literally get the relationship you pay for. The contractual relationship is the source of the idea that "The individual should give up what is good for him for the good of the team." That idea doesn't make any sense in the covenant relationship.

The modern concept of contractual relationships doesn't just apply to employment relationships, but to all relationships in the Modern Paradigm. Your relationship with your business partners, your clients, your doctor, attorney and accountant, and even the relationship you have with your family are all, at their core, understood to be contractual relationships.

A covenant relationship is successful when it maximizes the good of all those in the relationship. A contractual relationship is successful when it maximizes your self-interest, almost always understood to be at some expense to the other party.

THE PURPOSE OF COMMUNITIES

In the Wisdom Paradigm, the purpose of all communities and teams is to become good by helping the people within the community or team become good. This includes all communities, even businesses, governments and the military.

The Modern Paradigm rejects the idea that there is some underlying, shared purpose for all communities and teams.

Instead, because communities are formed through some version of a social contract, the purpose of the community depends on the reason the community was formed by its participants.

So the purpose of a business is to make a profit. The purpose of a non-profit is to provide a service to the community. The purpose of the military is to defend the nation. The purpose of an athletic team is to win games. The purpose of a church is to worship. The purpose of a family is to raise children.

MOTIVATION

In the Wisdom Paradigm, people are motivated by their desire to become good and achieve Happiness.

Since the Modern Paradigm can't talk about purpose on the public side of life, it must develop a new understanding of what motivates people on the public side. The motivation selected must be quantifiable so it can be easily measured in terms of reason.

The obvious answer to the modern issue of motivation is *money.*

So the Modern Paradigm understands human motivation primarily in terms of money, power or fame. Other motivations, like a search for meaning or Happiness may exist, they just aren't easily quantifiable. So these motivations are placed in the private sphere of life and not examined very seriously in the public sphere of life.

Think about the job advertisements you see. The key elements are a description of the position and compensation. Except for non-profits and the military, how often do you see employment advertising talking about fulfillment?

MORALITY

In the Wisdom Paradigm, morality is objectively true because it is a fact that virtues like honesty, justice, courage and integrity, help us become good and achieve Happiness. Morality, in the Wisdom Paradigm, rests fully on the concept that all humans have the same purpose.

When those bringing in the Modern Paradigm eliminate purpose, there are two big impacts on morality.

The first impact is on the focus of morality. In the Wisdom Paradigm, the focus is on your *character*—the *person you become*—as the result of practicing the virtues. Developing good character is, after all, the purpose of all actions in the Wisdom Paradigm.

When purpose and character are dropped by the Modern Paradigm, the only thing left to focus on are the actions themselves. What makes an action right or wrong? So we move from a wisdom-morality focused on *character* and becoming good to a modern ethics focused on the *right action in a given situation*. Which is why so much of contemporary, modern morality focuses on case studies.

Second, even though they dropped the idea of purpose, those advocating the Modern Paradigm didn't stop believing that honesty, justice, courage and integrity are moral facts. But they had to develop a new understanding of why these behaviors are factually true, an understanding that depended on reason alone and not purpose.

To put it in the terms of our New York City to San Diego metaphor: Even though San Diego has disappeared as our destination, we continue to travel southwest while the Modern Paradigm searches for an objective justification based on reason for going in that direction.

It is neither the purpose of this book nor do we have the space available to examine all the attempts in the Modern Paradigm to justify an objective morality using reason alone. Two of the most notable and representative attempts are deontological ethics, perhaps best exemplified by Immanuel Kant in the late 1700's, and consequentialist ethics, best exemplified by John Stuart Mill's utilitarianism in the mid 1800's.

While strong efforts, both these approaches, at least according to Wisdom and Postmodern moral philosophers, are ultimately unsatisfactory.[4]

Perhaps the biggest problem is that a system based on reason alone requires a starting point from which the entire system is constructed—like the axioms from which Euclidean geometry is constructed.

But what is the "reason" for selecting one set of axioms as a starting point for the reasoning rather than any other set of axioms? Let's say that the "reason" we choose the Euclidean axioms to start is that they

---

[4] For an outstanding and well-accepted critique of the problems in modern attempts to establish a rational foundation for morality/ethics, read *After Virtue* (MacIntyre, After Virtue 3rd Ed. 1981) and *Three Rival Versions of Moral Enquiry* (MacIntyre, 1991)

seem to be self-evidently true. If so, then we didn't start our system using pure reason, but with an act of faith that the axioms selected as the starting point really are self-evidently true.

If we have any other reason for choosing the axioms, then we must ask ourselves what is the reason we chose that reason that gave us those axioms? We can ask the reason for the reason for the reason for the reason as far back as we want and never get to an un-reasoned reason that doesn't involve an act of faith.

Indeed, what is the logical reason for believing that reason itself will lead us to objective Truth?

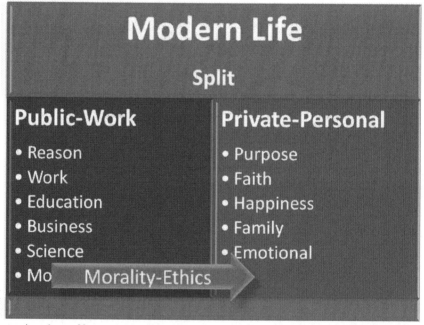

As the effort to establish an objective morality based on reason alone gets increasingly problematic, it becomes more difficult to discuss morality in public as a community. Morality begins to move from the public side of life to the private side of life. And when morality moves into the private side of life, morality is increasingly understood to be a matter of opinion and not fact.

Modern morality attempts to find objectivity by turning to reason alone, but fails because reason cannot give itself its own justification.

YOUR LIFE

In the Wisdom Paradigm, your life is your unique story of how you become good and achieve Happiness. Everything you do in life is focused on helping you become good.

In the Modern Paradigm, the separation of life into public-work and private-personal spheres means there is no overall unity in life. You are expected to keep your private-personal life isolated from your public-work life. Your pursuit of fulfillment or Happiness, however you define or reject that, is a matter for your personal life.

NATURE OF TRUTH AND KNOWLEDGE

The Modern Paradigm believes in an objective Truth, but generally understands that objective Truth can only be guaranteed through the proper and careful cultivation of reason combined with quantifiable sense data, as in science.

In the Wisdom Paradigm, the emphasis is on the development of wisdom—right knowledge coupled with right action—to help us become good and achieve Happiness. The Book of all Wisdom is Scripture because it contains the truth and knowledge you need to live a good life and become a good person. In the Wisdom Paradigm, knowledge and education are not pursued for their own sake, but exist to serve people by helping them become good. The *search for knowledge* must be accompanied by *character formation* to result in *wisdom*. The process of developing young people is known as *formation*.

In contrast, the Modern Paradigm focuses on the intellect, knowledge and the systematic collection of information. The point is to use reason to learn all there is in the universe, to gather all the information that is available, to know all that is knowable.

If we understand knowledge as information, then we can divide the totality of knowledge into a spectrum of subjects like history, sociology, literature, chemistry and physics. Then we can break these subject areas down into thinner and thinner slices.

For instance, we can subdivide chemistry into:

- Analytic chemistry
- Biochemistry
- Inorganic chemistry
- Materials chemistry
- Neurochemistry
- Nuclear chemistry
- Organic chemistry
- Physical chemistry
- Theoretical chemistry
- Agrochemistry
- Astrochemistry
- Atmospheric chemistry

Then we can assign people (we'll call them scientists and PhD candidates) to research each area or thin slice.

So instead of looking at how all areas of life might fit together with a focus on wisdom, the modern PhD candidate is going to focus enormous energy on a small slice of knowledge and produce a dissertation like the *Stereochemistry of the Vicinal Hydride Shift* (McRowe 1966).

The idea is that given enough time, dedication, diligence, scientists and PhD candidates, we can simply collect all the information that exists. Then we'll have all-knowledge.

We'll collect all that information and publish it in the Modern Paradigm's book of all knowledge—the *encyclopedia*. Scripture, the book of wisdom, is replaced by the encyclopedia, the book of knowledge and information.

While the Wisdom Paradigm uses *formation* to develop both knowledge and character in young people, the Modern Paradigm uses a different method—*education*—to focus almost exclusively on developing the intellect and knowledge.

Research in the Wisdom Paradigm is focused on helping us gain knowledge and wisdom, and become good. In the Wisdom Paradigm, it is understood that research topics or research methods that lead us away from wisdom and goodness should not be pursued.

Research in the Modern Paradigm contains no such overall restriction. Indeed, the Modern Paradigm's approach to knowledge contains a strong predisposition for researchers to study and learn as much as they can no matter where it leads—all in the name of collecting information. The lack of fundamental restrictions on the pursuit of research also applies to science and technology. The only significant restrictions to the pursuit of research, science or technology are the individual researcher's/scientist's morality and the social conventions of the time.

In the Modern Paradigm, knowledge, science and technology do not exist to help us become good, but for their own sake.

HISTORY

For Christians, history is the story of God working out humanity's salvation through a succession of covenants between God and humanity. The highlight of all this is the final covenant God established with humanity by sending his Son to die on the cross for the sins of all. The culmination of history will come when Christ returns during His Second Coming and the Final Judgment.

For the Modern Paradigm, history is not the story of God working in the world, but generally the story of humanity's development of science and technology. *Progress* is a term generally referring to *technological progress*. Our schools don't talk about history in terms of the Patriarchs of Israel, but they do teach kids about the Stone, Bronze, Iron and Industrial ages—all references to the technology of the people of the time.

MEASURE OF SUCCESS

In the Wisdom Paradigm, the measure of success is *honor*. Are you a good person who possesses the qualities of character worthy of honor? To what extent do you embody virtues like love, honesty, justice, wisdom, courage and integrity? The successful person is one who is honorable and good, and therefore achieves his purpose in life—Happiness.

While that sounds nice, we know that in the Modern Paradigm anything having to do with Happiness or purpose belongs in the private side of life. It's personal. That means the *measure of success* is properly a private or personal issue. You may well have a measure of success according to how you understand life, purpose or faith that is different than mine.

All that said, people in the Modern Paradigm will naturally desire to measure success in some way in public life. Because they are discussing success in public life, the more quantifiable the measure is, the easier it is to talk about it. The most obvious measures of success in public life are wealth, power and fame. They are easy to measure and easy to talk about, and they are consistent with the most visible and discussed motivation in the Modern Paradigm: money.

WORK

In the Wisdom Paradigm, work is fully integrated with the rest of your life, part of the seamless opportunity you have to practice and develop virtues to become good and achieve Happiness. Your work product is understood to be connected to you as *your product* and a reflection of who you are.

> American business theory is firmly based in the Modern Paradigm and understands all human relationships as contractual

With the Modern Paradigm's division of life into public and private spheres, all that changes. Work is obviously in the public part of life and normally effectively divorced from our fulfillment and Happiness.

In the Modern Paradigm, we talk less about our work and more about our *job*. Our job isn't for fulfillment, but to earn enough money to make a living. Hopefully, we save enough money so that we can retire from our job and do something in life that we find truly fulfilling. The work product is rarely connected to the worker and is not understood to be his product, but the product of the employer.

It is not impossible to find one's job fulfilling, but fulfillment in a job is considered an extraordinary benefit, not a fundamental part of work.

Contemporary American business theory is firmly based in the Modern Paradigm and understands human relationships as fundamentally contractual, not covenant. Most of us have had jobs where we've been heavily discouraged from ever mixing the personal and the public. Our jobs aren't supposed to be fulfilling or contribute to Happiness.

COSMOS: UNIVERSE VS. CREATION

In the Christian understanding of the Wisdom Paradigm, Humanity is at the center of God's Creation. By *center* we mean that Humanity is, at a minimum, at the metaphorical center of Creation, for Humanity is the purpose of Creation.

When the Modern Paradigm rejects purpose and faith as part of the public discourse, it necessarily removes the focus on Humanity (the purpose) from the discourse as well. Since we can no longer talk about the purpose—the *why*—of Creation, we are left only with the *what* and the *how* that reason and science can consider.

That means our entire view of the cosmos changes—at least in public discourse. We no longer talk about *Creation* (which implies purpose), but talk about the *universe.* We go from *Humanity is special because it is the purpose of Creation* to a view that *homo sapiens* is just one of many species competing and living on planet Earth, which is one of hundreds of billions of spheres on the edge of our galaxy, itself one of hundreds of billions of galaxies in the universe.

It is a switch from "God created all of this because He loves us" to "humanity is just another species on an insignificant speck of dust in an insignificant corner of the vast universe."

It is a completely different way of understanding the nature of reality and a completely different answer to the age-old question, "Where do I fit in the cosmos?" The new answer has an enormous impact on how we think and live.

WHAT ARE RULES FOR?

Rules in the Modern Paradigm function much as rules do in the Wisdom Paradigm. Rules help us become better at things faster than if we tried to figure them out on our own.

LEADERSHIP

Leadership in the Modern Paradigm is different than leadership in the Wisdom Paradigm because the understanding of human nature and motivation, the nature of human relationships and community, and goals are different.

In the Wisdom Paradigm, leadership is fully integrated through your work, family and life because all of them come together as seamless opportunities for you to practice the virtues, become good and pursue Happiness. Whether you are the leader or the follower, leadership in the Wisdom Paradigm focuses on developing virtues, becoming good, and achieving Happiness. Improved individual and team performance flows from that structure.

In the Modern Paradigm, the rejection of purpose, the separation of the private from the public, and the understanding of human relationships as contractual, changes everything. Leadership in the workplace is separated from the development of virtues in life. Workplace leadership becomes focused almost solely on achieving workplace goals with little or no regard for the impact on private life, fulfillment or Happiness.

Because all relationships are understood to be contractual, modern leaders tend to treat subordinates as a means to an end rather than as an end in themselves. Employees tend to be treated as objects, cogs in the machine, rather than as people. In the Modern Paradigm, companies have human resources offices because people are understood as just another commodity or resource in the corporation.

In the Wisdom Paradigm, all leadership is basically the same because all organizations, communities and teams have the same purpose—to become good and achieve Happiness. Singularity of purpose means singularity of motivation and singularity of leadership.

In the Modern Paradigm, all teams and organizations have their own different purposes. That means that motivation and leadership will be different because people are motivated to participate in teams and organizations by different things. Most people take jobs for the money. Some people may join the military for the money, but most do it to develop themselves with honor through service to their nation. Those who work in non-profits often forego higher salaries for the sense of fulfillment that comes with providing non-profit services. Different purposes mean different motivations and different leadership. What works leading a business might be disastrous if applied in leadership of a non-profit.

MODERN WRAP UP

The religious wars and deep suffering in 16th and 17th century Europe caused philosophers to attempt to reconstruct how people understood and explained all areas of life. They dropped faith/purpose to eliminate what they believed to be a core cause of the war and suffering.

Redefining life in terms of reason and empiricism caused a separation of life into two areas. One area, public life, is easily measurable and quantifiable by reason. The second area, personal life, contains all those things like faith, love, fulfillment and feelings that aren't easily measurable. We are supposed to keep our private life separate from our public life.

The Modern Paradigm isn't a framework that helps people understand how they achieve Happiness. It is an arrangement that allows people of different religions to live together without killing each other. Except for churches, people and communities generally no longer pursue wisdom, goodness and Happiness together, but only come together in contractual relationships where the self-interest of the individual often conflicts with the self-interest of the community or team.

Because faith/purpose has been eliminated and reason likes the measurable, money becomes the most common motivation and measure of success in public life.

Work is separated from purpose, Happiness and the person, and becomes a *job* focused on earning money.

We no longer pursue *wisdom* to achieve Happiness; we pursue *knowledge and information* either for technological application, the prestige of the researcher, or for its own sake.

MODERN AFTERMATH

Given the suffering and religious wars, eliminating faith/purpose and depending on reason and quantifiable sense data (empiricism) seemed like a reasonable thing to do. It seemed to eliminate what may appear to be the more subjective elements (faith) of the Wisdom Paradigm and to establish the Modern Paradigm on a solid foundation of objectivity.

But there is a price to pay. A very big price.

Going back to our analogy of the generations-long journey from New York to San Diego, it is a fact that southwest is the right direction to travel because that is the only direction that will get us to our destination, San Diego. It is also a fact that traveling in any other direction is wrong because it won't get us to San Diego. In the same way, in the Wisdom Paradigm, honesty, justice and courage are objectively right and true because they help us get to our destination of Happiness.

The Modern Paradigm removes the purpose—the destination—of our journey. Nevertheless, even with our purpose/destination removed, we continue to travel southwest and we continue to practice honesty, justice and courage. We do this because, deep down inside, it seems self-evident that southwest is the right direction and that honesty, justice and courage are right behaviors even if we can't fully explain why.

All we need is a new justification, based in reason alone, to travel southwest and believe in honesty, justice and courage.

But that turns out to be an enormous problem and, eventually, a fatal flaw.

Throughout the 18th and 19th centuries, the moral philosophers like Kant and Mill try to reestablish behaviors like honesty, justice, wisdom and courage as factually and objectively true based on reason alone. To make a long story short, Nietzsche and other philosophers of the late 19th century argue convincingly that those attempts failed.

According to these new philosophers, the fact that Modern attempts to justify these behaviors as factually true failed was an indication that these behaviors had never really been factually right or true in the first place. They essentially argued that morality really is *subjective*, a matter of personal opinion. These new philosophers replaced the *virtues*—the idea that morality is factually and objectively true—with *values*—the idea that all moral beliefs are subjective or personal opinion.

Honesty is not factually right or correct; many people simply *like* honesty. Honesty isn't true; people just put a lot of *value* on honesty.

In a world of values, there is nothing objectively better or more true about honesty than dishonesty. People just prefer, or value, one more than the other.

You might value honesty and I might value dishonesty and neither one of these values is better than the other. You like vanilla ice cream. I like chocolate. It would be weird to claim that chocolate is "right" and vanilla is "wrong"; they are just matters of taste.

So, these philosophers argue, there is no objectively true or right reason to travel southwest. There is nothing objectively better or more true about that direction than there is about any other direction.

Without a destination, the direction you take is subjective, simply a matter of personal opinion or taste. Any direction is just as good as any other direction. What Hume and the modern philosophers argued is that reason can only provide a direction; it can never provide the destination itself.

Without a destination, any direction or road will get you there. Without purpose in life, any behavior will get you there.

These new philosophers argue that we haven't been traveling southwest because it is factually right, but because that is what we have been trained to do by our parents, churches, schools, media, culture, etc. It is what we have been trained to do by those who are powerful in our society.

From a practical perspective, if anyone tries to travel in a different direction, the rest of the community will put enormous social pressure on that person and force him to travel southwest. The community will do that because anyone traveling any other direction is disruptive and the community doesn't like that.

No Purpose—No Destination

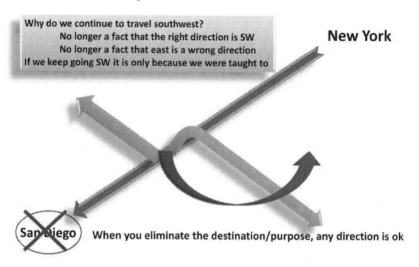

Why do we continue to travel southwest?
No longer a fact that the right direction is SW
No longer a fact that east is a wrong direction
If we keep going SW it is only because we were taught to

New York

San Diego

When you eliminate the destination/purpose, any direction is ok

But over time, more and more people will attempt to travel in other directions. They will argue more forcefully that reason doesn't give us any compelling justification why southwest is right. They will argue that attempts by society to get them to travel "society's direction" are unjust oppression.

For isn't it a matter of personal freedom that I be allowed to choose my own direction in life? Who are you to tell me what I can or can't do with my life? Who are you to tell me that honesty, justice or courage is right and whatever I value different is wrong? Who are you to force your definition of love on me?

Why are you being so judgmental?

The Modern Paradigm eliminates *purpose*, the destination of our lives, as a matter of Truth and public discussion to try to get past conflicts of faith and enable us all to live together without killing each other.

Paradoxically, when the Modern Paradigm eliminates *purpose* from the paradigm to better seek objective Truth, the Modern Paradigm inevitably degenerates into subjectivism. There are no facts, just opinions. Everything is in the eye of the beholder.

The Modern Paradigm inevitably degenerates into the Postmodern Paradigm

The Postmodern Paradigm

In many ways, the 20th century can be understood as the century in which postmodern thinking challenged and undermined thinking about the Truth in every dimension of our culture and society from politics, history, ethics and education to art, music and theology.

The Wisdom and Modern paradigms do not have a problem questioning what is understood as truth today so long as it is an attempt to get to a better and deeper understanding of the Truth.

The postmodern questioning of what is understood to be the truth today is very different. The postmodern questioning is not an attempt to get at a deeper Truth, but is a challenge to the notion that there is any Truth at all.

> The Postmodern Paradigm is best characterized by its subjectivism. There is no objective "Truth", just personal "truths", opinions, preferences, matters of taste and values

And so, from the Modern Paradigm we inevitably arrive at the Postmodern Paradigm, a view of life in which there is no Truth (with a capital "T") and no objective morality. There are no objective yardsticks by which we can measure anything. Everything is measured, everything receives its value, from you. In the Postmodern Paradigm, everything is subjective even if we try to pretend otherwise. The Postmodern Paradigm is best-characterized by its subjectivism.[5]

For example, if I tell you that people who like chocolate ice cream are *right* and those that like vanilla ice cream are *wrong*, you are likely to tell me that this is a poor way to think of ice cream flavors because neither one is objectively or factually right or wrong. You would likely

---

[5] It is important to note that, like the Wisdom and Modern Paradigms, the Postmodern Paradigm isn't a single orthodox viewpoint, but a collection of varying viewpoints that share common postmodern characteristics.

say that talking about chocolate and vanilla ice cream is a matter of personal preference, not objective Truth. Preference of one over the other is nothing more than a matter of personal taste. A value judgment.

But if I tell you that there is nothing wrong with killing people for pleasure, you are likely to respond that murder (unjustified homicide) is wrong. And you will likely mean *murder is wrong* in a different way than we used *wrong* with regards to ice cream. Most people think that *murder is wrong* is true in some deeper, objective, factual sense as in "It is a fact that murder is wrong".

But in the Postmodern Paradigm, the statements that *vanilla ice cream is wrong* and *murder is wrong* are the same thing. Neither is a statement of objective Truth or fact. Both are really statements of personal preference. They are *value* statements.

> **It is important to remember that postmodern subjectivism is the inevitable price of dropping the idea of purpose from our understanding of life.**

In the Postmodern Paradigm, saying that something is *wrong* is not saying anything about whether it is True or a fact or not; it is simply using a term ("wrong") that means the same thing as *like* or *prefer* or *feel*, but carries more persuasive or rhetorical weight.

It is important to remember that this subjectivism is the inevitable price of dropping the idea of *purpose* from our understanding of life.

In the Wisdom Paradigm, honesty is objectively true and right because it is a fact that practicing honesty helps us achieve our purpose—arrive at our destination—of becoming good and achieving Happiness.

The Modern Paradigm drops the idea of purpose, but still attempts to justify honesty through reason alone.

When that modern attempt fails, we are left with the postmodern realization that there is nothing objectively true about honesty.

When we drop purpose, we lose the ability to claim that any behavior is objectively right or wrong. In the postmodern way of thinking, murder isn't objectively any worse or better than giving someone a hug.

Those who embrace the Wisdom Paradigm argue that the fact that dropping *purpose* from understanding life leads to such obviously horrifying results shows that dropping purpose was a big mistake.

Those who embrace the postmodern view of life argue that we may not want to acknowledge that life is fundamentally subjective, and it may be uncomfortable and terrible, but they argue that this is the way life really is. This is the reality.

Though we may pretend otherwise and though we may want something different, there *really is no purpose*. There really is no right and wrong. There is no objective Truth. No objective Beauty. No deeper meaning. It's a horrifying realization, but that's just the way the universe is.

Indeed, the postmodern advocates argue that accepting this understanding of reality requires a special kind of courage that few people possess. The vast majority of people simply don't have the courage to acknowledge this postmodern reality and prefer to live in an illusory world where they can believe in meaning and Truth.

HUMAN NATURE CAN CHANGE

The Wisdom Paradigm regards human nature as essentially the same across cultures and throughout history. That's why today we can read and share experiences of love, betrayal and courage across the ages in Shakespeare, Scripture and the Epic of Gilgamesh.

In contrast, the Postmodern Paradigm argues that human nature is not constant or the same.

Instead, we are totally shaped by many factors in life including our parents and families, schools, ethnicity, religion, government, television and the media. These factors are ingrained so deeply in our lives that we aren't even aware of them. These factors are brought together, under the influence of our parents, schools, churches, government and media, to "construct" our understanding of life, reality and ourselves.

Depending on when and where you are raised, who raises you, your ethnic background, and your culture, schools and churches, your *construct*—your understanding of life—will be different from those of people from different backgrounds.

> There is no "real reality", but only *constructs* of reality taught to us by our parents, schools, churches, media, etc.

So there's no "real reality" out there that we can come to know if we just figure it out. Instead, there are a bunch of competing, subjective *constructs,* or understandings of reality, that dominate our lives.

These constructs may include a male-dominated patriarchal construct handed down through time that tells us that men should be in charge of families and business, and that women should be preparing food, raising kids and keeping the house clean.

Another construct may be that *marriage* can only be between a man and woman, not between a woman and woman or man and man, or even between three women and two men.

Another construct may be that the species homo sapiens is somehow better or should be privileged compared to other species on our planet.

Still another construct is that there is such a thing as objective Truth, and we all have a common purpose in life: to seek goodness and Happiness.

Those who embrace the Postmodern Paradigm argue that the Wisdom Paradigm is nothing more than a construct handed down to us from previous generations through our parents, churches and schools. There is nothing better or more true about the Wisdom Paradigm/construct than other constructs.

Indeed, many postmodern advocates argue that the Wisdom construct is worse because it pretends to be objectively true when it is not.

So, while it may appear that we all have the same human nature, the apparent commonality is really the result of our parents, schools, governments, etc. teaching us the same things and infusing in us the same beliefs and constructs over time—not that we really have the same nature.

The postmodern argument is that none of these constructs are objectively true or real, but simply our own created understandings. Change the outside factors, and we change the constructs and nature of the people.

LIFE IS ABOUT CHOOSING YOUR OWN DESTINATION FOR YOUR OWN REASONS

In the Postmodern Paradigm, the bad news is that in most ways we are the product of outside factors in our lives: of our parents, churches, schools, etc. They shape us and our construct of life so deeply and fundamentally that it is impossible to fully escape them.

Nevertheless, despite all these outside factors that so deeply shape us, we may be able to achieve some freedom. Certainly, the more these outside factors impact our construct of life, the less we can choose freely. But what we can do is try to understand how all these outside factors impact us, be aware of how they shape our construct, and then try to make free, informed choices among them.

Since there is no purpose or destination that all humans share due to a common human nature, the most you can make out of life is to attempt to choose your own purpose—your own destination—for your own reasons.

Since there is no objective right or wrong, and no objective Truth, no purpose or destination chosen is any better than any other. The purpose you choose is only better than the others because it is *your* choice. So in many ways, in the Postmodern Paradigm, life is about "deconstructing" the constructs that society has forced upon you, thereby becoming free to choose your own way for yourself.

What is the meaning of life? About all that can be said in the Postmodern Paradigm is that there is no true point or meaning in life, but you are free to choose your own meaning for whatever reason you want.

COMMUNITIES AND POWER

In the Postmodern Paradigm, the reality is that we all live in a variety of communities that include family, schools, ethnic and religious groups, clubs, neighborhoods and HOA's, and even nations. We've already talked about how, according to the Postmodern Paradigm, these communities shape your construct, your understanding of life.

When you live in a community, you must live with other people. In the Wisdom Paradigm, since all people are working to achieve the same thing—Happiness—and since all people believe that there is such a thing as objective Truth, one can expect that most people will be able to live together in general harmony because they are all focused on the same purpose.

When there are disagreements in the Wisdom Paradigm, they are solved by figuring out which side is closer to the Truth.

For instance, in a deep disagreement that might involve the courts, each side presents its best case to the judge and jury. The judge or jury decides which case is closer to the Truth (as expressed in the law) and makes a ruling in that side's favor.

In the Wisdom Paradigm, the objective Truth, however imperfectly known, is the objective yardstick against which issues are measured and decided. The process is not always perfect and is sometimes corrupted, but at least there is a process with a purpose and an objective measure.

Things are very different in the Postmodern Paradigm. Because each person gets to create his own purpose for himself and because those self-established purposes can be anything from love to hate, from empowerment to oppression, there is a high likelihood of conflict. So how are those conflicts resolved?

> There is no right and wrong, no good or bad, just *power*. Resolution of conflicts comes down to who has more power.

Since there is no objective Truth, no objective yardstick against which conflicts can be measured, resolution of conflict all comes down to who has more *power*. Those with more power are going to prevail over those with less power. There is no right and wrong, no good or bad, just *power*.

Power can be expressed or exercised in a wide variety of ways. It can be something as obvious and crude as making a threat or using violence. It can be something as subtle and nuanced as using schools to teach toddlers how you want them to think. Power is exercised through churches, politics, advertising, news coverage (or lack of it), fashion, media and internet search results. Power is exercised by what questions are asked and not asked, and how those questions are structured to emphasize certain viewpoints and deemphasize others.

In the Postmodern Paradigm, courts are no longer about two sides presenting their case to see which is closer to the Truth, but become just another way to exercise power by persuading judge or jury to choose your side. Those with more money and better rhetoric—more power—often prevail over those with less.

While *marriage and family* may have the appearance of being about love (which is simply a chemical reaction in the brain), *marriage and family* are little more than a camouflaged power relationship between people. The husband exercises power over the wife. Parents exercise power over how their children think and develop.

In the Postmodern Paradigm, same gender relationships may be better than mixed gender relationships because male-male and female-female relationships reduce the inherent power differential that exists in male-female relationship constructs.

Imagine that a person goes into a school and massacres 50 children. In the Postmodern Paradigm, while many people might not like the massacre, there is nothing objectively wrong with the massacre. When the police capture the killer and the state puts him on trial, they don't do so because they are objectively right and the killer wrong. They do so because they are exercising power over the killer just as the killer exercised power over the children he murdered.

The police and the state may talk a lot about how the massacre was "unjust" or "evil", but (in the Postmodern Paradigm) that is just rhetoric to get people riled up. That rhetoric hides the reality that there is no objective evil or justice.

With no Truth, it's about power in every dimension of life. If you are a cunning leader, you get control of the schools, the media, the churches and other influential aspects of life, and use them to control the constructs of the mass population. If you can achieve that, then you don't need to use violence or the threat of violence to keep control. You keep the masses under control by convincing them, perhaps through religious beliefs, education and media campaigns, that it really is "wrong" and "bad" to do (*insert undesired belief or behavior*) and "right" and "good" to do (*insert desired belief or behavior*).

As the ruler, you understand that the people really don't want to understand the nature of reality. They don't want to know that there is no purpose or meaning. It is too terrible and depressing. They would rather live under the illusion that there is meaning and will embrace the leader that cultivates that illusion.

The bottom line in the Postmodern Paradigm: It is all about power. The Postmodern Paradigm calls us to understand life in terms of who has power, who doesn't have power, and how power is exercised by the powerful over the weak.

This is where we get the term *empower*. Some people and groups have power. Others do not have power. Some people want to empower those who don't have power by helping them recognize how power is being exercised over them. They can then use education, activism and political avenues to gain power themselves. There is nothing objectively better about empowering others than using power to dominate others, though empowering others might sound good or have an emotional appeal for some.

TRUTH AND BEAUTY

There is no absolute or objective Truth or Beauty in the Postmodern Paradigm, only subjective truth and beauty. The postmodern approach to truth and beauty is best captured by the statement we have all heard: *beauty is in the eye of the beholder.* It means that there is no such thing as *Beauty* "out there" with an independent, objective existence. Beauty only exists in the mind of the person viewing.

There is no real beauty inherent in the Grand Canyon. The "beauty" of the Grand Canyon is something that exists only in our minds. Beauty is a value that we put on the Grand Canyon; it is not a quality the canyon possesses on its own. In the Postmodern Paradigm, the same is true of truth and art. If an elephant picks up a brush full of paint and puts it on a canvas, whether it is "art" or not depends on how *you* want to value it.

In the Wisdom Paradigm, art is about capturing Beauty. In the Postmodern Paradigm where there is no Beauty, art is about the self-expression and self-becoming of the artist. Art provides the postmodern artist a way to become what he does and clearly show others that he chooses his own way in life for his own reasons.

Immersing a Christian crucifix in a jar of urine is meant to shock people and demonstrate decisively that the "artist" is not bound by the constructs of Christianity or the community. Insulting Christianity and the sensibilities of the community is a way to assert freedom from other people's contemporary constructs.

This radical subjectivity applies to "truths" we take for granted, like physical health.

Most of us accept without thinking that it is a Truth that we should be physically healthy, including maintaining an appropriate weight.

In contrast, those embracing the Postmodern Paradigm would properly understand that choosing to be overweight, trim or anorexic is neither right nor wrong. They are simply different lifestyle choices.

> *"Healthy"* is nothing more than a construct foisted upon people to get them to live according to a particular, desired body image.

"Healthy" is a powerful term that has the illusion of objective Truth (that there is such a Truth as *health*) that others use to exercise power over you—and sell you things like diet plans and health club memberships. *Healthy* is nothing more than a construct foisted on people to get them to live according to a particular body image. This type of postmodern thinking can be seen on websites that advocate anorexia as a viable lifestyle choice. Go to the Internet and search for "pro-ana" or "thinspiration" or "thinspo".

MORALITY

When the Modern Paradigm dropped the concept of *purpose* from its understanding of life, it needed to develop a new justification for objective morality based on reason alone. Over time, as the postmodern philosophers pointed out, the attempt to provide that new justification for objective morality failed. When you eliminate the destination, all roads are the same. When you eliminate purpose, anything goes.

When the modern philosophers reject purpose, morality degenerates from the idea that there are moral facts—the *virtues* like honesty, courage and justice—to the idea that morality is nothing more than personal opinion, or values. We call this *moral subjectivism*[6].

In the Postmodern Paradigm, there is nothing truly right or wrong in any objective moral sense. Behaviors aren't right or wrong in themselves; they only have the value that you assign to them.

Some postmodern advocates, moral nihilists, argue that if all morality is subjective, then morality really doesn't exist in any meaningful way.

DEVELOPING YOUNG PEOPLE

In the Wisdom Paradigm, *formation* is the process used to develop knowledge, character and wisdom in young people. In the Modern Paradigm, *education* is the process used to emphasize intellectual/academic development in young people. In both formation and education, pursuit of objective, true knowledge is an important goal.

In contrast to formation and education, the Postmodern Paradigm uses *indoctrination* to shape the constructs of young people in whatever way those in power desire. School is not about helping young people pursue Truth or knowledge, but to get young people to think the way you want them to.

MOTIVATION

In the Wisdom Paradigm, we know that the desire for Happiness is the motivation to practice the virtues and become good. In the Modern Paradigm, we talk about being motivated—at least in our public lives—by money or wealth.

In the Postmodern Paradigm, motivation is all about the purpose a person creates for himself and the desire he has to achieve it.

One person may be strongly motivated to help the poor. Another person may engage greed and be motivated to become rich. A third

---

[6] *Objective morality* is the idea that there are moral facts (virtues). *Moral relativism* is the idea that there is no objective morality, but that morality is relative to a culture and time period. *Moral subjectivism* is the idea that there is no objective morality, but that morality is a matter of individual or personal opinion.

person may be strongly motivated to develop sexual relationships with children because he finds it pleasurable. A fourth person may strongly desire to uncover and become aware of all the factors that influence their construct of life, feeling that this knowledge will give them a sense of freedom from the oppression of that construct.

In the Postmodern Paradigm, none of these goals is any better or worse than the others. They are simply different goals or values. Motivation is simply a discussion about the depth of an individual person's desire to achieve their self-defined goal.

The big question is this: Do you have the motivation and courage to choose what you believe for your own reasons—no matter what others say or do—and fully pursue your choice? When your purpose conflicts with others, what price are you willing to pay to achieve your goal? Do you have the courage to crush those in your way to achieve your desire? Are you brave enough to confront the powerful to achieve your self-selected purpose?

RULES AND FREEDOM

In the Wisdom and Modern Paradigms, *rules* guide us and help us get better at things faster than we would trying to figure them out on our own. As we all travel the road to becoming good, we need the *freedom* to make and learn from mistakes. To become good, we must be free to choose Truth because embracing Truth under coercion is to not really embrace Truth at all.

Rules and freedom play a very different role in the Postmodern Paradigm.

In the Postmodern Paradigm, all you have is your own self-created sense of purpose, your own self-selected destination and meaning. All that you have in life that might have dignity is the opportunity to dig out from beneath the construct you have been given by your parents and society, and gain some understanding of the factors that dominate your understanding of life.

Understanding those factors gives you the freedom to accept or reject those factors that dominate your life. It is the freedom to reject the construct that was imposed upon you, so you can embrace something of your own choice.

In a world in which our constructs are imposed upon us by others, where everything is based on power, only freedom might bring dignity. The more freely you choose your own destination for your own reasons—and not because someone else told you so or because you were duped by ignorance of the construct—the more dignity you have.

Of course, that assumes that you value dignity.

Personal freedom to choose your own destination for your own reasons is what many value most.

Now we can understand *rules* in the Postmodern Paradigm. Rules are generally bad. When you follow other people's rules, you are surrendering yourself to their purpose, not your own. You are listening to them tell you what to do. You are giving them control. Rules are ways that others exercise their power over you.

That is why *rules are made to be broken*. The most visible way to demonstrate to everyone that you have the courage to choose your own destination for your own reasons is by breaking the rules established by others to control you. It's like choosing the red pill and freeing yourself from the Matrix. Rules are the blue pill.

When you break the rules, you prove that the rules of others don't apply to you. You demonstrate courage by choosing your own rules for your own reasons. You empower yourself by showing them that you are willing to pay the price for your own purpose.

> When you follow other people's rules, you let them exercise their power over you.
>
> *Rules are made to be broken* demonstrating your freedom from their power and your freedom to choose your own way for your own reasons.

In the same way, *freedom* is understood very differently. In the Postmodern Paradigm, freedom is a *radical freedom* to choose your own purpose, your own meaning, for your own reasons. It is freedom to reject becoming good as just another construct imposed on you by others. Freedom to choose to become whatever you want. Freedom to pursue whatever you desire in whatever way you desire. But that also means that establishing your own freedom may often require breaking the formal and informal rules established by others.

WORK

In the Wisdom Paradigm, our work is an opportunity for us to practice all sorts of virtues that help us become good. Work is essential to help make you who you are.

In contrast, the Modern Paradigm understands work to be more of a *job* that enables you to make a living. Your job is part of your public life kept separate from your private life.

Like the Wisdom Paradigm, the Postmodern Paradigm recognizes that work is vital in making you who you are, but with a big twist. Instead of work providing you an opportunity to become good, the Postmodern Paradigm sees work, like art, as an opportunity for you to express yourself in whatever way you want, to *become* whatever you want—especially by breaking other people's rules.

MEASURE OF SUCCESS

Since everything is subjective in the Postmodern Paradigm, the only real measure of success is yourself. Did you accomplish your self-selected purpose or desire?

If your desire was to help the poor, did you accomplish that?

If your desire was to become rich, did you accomplish that?

If your desire was to hurt people, did you accomplish that?

If respect is one of your goals, then success could be measured by the respect earned for your tenacity in pursuing your self-selected purpose. What price are you willing to pay to achieve your goal? What rules are you willing to break, and who are you willing to hurt and how much? How much pain are you willing to endure from those who have power and oppose you?

Or perhaps *success* itself is just another construct imposed upon us by society.

LEADERSHIP

Postmodern leadership means fully understanding that all relationships are really power relationships. Your goal as a postmodern leader is to use your power—whether it is persuasive, manipulative, influential, contractual, "love" or the threat or use of violence—to get others to do what you wish them to do.

In the Postmodern Paradigm, leadership is about getting other people to help you achieve your goals using whatever techniques work to achieve your goals. Your ends justify whatever means you desire.

Obviously, the best leadership technique to use depends a lot on the people being led, the goal and the situation.

> An effective postmodern leader knows there is no "moral" difference between using positive encouragement or torture to motivate a follower. He does not let hindrances like conscience, scruples or compassion weaken his resolve to accomplish his goal.

Nevertheless, an effective postmodern leader understands that there is no good or evil, and no purpose in life, and courageously embraces that understanding. The leader knows that there are no moral differences between using positive encouragement and threatening death in motivating a follower to accomplish the leader's goals. He does not let hindrances like conscience, scruples or compassion weaken his resolve to accomplish his goal.

The most skillful postmodern leader keeps the people deceived for their own benefit. He knows that they do not want the burden of realizing that life really has no morality, no meaning and no purpose. Perhaps his greatest gift to those he controls is keeping them safe from the horror of reality.

POSTMODERN WRAP UP

Those who consciously embrace the Postmodern Paradigm understand it simply as the recognition and acceptance that everything really is subjective. There are no moral facts, and there really is no objective Truth or Beauty, and no real meaning or purpose in life. They believe that the understanding of life that we have been taught is not true in any deeper sense, but is just a *constructed* understanding of life in which we have been indoctrinated by our parents, society, schools, religion, media, etc.

With no Truth or objective purpose against which we can measure things, we are left to admit that there is no right or wrong in life. Our relationships and potential conflicts with others are not settled by measuring them against a deeper Truth, but by the exercise of power.

With no overall purpose in life that applies to all humans, we are left to invent our own meaning for life. The only real dignity is to choose our own purpose for our own reasons—not because society told us to. No purpose is objectively better or worse than any other purpose. Rules are made to be broken because it is in the in breaking of rules that we prove to all that we freely choose our own destiny for our own reasons.

We develop our youth not through formation or education, but through *indoctrination*.

Of course, the vast majority of people don't want to know any of this. They embrace the convenient bits and pieces of postmodern thinking that give them the freedom to do whatever they want without thinking about what the deeper, darker implications are. The vast majority of the people would prefer to stay comfortable in their current construct of life and remain plugged into the matrix.

It requires an enormous amount of strength and courage to embrace the Postmodern Paradigm and face the vast meaningless universe head-on.

A Few Important Things

Everyone experiences life in terms of these paradigms. These paradigms are literally how we all see, understand and make sense of the world. They are the sources of the narratives and metaphors that we encounter throughout our day, every day of our lives. They tell us who we are, what life is about, and what our relationships with others are.

The paradigms provide the basic understanding one needs to answer the most fundamental questions in life. The paradigms allow you to take your everyday experiences and transform them from a meaningless collection of separate experiences into a set of meaningful, related experiences that are the story of you and your life. Without a paradigm, people cannot understand or function in life, and experience deep angst and psychological problems.

Besides fully understanding each of these paradigms and the story behind them, there are a few very important things to remember:

1. The Modern Paradigm inevitably degenerates into the Postmodern Paradigm
2. Our leadership mess is the result of conflicting paradigms operating in our society
3. Despite our notions of tolerance, it is impossible for the Wisdom and Postmodern paradigms to co-exist

The Modern Paradigm inevitably degenerates into the Postmodern Paradigm

The Wisdom Paradigm used *purpose* + *reason* as the foundation for pursuing knowledge and Truth. The Modern Paradigm dropped *purpose* from the foundation and sought to improve knowledge and objective Truth by depending on *reason* alone. As we have seen, when the Modern Paradigm drops the concept of *purpose*, it dramatically undermines the foundation for knowledge, morality, ethics and community, and begins the inevitable slide into Postmodern subjectivism. Without purpose—without a destination—any direction in life becomes ok.

So, while there are three paradigms when it comes to the story of the paradigms, as the story plays out there are only two paradigms in the end: the Wisdom and the Postmodern. The key to remember: *Once the Modern Paradigm eliminates purpose, it inevitably degenerates into the Postmodern Paradigm.*

Our leadership mess is the result of conflicting paradigms operating in our society and individual lives

On one level, within our society we have many people who think in terms of each of these paradigms. People born before 1950 are more likely to think primarily in terms of the Wisdom Paradigm with some elements of the Modern Paradigm. The younger the person, the more likely it is that the Postmodern Paradigm is highly influential in that person's understanding of life.

On another level, it is very common for individual people within our society to think in terms of the different paradigms in different parts of their lives without realizing that they are being fundamentally inconsistent.

A person may have a wisdom approach to raising his children, sports and physical fitness. He may take a modern approach in his work, understanding the purpose of business to be making money instead of becoming good.

He may embrace wisdom in understanding his family as a covenant relationship while taking a modern, contractual view of relationships at work.

He may take a postmodern approach to social and moral issues, believe that *beauty is in the eye of the beholder,* think of morality in terms of *values* instead of virtues, and fear ever being accused of being *judgmental.*

We are back to wearing a helmet and pads while shooting baskets with a small, white dimpled ball or teeing up the big orange ball to hit it with a club to a wide receiver on the fairway. We are back to playing the game to score the most points in some areas of our lives while playing a different game to score the least amount of points in other parts of our lives, and then wondering why our lives lack consistency.

We often embrace these different paradigms in different areas of our lives and then wonder why our lives seem fractured. If we pursue a wisdom approach in our home life and a modern approach in our business or professional life, then we're not going to grow in our relationships with others. Any progress made becoming good while embracing the Wisdom Paradigm's covenant relationship in our private-personal life will be undone by our treatment of people as objects in a modern contractual relationship in our public-work life.

We cannot make progress in shaping the character of the next generation when we tell our children that some things really are *objectively right* (like honesty) and *objectively wrong* (like the Holocaust) in accordance with *virtues* and the Wisdom Paradigm, while at the same teaching them in our schools that morality is nothing more than personal opinion, or subjective values, coming from the Postmodern Paradigm.

Either Wisdom *virtues* are True or Postmodern *values* are true, but it cannot be both. And when we try to live both at the same time, it is no wonder that we don't improve or make progress in leadership or our lives.

When we allow conflicting paradigms to operate in our society and lives, it cripples leadership, our trust and confidence in our leaders, and prevents us from making progress. Conflicting paradigms paralyze us, keeping us in the very dangerous status quo where we have enormous power but don't have the good, consistent leadership to wield it safely.

Despite our notions of tolerance, it is impossible for the Wisdom and Postmodern Paradigms to co-exist

We went into this a bit earlier in our text when we discussed the football-basketball-golf sports analogy, why they shared no common ground, and could not co-exist or tolerate each other. Let's go deeper.

The Wisdom and Postmodern Paradigms are mutually exclusive and cannot co-exist. Like matter and anti-matter, the existence of one by its very nature destroys the other. This can be a difficult thing for us to grasp. As Americans, our understanding of *tolerance* predisposes us to believe that groups with different beliefs can co-exist if they just work hard enough at it.

But the word *tolerance* has very different meanings in the Wisdom and Postmodern Paradigms.

It is possible for people of different belief systems that exist *within* the Wisdom or Modern paradigms to tolerate each other. Catholics, Protestants, Buddhists, Jews, Muslims and many other belief systems *within the Wisdom Paradigm* can coexist because they all share a similar understanding—common ground—that human nature is constant and human beings have a purpose. They may disagree about exactly what that human nature is and have different articulations of the purpose, but at least they share that fundamental understanding. While they have different understandings of what the Truth is and how people can arrive at it, they do share an understanding that there is Truth. They share the idea that certain behaviors—honesty, justice and courage—are objectively good and true. There is common ground upon which the different religions can find mutual understanding and tolerance.

In the Wisdom Paradigm, tolerance in many ways is the understanding that to develop wisdom, people need the freedom to be able to make, recover and learn from their mistakes. A person from one religion can tolerate what he perceives to be the mistaken ways of a person from another religion because he can understand that the other, while mistaken, is striving for the Truth. As long as everyone is pursuing Truth, it is possible to tolerate those pursuing the same goal but taking different paths.

But *tolerance* in the Postmodern Paradigm means something very different. In one sense, because of the overwhelming emphasis on subjectivity, the Postmodern Paradigm appears to tolerate anything and everything.

But there is a critical exception that makes it a lie. Because it is subjective, the Postmodern Paradigm cannot tolerate anything that says there are absolutes—like Truth. Belief in absolutes—by its very existence—attacks and denies the very foundation (subjectivism) of the Postmodern Paradigm.

In the end, the apparent tolerance of postmodernism is an illusion. If everyone is pursuing their own self-created purpose, then there will be inevitable conflicts. When those conflicts happen, the desires and directions of the more powerful will prevail over those of the less powerful. The desires of the less powerful will be effectively non-tolerated and eliminated.

Paradoxically, the postmodern concept of tolerance of everything is less tolerant than the wisdom understanding of tolerance. The postmodern freedom to do whatever you want means that the more powerful are free to use their power to force others to do what they wish.

Just as golf and football have fundamentally incompatible understandings of scoring and winning, the Wisdom and Postmodern Paradigms, at the very deepest levels, have fundamentally incompatible ways of understanding life.

> Tolerance is not possible between the Wisdom and Postmodern because there is no common ground.
> When there is nothing shared, community is not possible.

The one thing that unites all those in the Wisdom and Modern Paradigms—that search for Truth—is explicitly denied by the Postmodern Paradigm. The whole way one embracing wisdom understands and lives life actively negates the whole way the postmodernist understands and lives life at the most fundamental levels. The whole way the postmodernist lives life actively negates the whole way one embracing wisdom lives life at the most fundamental levels. As postmodernism grows, wisdom is destroyed, and vice-versa. They are literally cancers to each other.

There is no "both-and", tolerance or co-existence possible. When it is between the Wisdom and Postmodern Paradigms, it is "either-or".

The concept of *tolerance* (at least the wisdom concept of *tolerance*) implies that two different things in one community or society can co-exist or live together.

But because wisdom and the postmodern have no common ground, no shared understanding of life, they cannot be one community or society. They share nothing that unites them in any sense of community. Tolerance is not possible between wisdom and postmodern because community is not possible.

Remember, the Modern Paradigm inevitably degenerates into the Postmodern Paradigm. Despite our notions of tolerance, it is impossible for the Wisdom and Postmodern Paradigms to co-exist. Finally, the conflict between these paradigms prevents us from making any improvement or progress in leadership studies. To develop the next generation of leaders, we need to make a commitment to the right paradigm and move leadership forward.

Which Paradigm is Right?

We've taken an in-depth look at each of the paradigms. We know that we're down to considering two paradigms, Wisdom and the Postmodern, because the Modern Paradigm inevitably degenerates into the Postmodern Paradigm. We know that these paradigms cannot co-exist.

So which paradigm—Wisdom or Postmodern—is right?

The Wisdom Paradigm is right. This is true in several ways.

First, the Wisdom Paradigm provides us with the most powerful and highest performance people and teams. That means the Wisdom Paradigm is the right choice if we want the leadership understanding that maximizes performance in our economy, communities, families, government, non-profits, etc.

The Wisdom Paradigm produces people who are more deeply committed and motivated—and therefore will perform at higher levels—because they are motivated by fulfillment rather than just money. Teams based on the Wisdom covenant relationship are the highest performance teams because the covenant relationship has much deeper trust, is more stable and develops stronger bonds under pressure. People and teams in the Wisdom Paradigm will outperform similar people and teams living the Modern or Postmodern Paradigms.

Second, the fact that the Wisdom Paradigm yields the most powerful and highest performance people and teams is a powerful indication that the Wisdom Paradigm best matches, maximizes and fulfills human nature. It is an understanding that enables human nature to flourish by maximizing the most noble aspects and best qualities of being human: love, wisdom, honor, courage, integrity, etc.

Third, the Wisdom Paradigm is correct because we know that the Postmodern Paradigm is inherently contradictory. How so?

At its very core, we know that the Postmodern Paradigm is subjective with no objective Truth. The Postmodern Paradigm essentially asserts that:

There are absolutely no absolutes

While that logical contradiction clearly demonstrates that the Postmodern Paradigm is wrong in its understanding of the world, there are some who will acknowledge the logical contradiction but still hold firmly to the Postmodern Paradigm. They are too deeply invested in the Postmodern Paradigm as the way they understand reality for them to abandon it.

Indeed, those truly committed to the Postmodern Paradigm think that those embracing the Wisdom Paradigm are wrong. They think those who understand life in terms of the Wisdom Paradigm are wishful and deluded, creating a way of understanding reality that makes them feel good (don't we all want to believe in Truth, Beauty and Love?) rather than accepting the cold hard reality that there is no Truth, just personal truth and power.

Let's dig a little deeper into our first reason—that the Wisdom Paradigm is right and true because it provides us the most powerful and highest performance people and teams. Remember that the most powerful, highest performance teams are going to be founded upon high-trust relationships. As we discussed earlier, we will get the highest performance and generate the most power when we have *people and teams that we can trust to make good decisions in fast-paced, complex situations with minimal supervision.*

Let's contrast the understanding of human relationships in each paradigm and the trust levels each paradigm will generate. That will tell us a lot about the performance potential of each paradigm.

The Modern Paradigm understands human relationships to be contractual at their core. Remember the relationship between the company and the employee. It is in the company's best interest to get as much work as possible from the employee while paying the employee as little as possible. It is in the employee's best interest to get as much money as possible from the company while working as little as possible. The self-interest of the company and employee stand in direct opposition to and in conflict with each other. By its very nature, the contractual relationship at the core of the Modern Paradigm is low trust and unstable. The modern contractual relationship will shatter if you put much pressure on it. With low trust, the modern contractual relationship will only get you the commitment and performance you pay for.

In the Postmodern Paradigm, relationships may appear to be familial, contractual, legal, loving or even violent, but at their core, all relationships are based on *power*. Any appearances that a relationship may possess, like love, are not real. The relationship appearances are little more than a façade for the actual power relationship that lies underneath.

Do not underestimate or quickly dismiss the performance, effectiveness or power of teams bound through power relationships.

A clever postmodern leader may be able to create a very effective illusion—perhaps a compelling "cause", a "higher meaning" or even the illusion of love—that motivates people to make a deep commitment to the leader and team. Individual and team performance, at least in the short term, will match the commitment the illusion inspires.

Advocates of the Postmodern Paradigm understand religious fanatics as outstanding examples of a clever leader getting total commitment and high performance from followers by using a false religious motivation to exercise power over the followers. At some point, when the illusion collapses, the power and performance will collapse as well. But until that happens, the postmodern leader can get high power and performance.

Violence and fear can be a very effective postmodern motivator. If a postmodern leader puts a gun to your head, I bet he can scare you into a relatively high level of performance. Even more effective, if that leader can convince you that he will kill your entire family unless you accomplish the goals he sets, he can be confident—he can "trust"— that you will perform at very high levels out of fear. Using these kinds of techniques, the postmodern leader can produce higher-performance and more powerful people and teams than a modern leader.

But the postmodern approach to high-performance teams has a catch. You will perform for the leader so long as he can maintain the illusion that has captured your commitment or so long as you fear him. If he fools you into a deep commitment to him, his team and his "cause" by disguising his power relationship as something more inspiring (We're saving the planet!), when the illusion collapses he can count on a collapse of your commitment, motivation and performance. He can also expect to pay a heavy price for the deep resentment he causes in you for being fooled.

If a leader motivates your high performance through fear, he automatically creates within you a compelling motivation to destroy him if you ever get the chance. As leader, he must be on constant guard for those who might overthrow him when they find a weakness. If the leader is ever in extremis or his ability to generate fear is compromised, he can be confident that he will not be helped by others.

History has many examples where people and teams have performed at very high levels in power relationships while motivated by fear. Adolf Hitler, Joseph Stalin and Mao are three easy examples of people ruling through fear in Germany, the Soviet Union and China, respectively.

A good recent example is Saddam Hussein in Iraq. Hussein clearly ruled Iraq through fear. Multiple attempts to overthrow Hussein were unable to overcome the fear in subordinates that he would not only kill them and their families, but also massacre extended members of their tribe. It was only when it was clear that a US invasion and overthrow of Hussein was imminent—and that Hussein could not somehow return to power—that members of the Iraqi military and government renounced Hussein. Hussein's subordinates abandoned him quickly when it was clear that he would not be able to continue hurting them.

The Postmodern Paradigm is logically self-contradictory, provides lower-trust relationships based in *power*, and maintains that there is no Truth, Beauty, love, or moral right and wrong.

Pursued and explored, it inevitably leads to the dark, hopeless, depressing and nihilistic. Over time it denies all that makes us special or gives us inherent dignity as human beings.

Because everyone is pursuing their own self-defined goals for their own reasons, the Postmodern Paradigm is profoundly fragmentary and never provides common ground for unity.

In contrast, the covenant relationship in the Wisdom Paradigm is high-trust because the good of the individual and the good of the team are the same, and the relationship is focused on the fulfillment of all. People offer themselves for others because that offering and building trust helps each person become a better person, achieve fulfillment and Happiness.

The Wisdom Paradigm is right because it provides the foundation for the highest trust relationships, and the most powerful, and highest-performance people and teams. It integrates the "public and private" divisions of life, uniting them to focus everything on human fulfillment. It is logically consistent, and includes Truth, love, wisdom and objective morality. It provides the foundation for high-trust, high stability leadership emphasizing *wisdom* and integrating right knowledge (Truth) with right action (character).

Our nation and world possess enormous power and face tremendous challenges. We need the best leaders possible to ensure that our future, the future of our children and the future of our nation remain bright. We need wise leaders in our government, our business and economy, our military, and our families and local communities.

We can only achieve these things if we—as individuals and as society—make a full and deep commitment to the Wisdom Paradigm, eliminate modern and postmodern influences, move forward with a well-developed understanding of leadership, and form the next generation of good leaders we so deeply need.

The Culture War

In our media, we often hear reference to an ongoing "culture war" in America.

The culture war is real and very important, but despite the way it is often presented in the media, the conflict is not between liberals and conservatives, or Democrats and Republicans. The real culture war is a conflict between the Wisdom and Postmodern Paradigms, two mutually exclusive, incompatible and irreconcilable understandings of life.

To this point, we have been talking about the paradigms in a rather intellectual way. In the culture war, we encounter the conflict between the paradigms in a real-world, life-changing manner that directly impacts you, your family, your kids and our future. It can be very emotional because people's lives and families are often deeply invested and impacted by the ongoing conflict.

The unfolding culture war is having an enormous impact on the future of our nation. It is very important that we recognize and address the culture war for what it is, and resist the temptation to categorize the conflict as left or right, Republican or Democrat, liberal or conservative. These categorizations will only distract us from deeper and more important tensions between wisdom and postmodern ways of understanding life.

We have three choices in the culture war:
1. We can make a commitment to the Postmodern Paradigm
2. We can make a commitment to the Wisdom Paradigm
3. We can refuse to make a commitment, fail to develop the good leadership we need, continue to fragment as a nation, and risk destroying ourselves with our own power

POSTMODERN COMMITMENT

We could make a commitment to the Postmodern Paradigm, but we will be embracing a way of understanding and living life that is cynical, dark, hopeless and eventually nihilistic. It provides a less effective understanding of leadership that is based on power relationships and does not acknowledge any objective moral facts or obligation. It will give people the apparent freedom to pursue whatever they want but, underneath it all, limit people to only what the more powerful will allow them. Trust relationships are low and it does not maximize leadership or team performance.

REFUSE TO MAKE A COMMITMENT

If we refuse to make a commitment and let the current predicament continue, we will remain stuck in the current leadership crisis, unable to make real progress or develop the leaders we need to guide us into the future. There will be no common ground for discussion between proponents of each of the paradigms.

Postmodern thinking will continue to gain influence and our nation will continue to fall apart, fragmenting morally, culturally, socially and politically into many separate and conflicting groups. The conflict between the paradigms will intensify and our nation will become torn apart, increasingly polarized between those supporting each of the paradigms. There will be increasingly bitter and irresolvable battles over control of important, fundamental social institutions like government, the military, schools, media and the courts.

Refusing to make a commitment one way or the other is much like a person with a drug addiction refusing to make a real commitment to get treatment and reform his life. Ignoring the drug addiction doesn't make life any better for the addict, or his family or friends. Life will continue to get worse and worse. Ignoring the problem doesn't avoid the tough decision; it just puts it off to a future time when the addiction will be much more malignant, and the conflict and damage much deeper. Drug addicts who don't eventually reform die. So will our nation.

Refusing to make a commitment prolongs the conflict, fragmentation and destruction, fails to produce the next generation of leaders we can trust, and dramatically increases our risk of poor leadership making catastrophic decisions.

COMMITMENT TO THE WISDOM PARADIGM

The more quickly and decisively we make a commitment to the Wisdom Paradigm, the more quickly we can focus our efforts on ensuring that the next generation of leaders is the best it can be, and the faster we can reestablish common ground to build a nation that is stronger and more unified in all dimensions. We can implement Wisdom covenant leadership and make the educational, cultural and social alignments needed to maximize leadership development. It will give us and our children the best chance in our future and greatly diminish the threat of future leaders making catastrophic decisions.

A decisive commitment to the Wisdom Paradigm will enable us to develop the most powerful, effective and efficient leaders, people and teams. That dramatically improved leadership will enable us to develop and implement better solutions more effectively and efficiently across all aspects of our society including the economy, government, science, technology, education, health care and the environment. We will improve our ability to prevail amid global competition. We can expect an increase in GDP and trust in major institutions, and a decrease in partisanship, polarization and social friction.

Note that a commitment to the Wisdom Paradigm ***does not mean*** going back to earlier social practices that oppressed women, permitted racism or divided society into strict economic or social classes.

It does not mean rolling back the clock on science or technology.

In contrast, the Wisdom Paradigm and its focus on individuals, communities and teams becoming good ***demands that we eliminate injustice*** throughout our society. It is only through embracing justice and investing in the people throughout our society that we can practice the individual and community virtues we need to succeed, become good and achieve Happiness.

Real movement forward on social justice issues—indeed justice itself—***is only possible by embracing the Wisdom Paradigm***.

Neither the Modern nor the Postmodern Paradigms call for or implement this type of justice.

The Modern Paradigm's contractual relationship subordinates justice to self-interest.

In the Postmodern Paradigm where there is no Truth, justice is nothing more than a rhetorical device used by those attempting to exercise their power over someone else. True social and economic justice is only possible through the Wisdom Paradigm.

A real commitment to the Wisdom Paradigm will incur a sharp, heated and potentially violent reaction from those who embrace the Postmodern Paradigm. There will be claims that the advocates of the Wisdom Paradigm are suppressing free speech, and being oppressive and intolerant of dissent.

A commitment to the Wisdom Paradigm does not mean going back to earlier social practices that oppressed women, permitted racism, etc. The Wisdom Paradigm demands the opposite: that we eliminate injustice throughout our society.

When this happens, we need to remember that postmodern advocates will be using words that carry powerful meaning in the Wisdom Paradigm—*oppression, intolerance, suppression, unfairness*—but mean something very different to the people using them from the Postmodern Paradigm.

We need to remember that the purpose of free speech and dissent *within the Wisdom Paradigm* is to put all ideas on the table for discussion as the best process to pursue the Truth. For postmodern advocates, freedom of speech and dissent are simply ways to exercise power for their desires; they don't even believe in Truth.

We must be careful not to let postmodern advocates attack the Wisdom Paradigm with wisdom-concepts in which they don't even believe.

Making a commitment to the Wisdom Paradigm means understanding what is going on in the culture war so that we can identify and eliminate the tentacles of postmodern thinking that are increasingly influential in our society.

UNDERSTANDING THE CULTURE WAR

Like many conflicts, our culture war has a history of contributing factors.

During the late 1800's and early 1900's, it was becoming clear that the Modern Paradigm's attempt to find objective Truth through reason and empiricism had fallen short.

Philosophers like Nietzsche wrote books like *Beyond Good and Evil* and *On the Genealogy of Morals* to point out that the old way of believing in an objective morality had broken down and to propose a new way of understanding life.

While it might be good for the masses of people to believe in an objective morality—that would be comforting to them and keep them pacified—those with real courage, the *Overman* (Ubermensch), would understand the deeper reality and choose their own values for their own reasons. The *Genealogy of Morals* described the story of the breakdown of earlier attempts to justify morality. Now that it was apparent that there was no objective morality, it was time to go *Beyond* [the old categories or constructs of] *Good and Evil* and embrace the new reality.

The justification for objective morality in the Modern Paradigm broke down because modern philosophers had rejected *purpose*. The same breakdown occurred throughout the entire Modern Paradigm and its understanding of community, art, language, work, philosophy, theology, education, government, music, architecture, science, health—every aspect of culture and society. The modern slowly became postmodern.

Nietzsche was still relatively unknown when he died in 1900, but his writings and ways of thinking became increasingly influential in universities through the 1920's.

Europe and America were recovering from World War I in which nations at the apex of the Modern Paradigm engaged in brutal "modern warfare" that destroyed an entire generation of young men. It was a horrible and wasteful war that seemed to find its roots in a modern approach to life, and found so much death in modern technology like the machine gun and chemical weapons. With the incredible death, destruction and loss, it is easy to understand why the prevalent Modern Paradigm was deeply undermined and why postmodern thinking found fertile ground in universities in the 1920's and 30's.

The incredible horrors of World War II, the Holocaust and the power of the hydrogen bomb undermined trust in older institutions—especially in Europe—and added momentum to postmodern thinking.

You can do the math and figure out that those going through college in the 1920's (about 20 years old) became the elders of higher education by the 1960's.

As they became college department heads and assumed leadership positions dominating the thinking and hiring practices of our universities, they brought with them the postmodern thinking to which they had been exposed in college, and which they further developed and published throughout their careers.

Postmodern thinking has increasingly penetrated our society and become much more influential. Postmodern concepts and terms are increasingly heard and accepted throughout our society like:

- Beauty is in the eye of the beholder
- Values (not virtues)
- Rules are made to be broken
- Gender
- Empower

Over just a few generations, we have lost our ability to articulate why elements of the Wisdom Paradigm—like objective morality, Truth and love—are true and why moral subjectivism is wrong.

The more we understand primary points of conflict between the Wisdom and Postmodern Paradigms, the more we can recognize and eliminate elements of the Postmodern Paradigm in our society.

Because the paradigms are entire ways of seeing, organizing and understanding every aspect of life itself, the conflict between the paradigms occurs in every aspect of life. Let's look at some areas of life where the conflict is more visible.

VIRTUES OR VALUES?

Today, we rarely hear talk about the objective moral truths—the *virtues*—like honesty, courage and wisdom. They have been replaced in our common talk by the postmodern moral subjectivism of *values*. Organizations don't talk about their *core virtues*, they talk about their *core values*. The move from a wisdom or even modern concept of an objective morality to a postmodern concept of subjective values has been gaining speed over the last generation.

Since 1995, the transition has been obvious in the seminars I lead.

In the mid 1990's, if I asked participants whether it is a fact that the Holocaust was wrong or evil, about 80% would assert that it is a fact that the Holocaust was wrong.

About half of the participants could give a fairly compelling reason why it is a fact that the Holocaust was wrong.

Of the people who thought the Holocaust was objectively wrong but could not give a compelling reason, the older participants (born before 1940), would eventually argue that while they couldn't personally articulate a compelling reason—perhaps they didn't have the formal education to do so—anyone who thought the Holocaust wasn't objectively wrong was simply "crazy".

Then there was the 20% who didn't think that it is a fact that the Holocaust was objectively wrong. They responded that while they personally opposed the Holocaust and thought it "wrong", they wouldn't say that it was wrong for everyone. If Hitler thought that the Holocaust was the right thing to do for him, then who were they to judge Hitler? These people used the term *wrong* as an expression of their personal feelings, not as an expression of a moral fact.

Since that time, things have gotten much worse.

Today, in a seminar of 25 participants, many with graduate degrees, it has become rare that anyone can give a reasonably compelling public argument why it is a fact that the Holocaust was wrong. The more highly educated the participants, the more reluctant they are to judge the Holocaust as objectively wrong.

The problem isn't that they don't believe the Holocaust to be wrong, but that they are not equipped to say why it is a fact that the Holocaust is wrong, and they are not comfortable talking about it in front of others. This is the moral fragmentation we discussed earlier.

Postmodern thinking has so influenced our moral thought that people are no longer equipped to make a compelling argument why it is a fact that the Holocaust is wrong, and they are afraid to attempt to do so publicly because they fear being accused of being judgmental.

Because they are ill-equipped to argue otherwise, most of the participants will nod their heads and passively accept the statement "It is not a moral fact that the Holocaust is wrong."

What does our future look like if our current and future leaders can't even tell us, in a compelling manner, why it is a fact that cheating, dishonesty, drug use or other behaviors are wrong?

In a 2011 seminar, I encountered the first executive that actively argued for a postmodern understanding of life. A well-educated young man, he strongly argued the postmodern idea of *constructs* and continually affirmed that there was nothing objectively wrong with the Holocaust or murder.

When pressed on issues like pedophilia, child rape and torture, it was very clear that he deeply disagreed with those behaviors, but he also argued that it was a matter of opinion, not fact, that these behaviors were wrong. Sharp, well-educated and the youngest executive in the seminar, he was the first of what is a rising wave of important young leaders increasingly embracing postmodern thought.[7]

Postmodern moral subjectivism is very alluring—especially to our young people—because it is fashionable and progressive, and appears to give them permission to pursue any desire they have free of apparent consequence or the judgment of others. It encourages them to prove their freedom and define themselves by breaking rules. It is

---

[7] I encountered the same young executive several months later in another seminar, and found that he had changed his position from a postmodern outlook on life to a wisdom understanding of life.

very much like Disney's Pinocchio heading to Pleasure Island where boys can do whatever they wish.

As we make the commitment to the Wisdom Paradigm, we must teach the next generation why the postmodern temptation of moral values and short-term pleasure are a lie and inevitably unfulfilling. We must teach the next generation why the virtues and objective morality are factually true and ultimately fulfilling. To complement that knowledge, we must work hard to develop their character so they can develop wisdom and live what they have learned.

MEANING OF LIFE AND THE LOSS OF HONOR

What happened to *meaning in life* and the concept of *honor*?

In the Wisdom Paradigm, it is very clear what life is about. You are called to become a good person, a person of honor, and find fulfillment and Happiness.

With the rise of the Modern Paradigm, the pursuit of fulfillment and Happiness (purpose) moved from the public discussion of life into the private area of life, and became increasingly personal.

Everyone assumed that everyone else was thinking the same things about *purpose* and *fulfillment* in their private lives, but because it was no longer discussed as part of public life, the idea that our purpose in life is to become good and achieve Happiness became fragmented. When people stop talking about *purpose* in common as a community, the community-shared understanding of *purpose* gets forgotten by following generations of individuals.[8]

---

[8] As discussed earlier, much the same thing is happening with the fragmentation of morality in our society today. In fragmentation, concepts will inevitably go from being shared, accepted and supported by the community to becoming a collection of increasingly divergent personal understandings. If we use the term *ball* and the community continually re-teaches and reaffirms that *ball* means an oblong leather object of a certain size and shape (i.e. football), then we will continue to all mean the same thing by *ball*.

But if *ball* drops out of public discussion and into the private side of life, if *ball* is no longer re-taught and reaffirmed and discussed publicly, over generations people will develop their own individual idea of *ball*. We will continue to use the same term and think it means the same thing, but in reality, one thinks golf *ball*, another basket*ball*, and another cannon *ball*. If we are called to come together and play in the big game (life), we will find it impossible to play together because our different understandings of *ball* will have an enormous impact on how

On the public side of life, the Modern Paradigm took meaning and fulfillment out of our work and turned it into a *job*. Science increasingly saw people as just another species. The idea of humans being special in Creation was lost to the new idea of homo sapiens as just another species on a tiny speck of matter in an unimaginably vast universe.

Instead of being fundamentally social beings in which our relationships of family and love are central, we came to be seen as individuals bound by social contracts. Science told us a lot about the *how* and *what* in our world, but because the Modern Paradigm rejected purpose, could never address the *why* in life. As science gained more influence in helping us understand the *how* and *what* in our world, the question of *why* moved to the private side of life and suffered.

As humanity began to be regarded more and more as just another species, as Creation lost relevance in a vast universe, as our relationships were sanitized of deeper meaning, our lives lost significance. At least on the public side of life.

As we lost our shared understanding of life, how we fit in our communities and how we fit in the cosmos, we have increasingly encountered what is a silly question to those in the Wisdom Paradigm: *What is the meaning of life?*

The *why* of life got lost in the *what* and *how* of science, the change of generations, a couple of devastating world wars and the rise of the Postmodern Paradigm.

Think of all the literature written and movies made in the last 100 years that pose that question—*What is the meaning of life?* —in a profound, heartfelt and often angst-ridden manner, seeking an answer.

We should not be surprised that when *purpose* is removed from discussion in our public life that, over time, we lose our sense of... purpose.

---

we understand and play the game. Carrying, pitching, passing, kicking and fumbling the *ball* mean very different things to people thinking of a football, basketball, golf ball or cannon ball. Failure to publicly discuss, re-teach and reaffirm the shared understanding of *ball* means that we forget the original idea of *ball* and are unable to play together in the big game (life) at all. If the community stops continually teaching something in common, the common idea will be lost and the idea will become fragmented.

Meaning in life—at least in the Wisdom Paradigm—is closely related to *honor*.

In the Wisdom Paradigm, people understand and seek *honor*: the respect you are owed for the person that you have become, for the character you have demonstrated. That is why people are *honored* at events. They are celebrated for their character.

But the concept of honor based on character has no place in a Postmodern Paradigm that celebrates achieving freedom by breaking the very rules and social understandings that contribute to honor. In the Postmodern Paradigm, *honor* is replaced by *notoriety*. Those in the Postmodern Paradigm often use the term *respect*, but the wisdom concept of *respect for character* is replaced by a postmodern concept of *respect* as *deferential acknowledgement (fear?) of another's power*.

> We should not be surprised that when *purpose* is removed from discussion in our public life that, over time, we lose our sense of... *purpose*.

Finally, we are confronted with the stark contrast between the Wisdom Paradigm's understanding of life that puts meaning and purpose at the very center of life, and the Postmodern Paradigm's understanding that there is no meaning, no purpose.

Wisdom emphasizes honor, fulfillment, Happiness, and virtues like love, courage, honesty and integrity, while the Postmodern cynically understands these concepts as empty promises and camouflaged ways to exercise power. Contrast the openness to hope in Wisdom that flows from meaning in life, and the postmodern hopelessness that comes with the realization that nothing in life or about your life really matters or has any enduring meaning.

The postmodern appears to offer license to do whatever you desire and become whatever you want, but the hidden price is a life that is meaningless, a life that replaces love with power, and a life that is eventually empty, dark and nihilistic.

As the Postmodern Paradigm gains influence in our culture, we should not be surprised that some 20%-30% of our teens will experience depression before adulthood (Teen Depression Statistics 2011).

According to the Suicide Prevention Action Network and the Center for Disease Control, suicide has become the 3rd leading cause of death for 10-24 year olds (SPAN-USA 2011). According to the National Council of Legislatures, suicide rates for 15-24 year olds are up 6% and suicide rates for 10-15 year olds have climbed 100% (National Council of State Legislatures 2011).

THE NATURE AND DIGNITY OF HUMANITY

In earlier times, people were called to respect the life, liberty and happiness of others because those others were human beings. That respect owed other humans might flow from respect for the other person as a creation of God. It might flow from a non-religious respect for all those who possess a human nature; special because humans alone can become good through the moral choices they make in life.

In either case, it was understood that humans possessed a special, inherent human dignity.

In the Wisdom Paradigm, we are called to respect other people because it is through that respect, that love of and commitment to others, that we become good people and achieve fulfillment ourselves.

With purpose removed in the Modern Paradigm, a new justification had to be found for respecting the inherent dignity of humans. Modern philosophers attempted to achieve that by translating that respect into the language of human rights. It is common today to say that all people possess human rights.

While the existence of rights is widely accepted in our world, a universally-accepted understanding of what human rights are and where they come from was never conclusively established. Different philosophers came up with different rationales explaining human rights and their origin. The American Declaration of Independence states that people are "endowed by their Creator" with human rights (Continental Congress 1776). Other modern philosophers argue that human rights are derived from natural law and our human nature (Locke 1689). Still others posit that human rights arise from the state of nature and social contract; in the state of nature we give up freedoms and gain security, rights, in return (Hobbes 1651) (Rousseau 1762).

Over the last 300 years, the idea and language of human rights has been largely accepted throughout the world.

But the lack of a universally accepted rationale for what rights are and where they come from is a big problem. It means that different people can have very different understandings of rights depending on what they think rights are and where they originate. We're back to using the same term, in this case *rights*, but meaning very different things by that term. As we have seen before, when a term like *rights* can mean different things to different people, people begin to believe that rights are not objective, universal facts, but a matter of personal opinion.

Because human dignity, in the Modern Paradigm, is expressed in terms of rights, when rights lose their status as objective, universal facts and become personal opinion, human dignity loses its status as an inherent, universal fact and becomes more a matter of opinion.

> Over time, rights have become a sort of taboo.
> We have the social demand that we respect rights, but we have forgotten the reasoning behind them.

As postmodern thinking became more influential, concepts of objective Truth, meaning and honor receded from life until we forgot what the term *honor* meant. The collapse of human dignity paralleled the collapse of objective morality. Once *purpose* is removed from public discussion, objective morality and respect for the special, inherent human dignity of people break down, fragment and eventually get lost.

So we should not be surprised that postmodern philosophers no longer view human beings as having any special, inherent dignity. Indeed, it has become acceptable to describe human beings as just another animal, or even a virus or scourge, on our own planet.

In a postmodern world where there is no right and wrong, no Truth or Beauty, and the foundation for human dignity has been eroded, people become objects that have no intrinsic value. Other people become little more than tools for our own desires, and human life loses dignity and value. Extreme pornography—the use of other people for sexual gratification—becomes acceptable, and further dehumanizes and objectifies people. It is a world in which people are used and become pawns of those with power, and the likelihood and acceptability of horrors like genocide, organ harvesting and euthanasia increase. If people are equivalent to animals or viruses, what is wrong with treating them like we treat animals and viruses?

In the end, rights without underlying, genuine respect for human dignity will not prevent genocide.

When there is no intrinsic dignity and value to being human, why wouldn't the people in power simply get rid of those they don't like or consider a burden?

OBLIGATION TO OTHERS

In the Wisdom Paradigm, loving service to others is an outstanding way to practice those virtues that will make us good and help us achieve Happiness. When care and love are practiced through service, we become more caring and loving ourselves. When justice, courage and wisdom are practiced through service to others, we become more just, courageous and wise ourselves. When we sacrifice in service to others, we gain freedom from the temptations of materialism.

When there is injustice in our community, we are called to help solve the injustice in cooperation with others so we can practice love of and justice for others. Practicing love and justice makes us better individuals and a better community.

To turn injustice over to the government to solve is to miss the opportunity for us as individuals and as a community to practice love and justice, and become more loving and just. When we feed the homeless, we don't just put calories in stomachs. We do something much more important. We develop human relationships with people. We honor their inherent value and dignity as humans. That makes both them and us more human and better people.

In the Postmodern Paradigm, there is no fundamental obligation to others; just competition for power with others. There is no obligation to feed the hungry or house the homeless.

Perhaps we cannot ignore the hungry in the park, because, if we don't feed them, they might starve and make us feel bad. Or perhaps they will even riot. Perhaps by feeding the hungry we can empower them and make them our allies in some power play. But there is nothing inherently good in feeding the homeless ourselves because they have no inherent dignity.

> To turn that injustice over to the government to solve is to miss the opportunity for us as individuals and as community to practice love and justice.

In the Postmodern Paradigm, why not turn the task of helping the poor, starving and homeless over to the government? Why not simply move the homeless someplace where they are no longer a problem for anyone?

For in the Postmodern Paradigm there is nothing objectively better about being helpful than being cruel. Social justice isn't about being or doing what is right, for there is no objective right. *Social justice* is a pretty term that makes the redistribution of power sound more attractive than the term *oppression*, but they are qualitatively the same.

In the Postmodern Paradigm, *social justice* is when you take power from others. *Oppression* is when others take power from you.

Do we want the next generation of leaders to serve us and others out of love and justice because they understand that practicing those virtues makes them better people too?

Or do we want them to see others as little more than pawns in the ever-changing dynamics that exist among the powerful, and between the powerful and the oppressed?

BUSINESS

Contemporary business is based in the Modern Paradigm, so the primary cultural conflict is between the Wisdom Paradigm and the Modern Paradigm.

In the Wisdom Paradigm, the purpose of business is the same as the purpose for any other community or team: to achieve excellence by helping people and our society become good. When business helps the community and participants become good, then business is good—both financially and morally. When business is pursued in ways that do not help the participants and community become good, then business is being used in bad ways.

When the Modern Paradigm moved purpose and morality out of the public sphere of life into the private sphere, it freed business from the purpose of becoming good, and effectively freed business from morality as well. The public purpose of business became money, and business became bound only by law and business itself.

We teach our young people the modern concept that the purpose of a business is not to become good or provide the employees an opportunity to become good, but to make money. We can argue whether it is short term profits or long term profits or shareholder value or whatever, but we teach our children that the purpose of business is money.

That is why a business is called a *for-profit* and it is what makes a business qualitatively different—at least in the Modern Paradigm—from non-profit and government organizations.

We tell our young people to aggressively push the envelope in the pursuit of money and we give them bonuses when they maximize profits. When we screw someone over with immoral but not illegal practices, we ignore the fact that we became worse people by what we did and rationalize our actions by telling ourselves "It's just business."

So, our business people do what we teach them to do; they attempt to maximize money. And they maximize money by aggressively playing in that gray area that lies between what one knows is right, and what is illegal, that exists in accounting and law and many other professions.

For example, imagine you are striving to make partner in an accounting firm. Your success depends on your ability to bring in new accounts. You encounter a potential client who is looking to attract big investors. That client needs to have the best-looking financials to maximize their chance at new investors, and will hire the accounting firm that can make their financials most attractive.

> After we teach our young people in school that the purpose of a business is to make money, and tell them that people are motivated by money, and reward their aggressive pursuit of money with money, we are surprised and horrified when they actually do what we told them to do. It's entrapment.

Now we all know that accounting rules are not black and white, but have gray area—room for interpretation. To get the new client, your firm goes into the gray area by aggressively interpreting the accounting rules to make their financials look the best possible.

Over time, to keep up with the competition, other firms are forced to do the same, and soon playing aggressively in the gray area goes from the exception to the norm.

And as playing in the gray area becomes the norm, "aggressively playing" in the gray area moves from the less risky to the riskier. All in the name of maximizing money.

Then when it goes wrong and things collapse (see the mortgage crisis of 2007), people get very upset and call the accountants or lawyers or businesspeople immoral, greedy scoundrels who should be thrown in jail.

After we teach our young in school that the purpose of a business is to make money, and tell them that people are motivated by money, and reward their aggressive pursuit of money with bonuses, we are surprised and horrified when they do what we told and incentivized them to do. It's almost entrapment.

There is more. Remember that the Modern Paradigm teaches us that all relationships—especially business relationships—are fundamentally contractual. But in these contractual relationships, by definition, the interest of the business and the interest of the employee are in opposition to each other. The business wants more work for less money. The employee wants more money for less work. The relationship is fundamentally low trust and unstable.

While attending a conference for corporate ethics officers, I once listened to a panel of senior corporate executives discuss how they could get employees to be more ethical. After all, unethical employees were costing their businesses lots of money.

These senior executives were trying to figure out how they could get employees—with whom they had low-trust, contractual relationships—to "put aside what was good for the employee for the best interest of the team [company]. "

> If we treat those with whom we work as co-creative partners in a calling, a vocation, that honors them as a real person and helps them find fulfillment in their work, we will get a completely different level of performance.

It was surreal. Corporate executives said these things with a straight face as some were compensated at 100 or more times the rate of their average employee. And they seemed genuinely surprised when employees didn't make a big sacrifice and act "in the best interest of the company." They couldn't seem to understand that few employees feel inspired to give up their own self-interest to promote the opposing self-interest of a business that, no matter how many corporate picnics it throws, essentially regards employees as cogs in the machine.

When we treat people as contractual employees—as objects in a machine—that have an 8 to 5 job that simply gives them money, we will get a certain level of performance. Most of the time we will simply get what we pay for.

But if we treat those with whom we work as co-creative partners in a calling or vocation that honors their dignity as real people, and helps them find fulfillment in their work, we will get a completely different level of performance. We will get trust, commitment and performance that you couldn't buy with any amount of money.

Many American companies—especially small to mid-range companies—already operate in accordance with the Wisdom Paradigm. They are obvious in the "success stories" of American business.

It is <u>impossible</u> to develop the high trust, high-performance people and teams that we need to succeed in the future within a Modern Paradigm that only knows low-trust, low stability, contractual relationships. No matter how hard we hammer, the square peg will never fit in the round hole. It is insanity to think otherwise.

The gap between the economic-business performance we can get by engaging the Wisdom Paradigm and the performance we actually get with the Modern Paradigm is enormous. This conflict probably costs American business trillions of dollars in lost productivity, trust, performance, creativity and commitment.

Do we want our next generation of business leaders to prevail in global competition by maximizing individual and team performance through the Wisdom Paradigm and high-trust, highly stable covenant relationships?

Or do we want to continue to sink, tying our business performance and power to the anchor of modern contractual relationships?

SCIENCE AND TECHNOLOGY

In the Wisdom Paradigm, science and technology exist to help people become good in several ways. As people practice science and develop technology, they get better in developing scientific skills and virtues like discipline, persistence and attention to detail. People who are passionate about science and technology find fulfillment in their work. Science and technology yield knowledge and practical devices that can extend life, make life easier, and improve the community and the economy.

Within the Wisdom Paradigm, science and technology are never permitted to run free on their own, but must always operate within the boundaries of serving the purpose and good of the community.

With the introduction of the Modern Paradigm, and the division of life into the personal/private sphere and the public sphere, science and technology (in the public sphere) were effectively freed from purpose and morality (in the private/personal sphere).

Scientists became free to pursue science in whatever ways and directions they desired. Those who created technology gained the same freedom. The study of science for its own sake with the aim of simply increasing scientific knowledge, became permissible.

In the beginning, the personal morality of scientists and societal morality expressed in law prevented scientists from studying anything too outlandish. But over time, the moral fragmentation that occurred in society impacted the scientific community. Scientists, no longer feeling bound by personal morality, began to extend the boundaries of acceptable research.

As morality moved to the private side of life, society became less comfortable expressing morality in the law, and legal proscriptions against certain kinds of scientific research were relaxed as well. Eventually, society lost the ability to make a compelling argument that science should have any moral or ethical restrictions at all.

What was prohibited yesterday by the personal morality of scientists and the law is permitted today because personal morals have fragmented and degenerated, and the law has gotten out of the way.

What was once unacceptable—like cloning and the creation of human-animal hybrids called *chimeras*—is becoming increasingly routine. In 2011, the UK's Daily Mail reported that British labs had produced 150 human animal hybrids in three years after prohibitions against the research were relaxed (Martin 2011).

That is how we have found ourselves in a culture war that pits the Wisdom Paradigm's idea that science and technology exist to serve the community good, and the Modern Paradigm's assertion that science essentially serves and is responsible only to itself.

Parallel arguments are made for those pushing the limits of technology in the Modern Paradigm. With technology on the public side of life and morality on the private, technologists can simply claim that morality has no authority over technology. Who are you to tell me what technology I can create in my own lab? If I don't invent it, someone else eventually will anyway.

None of this is particularly new. Mary Shelly's *Frankenstein*, published in 1818, was already exploring the problems with unfettered scientific research and the technological creations that follow.

Certainly, we want science and technology—and our world—to continue to benefit from open and creative research. That openness and creativity have provided our society with vast scientific and technological benefits.

At the same time, however, do we really want to say there are no objective moral limits on science and technology?

While the cultural conflict between the Wisdom and Modern Paradigms in science has been around for a while, more recently we have seen an increasing postmodern influence in science.

It has been argued that some scientists, scientific organizations and even government policymakers have blurred the distinction between scientific research and political advocacy.

In these cases, the problem isn't politicians using science to advocate a policy or scientists making use of science to advocate a scientific position. Rather, the danger is that scientists who advocate particular political policies may "massage" the scientific data or conclusions to make desired socio-economic-political changes happen. The possible falsification or massaging of scientific data to impact policy debates on endangered species, vaccines and global warming has been controversial.[9]

People give substantial weight to scientific results because—according to the Wisdom and Modern Paradigms—scientific results are supposed to be objective, factual and true.

In the Postmodern Paradigm, however, where everything is about power, science isn't used in arguments because it is objectively true. Science is used in arguments *because it appears to be objectively true* and therefore carries persuasive weight in arguments.

> In the Postmodern Paradigm where everything is about power, science isn't used in arguments because it is objectively true. Science is used in arguments because it appears to be objectively true and therefore carries persuasive weight in arguments.

It isn't important whether the scientific data is valid or true. It is important whether the data can be used persuasively to exercise power and achieve the desired goal. That is why, from a postmodern perspective, there is nothing wrong with changing the data if it achieves the goal.

Will our next generation of leaders embrace the Wisdom Paradigm and ensure that while scientific and technological research is open and creative, it is also objective and responsible to the societal good?

Will our next generation of leaders continue down the modern path where science and technology exist for and control themselves, outside of our community good?

Or will our next generation of leaders embrace a postmodern understanding where science and technology are just another way to exercise power over others?

---

[9] For more on falsification of data regarding vaccines, refer to (CNN Wire Staff 2011); for endangered species see (US Forest Service 2002) and (Williams 2002)

MAKING THE COMMITMENT

We are in a brutal culture war that is increasingly dividing, fragmenting and polarizing our society, and making discussion of very important issues difficult and vitriolic. Every day there seems to be less common ground for discussion, and more demonization and dehumanization of the other side.

America has battled through massive challenges in our past like independence, slavery, civil war, industrialization, the Great Depression, civil rights and two world wars. Each time, we overcame these challenges because good leaders brought good people together in a common, shared understanding of life.

Our culture war today is fundamentally different because it is between two rival, irreconcilable and mutually exclusive ways of understanding life. We cannot solve this challenge by finding common ground with the opposition within a shared paradigm. There is, by definition, no shared paradigm, no common ground. It is either the Wisdom Paradigm or the Postmodern Paradigm, but it cannot be both.

This violent clash of these irreconcilable paradigms is also the reason our society has stalled in terms of future economic, social and political development. Until we make a commitment to one of the paradigms, we will not have the unity or shared vision required to progress in leadership studies or in any other area of our society.

We have three choices as individuals and as a society:

1. We can fully commit to the Wisdom Paradigm
2. We can fully commit to the Postmodern Paradigm
3. We can continue our current path and delay making a commitment

It is undoubtedly tempting and convenient to continue on our current path and avoid making a commitment to either paradigm. It is always easier to avoid facing the hard realities and put necessary changes and commitments off to the future.

We can simply let the paradigm clash and culture war continue to fester until things get so bad in all areas of our society that we hit rock bottom. Failure to commit will undermine and corrode our culture, deeply divide our society, and create intense distrust and polarization. It will leave us fragmented and weak economically, socially and in our national security.

At some point, not far in our future, it will be too late to recover.

It takes many years to form a generation of good leaders. Not only will we lack the time to form a generation of leaders that we can trust to guide us out of such a mess, we will likely have forgotten how to form the leaders we would need anyway.

We could make an individual and societal commitment to the Postmodern Paradigm, embracing moral subjectivism, emptying life of meaning and accepting that human beings have no more inherent dignity than a virus. We could embrace a postmodern life that understands all relationships, even family relationships, as ultimately power relationships. We could choose the Postmodern Paradigm or simply let it continue to infiltrate our society until it becomes the de facto paradigm.

Or we can step up, make an individual and societal commitment to the Wisdom Paradigm, and form the next generation of leaders that we can trust to guide our nation well. We can create a brighter future for ourselves and our families. A deep commitment to the Wisdom Paradigm is right because it:

- It is the only paradigm that can give us the next generation of good leaders that we need
- Fully engages trust and provides the highest performance people and teams
- Understands love, objective morality, Truth and Beauty
- Provides meaning, purpose and fulfillment in life
- Enables us to prevail in global competition
- Integrates our public/work life with our private/personal life in our journey towards fulfillment and Happiness
- Is True

Remember, a real commitment to the Wisdom Paradigm will incur a sharp, heated and potentially violent reaction from those who embrace the Postmodern Paradigm. There will be claims that the advocates of the Wisdom Paradigm are suppressing freedom, and being oppressive and intolerant of dissent.

We cannot forget that postmodern advocates will be using words that carry powerful meaning in the Wisdom Paradigm—*oppression, intolerance, suppression, unfairness*—but mean something very different in their own Postmodern Paradigm.

We cannot forget that the purpose of free speech and dissent *within the Wisdom Paradigm* is to put all ideas on the table for discussion as the best mode to pursue the Truth. For Postmodern advocates, however, freedom of speech and dissent are simply ways to exercise power for their own desires; they don't even believe in Truth.

We must be careful not to let postmodern advocates attack the Wisdom Paradigm with concepts in which they don't even believe.

We possess enormous power and face some very daunting challenges. Good leadership is the key to our future in every dimension of our lives.

With good leadership, we can develop the highest performance people and teams. We can dramatically improve our economy, our global competitiveness and our national security through improved efficiencies, better creativity, less corruption and higher productivity from people fulfilled in their work.

With good leadership, we can unite our nation on common ground, focus our tremendous power on the good and engage a very bright future.

What is stopping us?

By making a total commitment to the Wisdom Paradigm, we can move out of the leadership mess in which we have been stuck and derive an understanding of leadership that will enable us to:

- Understand how leadership works
- Develop the next generation of leaders we can all trust
- Create the most powerful people and teams that will enable us to prevail in global competition
- Help you become a better leader in your profession, community and family

So how does the Wisdom Paradigm work in all of this? Let's start with the four key areas we must consider when we discuss leadership. We'll rearrange the order here to make it more of a progression.

- Human nature
- Nature of human relationships/community
- Goal(s)
- Leader and follower

We'll use terms like *team, community, group, organization*, etc. interchangeably. They all refer to groups of people bound together in a *covenant relationship*.

Fundamentals of Leadership

HUMAN NATURE

Human nature has remained the same for all people throughout history and across cultures. We are united as human beings by our common human nature. We seek meaning in life. We seek to become good, pursue fulfillment and achieve Happiness. That is our purpose as human beings.

NATURE OF HUMAN RELATIONSHIPS AND COMMUNITY

Human relationships are naturally *covenant relationships*, not contract or power relationships. In the covenant relationship, the good of the individual and the good of the team are the same. The more the individual contributes to the team effort, the more the individual grows. The more the team invests in the individuals, the better the team gets.

The purpose of all human relationships, communities or teams, whether they are family, work or athletic relationships, is to become good and help those within the community to become good.

GOALS

The final goal or purpose of all people and teams is the same—to fulfill their human nature, become good, and achieve Happiness.

The beauty and strength of the Wisdom Paradigm is that all individual and team goals—whether they are described as primary goals, secondary goals, (etc) or as the mission, purpose or strategic purpose—align with the ultimate purpose of all people and teams: to become good.

We can evaluate any action or behavior against an ultimate standard:

Does this help us become good?

LEADER AND FOLLOWER

In leadership, there is always *one providing guidance to another*. With the Wisdom Paradigm, the highest trust and highest performance leader-follower relationships are possible because the good of the leader is fundamentally tied to and consistent with the good of the follower.

PURPOSE

As we begin discussing leadership in the Wisdom Paradigm, it is important that we reinforce the importance of *purpose*. It is at the very core of the Wisdom Paradigm. When we fail to keep the primacy of *purpose* at the forefront of our minds in all things in life, we lose the advantages of the Wisdom Paradigm and covenant teams, we lose focus on the meaning of life, and our performance levels will erode.

It is important to reinforce that we all have the same purpose in life—to become good so we can achieve Happiness—and that when we remove purpose as the center point of our understanding of life, we start down the road that inevitably leads to the Postmodern Paradigm.

Finally, it is important to understand the critical relationship between *activity*, *mission* and *purpose*. When we understand them and how they work together, we can use that knowledge to create very effective and efficient programs to develop the next generation of leaders.

The relationship is simple: we need some *activity* focused on some goal (the *mission*) that gives us the opportunity to practice the virtues and become *good* (purpose).

We know this in physical fitness. You can't get in good shape by sitting on the couch. We need an *activity* that exercises our muscles and elevates our heart rate (*mission*) and helps us get in good physical shape (purpose). It doesn't matter so much what the *activity* is—running, biking, swimming, dance—so long as it exercises our muscles and elevates our heart rate.

The same thing is true with our character and becoming good. You can't become a good person by doing nothing. You need some activity that enables you to exercise your character "muscles"—virtues like honesty, justice, courage, wisdom and love—and become good. Just as it doesn't matter so much what exercise you do (activity) to get your heart rate up for an extended period (mission) to get into good physical shape (purpose), it doesn't matter so much what activity or mission you pursue in life as long as it gives you the opportunity to practice virtues and become good.

A basketball team plays basketball (the activity) to win the league championship (the mission) so that it can become good (purpose).

A business makes a product or provides a service (the activity) to generate a profit (the mission) so that it can become good (purpose).

A military unit engages in combat (the activity) to win battles and defend our nation (the mission) so that it can become good (purpose).

Your kids are told to put away their belongings (the activity) so that the room is clean (the mission) to help them become good people (purpose).

In each of these examples, the activity is an opportunity for the participants to practice virtues like self-discipline, commitment, honesty, justice, courage, wisdom and love with other participants. The more that each of these teams—whether business, military unit or athletic team—practices the virtues and makes them a fundamental part of who they are—as a team and as individuals—the more trust and performance they will develop, and the more successful they will be.

Just about everything we do in life is an opportunity to practice the virtues and become a better person. The more intensely we pursue the mission, the more we develop the virtues within ourselves, and the better person we become. Mission must always remain second to our purpose of becoming good.

> Activity, mission and purpose must align and each be good in itself as well as focused on overall goodness.

It is very important to remember that all these levels—activity, mission and purpose—must align and each *be good in itself* as well as focused on helping you become good overall. For example, you can't perform a bad activity (i.e. hazing) as part of a good mission (i.e. team unity).

You can't pursue a bad mission (i.e. tearing down the reputation of a rival) and expect to become a good person. It doesn't work.

When you engage in a bad activity or pursue a bad mission, you are practicing or pursuing something bad, and that means you are becoming bad not good. This is why the *ends don't justify the means.*

The good activity must line up with the good mission and line up with helping you and the team become good. If you don't understand this or don't carry it through fully, little else in the Wisdom Paradigm will work for you.

Activity is literally the activity you are doing. The more challenging the activity, the more development will occur. In physical fitness, when you run further at a greater speed and steeper incline, you get in better physical shape faster. The same is true with your character. When you engage in activities that challenge you to practice honesty, justice, compassion, wisdom and integrity, you get in better character shape faster. Better character becomes the foundation for the high trust relationships that maximize performance in business, non-profits, public service or any other covenant team.

Mission is any single goal or set of goals associated with the activity. The mission of a basketball team is to help kids improve basketball skills (one mission/goal), win basketball games (a second mission/goal) and win the league basketball championship (a third mission/goal).

The mission of a business is to provide a service or product.

The mission of a family is to raise children and be a nurturing community for parents, kids and relatives.

Note that *mission* is almost always associated with the direct goals of the activity.

The **purpose** of any person or team is always, always, always *to become good*. We've emphasized that concept of purpose very hard, but unless it has become the center point around which you intuitively organize how you live and understand life, we haven't emphasized purpose hard enough. Purpose is not just an intellectual choice, but a way of life as well.

It is very important that we do not confuse *mission* and *purpose*. Bad things happen when we confuse mission and purpose, and sports in America provide us a good example.

It used to be that you played professional sports *for the love of the game*, and high school and college sports because it *builds character*.

Playing for the love of the game is about finding fulfillment in the sport, the competition and the kind of person playing makes you. *Building character* is all about using sport to identify and develop your talents; about learning what it means to be a teammate; and about the qualities of character you develop playing as part of a team.

Beneath these statements is the idea that sports are about the kind of person you become by competing—by giving 110% to your team mates and the game. It is a proper focus on *purpose* (goodness) above *mission* (winning games).

We participate in sports (the activity) and work hard to win games and the championship (mission) so that we can become good (purpose). We strive to win because that pushes us to develop the virtues associated with the sport, and helps us to become good. But the mission of winning is only valuable insofar as it helps us achieve our larger purpose of becoming good.

Today however, we've largely lost the idea that the purpose of sports is to build character and become good—even in youth sports.

> The mission of winning is only valuable insofar as it helps us achieve our larger and far more important purpose of becoming good.

We can see the influence of the Modern Paradigm as professional sports, and increasingly even college and high school sports, have become contract relationships between the athlete, and the team or school. The focus isn't so much on developing the athlete's character through team play, but the exchange of athletic performance for money and/or fame.

With the increasing influence of the Postmodern Paradigm, the concept of purpose has been replaced by an emphasis on winning for its own sake, "dominating" the competition, and pursuing fame, even notoriety, for athletic success. It has become all about the mission— *winning*.

In professional sports, playing *for the love of the game* has been replaced by playing for money and fame. Professional athletes are famous and popular, but many reject the idea that they have any obligation to be a good role model for others. They are supposed to win, be very visible and collect lucrative sponsorships, but developing character and becoming good are no longer part of the picture. Players who have poor character but have talent are heavily recruited. Poor behavior is tolerated unless it becomes a large public relations problem for the team. Only then does it receive condemnation.

Some athletes come to believe that because they win, the rules that apply to the rest of society don't apply to them. They can drive recklessly. They can sexually assault women. They can brandish guns. And though it can lead to extremely serious health problems and even death, some athletes use performance enhancing substances like steroids. Gaining an edge in their pursuit of money and victory is more important than their character, their honor or their health.

We shouldn't be surprised that when we make the mission (winning) more important than the purpose (becoming good), then anything that helps you win—even cheating—becomes acceptable.

> Accomplish your mission better by keeping purpose--*becoming good*--above your mission.

That's true because when you make *winning* the ultimate goal, winning becomes the most important thing. Even more important than playing fairly. When the ultimate goal is winning, cheating is only bad if you get caught and it hinders you from winning.

When mission becomes the ultimate goal, only a fool plays by the rules.

Some may want to reject that last sentence and argue that no, even if winning is the ultimate goal, people shouldn't cheat.

But they are wrong.

The whole point is that if you think "no cheating" is more important than winning, then "no cheating" becomes the ultimate goal, the purpose, and takes precedence over the mission of winning. Now we're back to *being good* as the ultimate goal or purpose.

If professional sports teams placed goodness over winning, if they treated players more like people rather than property, they would develop higher trust relationships with players and in teams, and improve overall performance.

How many times have we heard about prima donna players with lots of talent and bad attitudes who destroy team chemistry?

How many times have we heard about a team that had lesser talent, but won because they had better team chemistry and deeper commitment than more talented teams?

When we confuse purpose and mission, bad things happen. When we understand that mission always feeds our purpose of becoming good, we become better people and better teams with higher performance.

There are real and important benefits in always placing *purpose* higher than the *mission*.

First, placing purpose higher than mission ensures that *becoming good* is the highest standard against which all activity in life is measured as ethical, moral and/or professional:

If the activity and mission help you and the team become good, then go for it!

If either the activity or mission does not help both you and the team become good, don't do it!

There is a second big advantage. It may sound counter intuitive, but you will accomplish your mission most effectively if you put *purpose* above *mission*.

You will be more successful in business if you place *becoming good* (purpose) above *making money* (mission).

Our American military will win more wars and battles if they place *becoming good* (purpose) above *winning wars and battles* (mission).

The team you coach will perform better and win more games if you ensure that *becoming good* (purpose) is more important than *winning games* (mission).

When everyone on the team knows that everyone else is focused on the purpose of *becoming good*, they not only make a deeper commitment to achieving the mission (that's how we achieve our purpose), but also have deeper trust and commitment within the team than if they were merely focused on the mission.

That deeper trust and commitment means the team will perform at a higher level by focusing on the purpose than by focusing on the mission.

Never forget that the purpose of all people and teams is to become good. To become good, we need an activity focused on some goal or mission in which we can practice virtues like wisdom, love, justice, integrity, honesty and courage. It is critical that we keep purpose (becoming good) above mission so that:

- We can remain focused on becoming good
- All activities and missions align and help us to become good
- We have a standard—*Does it help us become good?* —against which we can measure our activities and missions
- We maximize commitment, trust and team performance

Covenant Teams

A covenant team is any group of people committed to each other, and focused on some good or noble goal. A covenant team can be your family, a work team or company, a neighborhood or community, an athletic team—any group of people that are committed to each other and focused on doing something good.

A gang cannot be a covenant team because while they are committed to each other, they are focused on a wrong goal and use wrong means.

In this text, you will read over and over about doing things as part of a team rather than doing as just an individual. While it possible to develop virtues and pursue goodness through individual, solitary activities, there are big advantages in pursuing the virtues as part of a team.

> **COVENANT TEAM**
>
> A covenant team is any group of people committed to each other and focused on some good goal.

A team will generally push you to improve further and faster than you would on your own. If you run distances with other people, they will tend to push you to run further and faster than you would on your own. When you lift weights in the gym, a workout partner will generally push you further and harder than you would push yourself. When you are part of a team in a pressure-filled situation, you will tend to push yourself further and hold on longer because you can't let your teammates down. Peer pressure can be a positive thing if it is focused on helping you become good.

Team participation also enables you to practice virtues like justice, teamwork, patience, honesty and love that require other people and that you cannot practice by yourself.

COVENANT RELATIONSHIP

Any time we are part of a group or team, our relationship with that team should be a *covenant relationship*. Any time we have an opportunity to build a relationship with another—a client or even a competitor—that too should be a covenant relationship.

The great thing about being part of a team is that it provides you the opportunity to become a better person by practicing the virtues in the context of the team and its activity. Whether the team is a neighborhood group cleaning up a park, a work team focused on a project or an athletic team competing in a sport, being part of the team means you can practice honesty, love, wisdom, justice, courage, perseverance, determination, patience and other virtues, making them more and more a part of your character and who you are.

Everything you do, every team you're on, provides you an opportunity to become good.

The more committed you are to your team, the more you put into your team and its activities, the faster and more effectively you will develop the virtues, and your character, skills and teamwork. The more you put into your team, the more you will gain from it.

Now place yourself as the leader of a team. Your team's success and your success as a leader are going to depend a lot on how good your people are: good in *skills*; good in *teamwork*; and good in *character*. The more the team invests in its members in each of these areas, the more you invest in your people, the better your people and team will become.

The covenant relationship is extraordinarily powerful and important. It is the highest trust and most stable relationship because:

1) The goals of everyone on the team are aligned with each other. This alignment runs from the *activity* up through the accomplishment of the team's task or *mission* (i.e. cleaning up the neighborhood or getting the work project finished) all the way to our *purpose* of becoming good. When everyone understands that their goals are aligned at all levels, they can build deeper trust with each other.

2) The goals of the team are aligned with the goals of the individual. This builds trust and confidence between the individual and the team.

3) The knowledge that the more I give to the team the better I become strengthens my commitment and relationship with the team

4) The knowledge that the more the team invests in me, the better the team becomes, gives me confidence that the team is committed to me, and builds trust and confidence

5) To use Modern Paradigm terminology, the team has a vested interest in helping me become good in terms of my teamwork, skills, character and leadership. I have a vested interest in helping the team succeed in its mission.

That commitment to the success of each other, individual and team, maximizes trust and makes the relationship very stable. When times get tough and pressure is put on the covenant relationship, the trust will deepen and the bonds will get tighter because the teammates will gain confidence in each other as they see each other perform well under that pressure.

As we look to develop the next generation of leaders, the Wisdom Paradigm and covenant relationship give us confidence that the leaders and their organizations—whether they are government, business, military or public service—are aligned with us and our community. Everyone striving to become good. While we won't all agree on all the decisions, we can have more confidence that good people are trying to make good decisions for the right reasons in the right ways. The common ground and shared sense of purpose will help us eliminate the demonization and partisanship that is currently undermining our society.

When you serve as a leader at work, the covenant relationship provides the context, and the people and teams that you can trust to make good decisions, professionally and morally, in the fast-paced, complex situations we face today. As a teammate, these are the kinds of people and teams that you can trust to be there when you put yourself at risk for your team.

These are precisely the kinds of highly-skilled, ethical and committed leaders and teams that we can trust to wield our tremendous power and navigate the tough challenges in our future as a nation.

Covenant relationships can be found at the core of many organizations. The US Marine Corps and other top US military units are very successful because they are, at their core, covenant teams. They are bound by something deeper than just their military mission or money; they are bound by commitment to each other and honor.

From time to time, we encounter stories about how a business owner has had such a good (covenant) relationship with her people that when one experiences hardship the other comes to the rescue.

We can't fully understand the extraordinary power, trust and stability of these covenant teams until we contrast them with teams as understood by the Modern and Postmodern paradigms.

The majority of our businesses are based in modern contract relationships[10] where the interest of the employee is, by definition, opposed to the interest of the company. One benefits at the expense of the other, so trust levels are low. When this relationship is put under pressure, it tends to fall apart and collapse. It is impossible to get the highest performance out of this low trust, low stability relationship.

In the Postmodern Paradigm, trust levels and commitment can be even lower because the relationships are based in manipulative power and individual goals.

Right now, the performance of American business is limited by its embrace of the Modern Paradigm's contract relationship.

We need creativity, innovation and high trust decision-making. These are not possible in contract or power-based relationships. These are only available with wisdom covenant relationships.

---

[10] By contract relationship, I mean a social contract relationship distinguished from a legal contract relationship. If we understand a legal contract to be a document that fully contains the mutual expectations between two parties, we can see that even covenant-based relationships may include a contract so everyone understands the explicit expectations. A contract in this case builds trust and enhances the covenant aspect at the foundation of the relationship.

If we wish to prevail in global competition, we must increase our performance by dropping the modern contract relationship for the wisdom covenant relationship. That can only occur if we fully embrace the Wisdom Paradigm throughout our society.

THE TEAM DYNAMIC

The *team dynamic* describes what happens within a covenant team as it grows and develops through time, pursuing its mission.

The diagram on the opposite page shows the relationship between teamwork, character and skills in the team dynamic.

Imagine that you are the coach of a basketball team. The activity of the team is obviously basketball. The mission of the team is to win games and the championship. The team will play basketball and strive for the championship to achieve their purpose of becoming good.

To win, you must have great teamwork. The more your players develop a team rhythm, understand each other's strengths and challenges, and know where each other are on the court, the better they will work together as a team. Good teamwork is critical to success.

Good teamwork depends on good skills, so to develop good teamwork you must also develop the skills of your players. The better your players dribble, rebound, shoot and pass, the better your teamwork and the more successful the team will be.

Good skills help build good teamwork, but the opposite is true as well. Good teamwork helps develop basketball skills. The more you practice passing to, and rebounding and dribbling against others, the better you will get at each of those skills. Good teamwork demands that you push yourself to develop other skills so you can play well as part of that team.

The same is true between teamwork and character—they feed each other's development.

Character builds teamwork because when you practice honesty, justice and courage with your team, you build higher trust, tighter bonds and deeper commitment with your teammates.

Teamwork builds character because the commitment developed through teamwork calls each player to go the extra distance for each other developing virtues like justice, courage, toughness, determination and perseverance.

Finally, character and skill development feed each other as well. The more you possess qualities of good character like self-discipline, courage, toughness, perseverance and endurance, the more you will push yourself to develop skills required for basketball like speed, endurance, ball handling and shooting. On the other side, the more you develop your skills, the more you will practice and develop virtues like commitment, dedication and discipline.

Team Dynamic

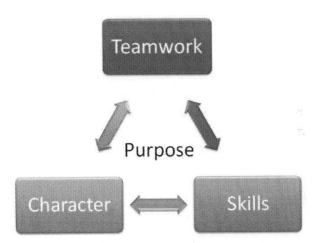

Over time, teamwork, skills and character build each other up in a self-reinforcing loop.

That is why most teams get better as the season progresses. Good teams gel as their teamwork, skills and character feed on and build each other.

We call this teamwork-skills-character self-reinforcing loop the *team dynamic*.

The team dynamic is not limited to a basketball team pursuing a league championship. It is true of any covenant team pursuing any mission from two of your children cleaning a room to a company introducing a new product. Every covenant team activity is an opportunity to develop teamwork, character and whatever skills are associated with the activity and mission.

We can express the team dynamic of increasing performance over time in a simple graph.

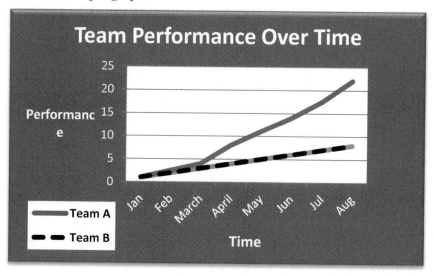

The chart shows the performance improvement of two teams over time. Obviously, since Team A's performance improvement is greater over the same period, we would all choose to be Team A over Team B. Assuming other factors being relatively equal, Team A shows a larger performance increase because they go through the team dynamic faster and more effectively than Team B.

So, what is the key to maximizing the increase in your team's performance? What is the key to going through the team dynamic as fast, efficiently and effectively as possible?

PERFORMANCE KEY

The key to high performance is *commitment*. The more deeply committed people are to the team, the activity, the mission and the purpose, the more deeply and quickly they will engage the team dynamic, and the faster their performance will improve.

Deeper commitment = better skills, character and teamwork.

So, what is the key to getting the deepest commitment from people?

What is the key to getting the deepest commitment from *you?* From a more personal perspective: *Why should I give you my deepest commitment? What's in it for me?*

These are the questions that must be honestly asked and answered to get the deepest commitment and highest performance. Commitment really boils down to *motivation* and *trust.*

What is my motivation for being part of your team? How much can I trust you?

What can you offer team members to get their maximum motivation, trust and commitment?

In the contractual relationships of the Modern Paradigm, money is the prime motivator. The leader gets the level of motivation, trust and commitment that he pays for. When the money runs out, so does the motivation, trust, commitment and the relationship.

> **People will pay to do things they find fulfilling.**

The Wisdom Paradigm offers a more compelling motivation: fulfillment. The Wisdom Paradigm offers the opportunity to become good and pursue honor, fulfillment and Happiness. Whether you are the leader or a team member, the more deeply you commit yourself to the team and its mission, the more you will develop your character and goodness, and the more you will find fulfillment in your life and your work.

Look at it from a different angle. How many people work at a job that they hate because they need the money? They must be paid to do the work. Many of them put in the minimum effort required because they don't find their job meaningful or fulfilling. Contract relationship.

How many of these same people take their hard-earned money and spend it on some activity which they find fulfilling?

How much will they spend doing something they find really fulfilling? Hundreds of dollars? Thousands? Hundreds of thousands of dollars?

No one is paying them to do what they find fulfilling. Instead, *they are paying others* for that opportunity.

When activity is meaningful and fulfilling, people will pay to do it.

If you can make their work fulfilling, how much will that add to your team productivity and performance?

Sometimes it is the very nature of the activity that people find fulfilling. Often it is also the culture and environment, the people they are with and the feeling that they are part of something that is meaningful.

Motivation. Commitment. Whether you are the leader or a team member, what's in it for you? The opportunity to pursue fulfillment and Happiness, and be part of something meaningful and good.

Of course, there are some people who are more deeply motivated by money, power, prestige or other things than they are by the opportunity to participate in something meaningful. Perhaps they are interested in the short-term pleasure money and power promise. Perhaps they believe that money, power and fame are the forces that ultimately drive the world.

In the end, they will find that money, fame and power are fleeting and their desire for them ultimately impossible to satisfy. The pursuit of money, power and fame will not lead them to fulfillment. Either they will figure this out and pursue the only road to Happiness, becoming good, or they will die never having found true fulfillment.

You don't want people who are primarily motivated by money, power or fame on your team. Their focus on these things will cause disharmony with the rest of the team and the team's goals, and you will lose performance.

Of course, money is always an important consideration. People must make enough money to take care of themselves and their families in a reasonable way. Pay people enough to take care of their families so they can focus, distraction-free, on pursuing goodness, fulfillment and Happiness in their work with you.

It turns out that you can make more money being motivated by and pursuing *goodness* than you can by being motivated by and pursuing *money* itself.

First, when you pursue goodness, you develop the high-trust and deeply committed relationships that will outperform the lower-trust and less committed relationships that follow from the pursuit of money. In the marketplace, that performance advantage translates quickly into a profit advantage as well.

Second, the deeper your commitment, the more you will develop teamwork, skills, character and eventually leadership. The more deeply you develop and embody these qualities, the more valuable you are in the workplace. That means increased compensation.

When you search for team members, subordinate leaders or a leader to follow yourself, seek out those who are well-prepared, motivated and committed to seek fulfillment, goodness and trust. These are the people who are best prepared to be our leaders and teammates. They will produce the highest performance people and teams. They will make the decisions we can trust to guide us through the tough challenges of the 21st century.

A covenant team is any group of people committed to each other and focused on some good or noble goal.

The covenant relationship is high trust and stable, and gives the best foundation for developing the next generation of leaders, and the highest performance people and teams.

With the team dynamic, we find that teamwork, character and skills all drive continuous improvement in each other in a self-reinforcing loop. That leads to individual and team improvement over time.

The more that team members are motivated, trusting and committed to the team, its activity and mission, the faster and greater the performance improvement.

Maximize team performance by maximizing the motivation, trust and commitment of your team by offering them the opportunity to find goodness, fulfillment and meaning in their work.

Understanding the covenant team and the team dynamic is critical as we develop the means to systematically and reliably develop the next generation of good leaders. The more the next generation understands the covenant team and team dynamic, the better and more effective their leadership. The more we—the current generation—understand the covenant team and team dynamic, the better leaders we can be and the more effectively we can teach and develop the next generation. They will learn something from what we say. They will learn the most and best by what we do.

The Leadership Components

Now that we have fully engaged the Wisdom Paradigm and its understanding of human nature, covenant relationships, and goals, we can more deeply examine the four leadership components. Every leader possesses these qualities in some greater or lesser amount:

- Skills
- Character
- Bearing
- Vision

The more people trust your skills, character, bearing and vision, the more they will follow you.

SKILLS

The more people trust your skills, the more they will follow you. The skills break down into four different areas:

1. Conveying meaning
2. Skills associated with the activity
3. People skills
4. Management skills

Conveying meaning

The more those working with you understand how their participation is meaningful, the more they will follow you. If you are a good leader, you will make the meaning of their participation tangible and present to them on several levels including how their participation contributes to:

- Their personal development: skills, character, teamwork, bearing, vision and leadership
- The success of the team's mission

- The team's pursuit of goodness
- The well-being and success of other people
- Their own development of goodness, and their pursuit of fulfillment and Happiness

It is about making sure that your people understand how their effort fits into and is important in the big picture. The importance of conveying the meaning and framework for understanding the team's work is hard to overstate.

There is the famous tale of the traveler who encounters three stonecutters at work and asks them all the same question "What are you doing?"

The first stonecutter, grumpy, replies that he is cutting stones. The second, without looking up, replies that he is helping to build a wall. Raising his eyes to meet those of the traveler, the third stonecutter smiles and says "I am part of a great effort that honors God with a cathedral!"

The more your people understand that they are building a cathedral in everything that they do, the deeper their commitment and the more they will follow you.

Skills associated with the activity

These are the skills associated with the activity that you are leading. If you are going to lead (coach) a basketball team, how good are your basketball skills? Can you shoot the ball and dribble well? Maybe you have played, but how much basketball coaching experience do you have? Ever been a head coach? As a coach, have you ever made tough decisions under pressure in a championship game?

It comes down to your professional credibility with those whom you are leading. The more your team members trust your skills associated with the activity, the more confidence they will have that you know what you are doing, and the more they will follow you.

Are you leading engineers? How is your engineering credibility? Are you leading doctors? How is your credibility taking care of patients? Are you leading law enforcement officers? How are you police skills?

People Skills

The more people trust your people skills, the more they will follow you:

- How well do you relate to people?
- Do those on your team feel like you listen to and care about them?
- When someone makes a big mistake, do you know whether that person needs a knowing glance, a pat on the back, a hug, or a direct conversation to correct their error and do better in the future?
- Do you praise in public and correct in private?
- What are your people capable of?
- What are their strengths and challenges?
- How fast and hard can you push them?
- What are their limits?
- Do you understand your people and know what motivates them?
- How does each of them understand life?
- What paradigm(s) are they living in?
- How mature are they?
- What is their family like?
- Where do they come from?
- Where do they hope to go in the future?
- What are the top three things they care about?
- What are they anxious about?
- What do they do for fun? What are their hobbies?
- What makes them joyful?

The deepest trust and commitment come when people understand that you are helping them achieve their dreams—achieve what fulfills them. That dream might be unrelated to the work or mission they are doing with you, but you can always contribute character and teamwork development to the journey to their dream. You can be someone with whom they share the excitement of their dream. But you can't do any of this if you don't know what their dream is.

Management Skills

The more people trust your management skills, the more they will follow you.

- How organized are you?
- Can you understand a mission and put together a good plan to achieve it?
- Can you execute that plan managing tasks, leading people, and hitting timelines and milestones?
- How many tasks can you mange simultaneously?
- Are you thorough? Do you always complete the task?
- Can we trust that you won't let some detail slip through the cracks?

CHARACTER

The more people trust your character, the more they will follow you.
- When times get tough, will you be there for them?
- Can they trust that you will be honest with them?
- Will you be courageous for them?
- Will you demonstrate integrity?
- Are you just and fair, or do you play favorites?
- Will you persevere with them or give up on them?
- When things go well, do you give your team the credit?
- When things go poorly, do you step in front and take the blame?

When people know that you are there for them in the toughest times for the right reasons and in the right ways, they will follow you anywhere.

BEARING

Bearing is how you conduct yourself and how well you make decisions while under pressure. In a stress-filled situation, do you make good decisions while demonstrating composure, and a calm and cool demeanor that gives everyone confidence that success is on the way? Do you lose your cool and undermine everyone's confidence?

Some examples of demonstrating bearing:

- The football quarterback who must lead his team down the field to score the winning touchdown at the end of the game
- The naval aviator landing his jet at night on the pitching deck of an aircraft carrier
- The law enforcement officer handling an emotion-laden domestic dispute
- The business executive making the pitch for the big deal
- The attorney arguing before the Supreme Court
- The school bus driver with 55 rambunctious kids in the back merging onto the freeway during rush hour
- The trauma physician working to keep a family alive after a brutal car accident

The more people trust your ability to maintain your composure and make good decisions while under pressure, the more they will follow you.

VISION

A lot of books and articles have made *vision* sound like a complex, hard-to-understand, rather esoteric concept. But it's not.

Vision is simply the ability to see down the road to accomplish your goals/mission and our purpose of becoming good.

The further you see down the road, the better your vision. The further down the road you see, the more people will trust and follow you because you know the route better than they do.

In the military, this idea is often referred to as *situational awareness* or by its abbreviation: *SA*. The fighter pilot or commander with the best overall sense of what is going on in the battle—who has the best vision or situational awareness—has a big advantage and will likely win the battle.

Imagine that your spouse is sending you and your 16-year-old child to the store to get some groceries and give your child some driving experience (your mission).

As an experienced driver, you see further down the road than your 16-year-old. You recognize potential problems much earlier. You see potential opportunities much earlier.

When you arrive at a four-way stop, you look at the other stopped drivers to make sure it is your turn and that they see you before you pull out. You see the kid on the bike on the driveway a block down, and already know whether he'll be going down the driveway toward the street when you go by.

You notice the young driver in the sports car approaching from behind way too fast just one lane over. You make sure that you're protected from another young driver in the other lane who is looking down, busy texting.

If you are a good driver, your vision extends down the street and out the sides and the rear of the car. You know exactly where everyone is and have a feel for the flow of the cars into the near future. The better your situational awareness, the better your vision, the further down the road and into the future you can "see" how things are unfolding.

> Vision is the intuitive knowledge of the flow of things around you so that you can best navigate obstacles and take advantage of opportunities to achieve your mission and purpose.

But that 16-year-old behind the wheel of your car doesn't see any of that. Her vision extends about two feet beyond the front of the car. A young driver must spend so much of their attention just handling the basic driving tasks that she is unable to see much down the road. Her situational awareness is low. With experience, her vision will gradually expand. She will see further down the block and begin to recognize potential problems. She will begin to get a feel for the flow of cars in other lanes.

Vision includes that intuitive knowledge that you develop for the flow of things around you.

One reason Michael Jordan was so successful in basketball was because he had an intuitive feel for the flow of everyone and the ball on the court.

In hockey, Wayne Gretzky's vision of the game enabled him to know—to "see"—where the puck was going to be before anyone else did.

The great football quarterbacks "read" the defense and recognize mismatches and opportunities much earlier than other quarterbacks.

The chess grandmaster has better awareness of the situation on the chess board, sees many moves ahead of opponents, and beats them.

The business leader who can anticipate customer desires and trends has vision.

Vision is the intuitive knowledge of the flow of things around you so that you can best navigate obstacles and take advantage of opportunities to achieve your mission and purpose.

Vision comes with experience. The more information you have and the better you are able to integrate that information into your overall understanding of the situation, the better your vision will be. The more you know what's going on, the further down the road you will see.

Using the driving metaphor, gaining more information might mean turning on the radio or using your GPS navigation system to avoid bad traffic. Vision also means recognizing opportunities before others do so you can take advantage of them.

While more information generally helps build and improve your vision, getting overwhelmed with too much information can reduce your vision. Leaders with good vision understand what information is important and what isn't, and use the best information to build the best picture of what is going on while discarding the rest.

When you see further down the road than others, you have an enormous advantage over them. You can take advantage of opportunities and avoid problems others can't see. You will literally be way ahead of the competition.

Those who see far down the road and have the greatest vision are called *Master*.

The more that people trust your vision, the more they will follow you. After all, you know the way to go better than they do.

CONTINUOUS IMPROVEMENT

Continuous improvement is a vital part of effective leadership. Leaders and teams should never be satisfied to remain where they are. They should strive for growth and continuous improvement.

A good leader will set standards that challenge the team members to excel. When the team members meet those standards, the leader should set new, higher standards. Optimally, this becomes a continuous improvement loop that improves the performance of the leader and team members.

INTEGRITY: 24—7—365

To maximize leadership, you need to maximize *your* skills, character, bearing and vision. The more deeply you develop each of these areas, the more people will trust and follow you.

Everything you do in life can either contribute to your development in these areas and your leadership, or undermine your development and leadership. If you want to become the best leader possible, it requires your attention 24 hours a day, 7 days a week and 365 days a year.

The good news is that everything you do to build your skills, character, bearing and vision—to become a good leader—also contributes directly to you becoming a good person, and achieving fulfillment and Happiness. Good leadership, a good life and fulfillment go together.

With all aspects of life—including your personal/private and work/public—integrated into a single, unified focus on becoming good, you can no longer practice vices in your private life and pretend that they won't undermine your leadership, character and goodness in the rest of your life. That might seem obvious, but many people think they can cheat in their private life and believe that the breach of character won't increase the likelihood of cheating in their professional life. They think that what happens in Vegas stays in Vegas. They think that they can go to church on Sunday and then live a different life the rest of the week. But life doesn't work that way.

It's akin to thinking that you can gorge yourself with food in your private life while keeping a healthy diet in your public life, and that it won't somehow impact your physical fitness or health. The fact is that gorging yourself in your private life undoes the self-discipline developed with a healthy diet in your public life, *and* it changes your fitness and health.

In the same way, when you cheat in your private life it necessarily impacts and changes your character. It doesn't matter if you did it secretly and no one else knows. It doesn't matter if you think it doesn't hurt anyone else. When you act poorly in any aspect of your life, it impacts and changes your character for the worse, and undermines your integrity. It directly and undeniably hurts *you*. It takes you away from your purpose, your goodness.

> The deepest trust and commitment (and performance) come when people understand that you are helping them achieve what fulfills them.

When times get tough, it means you won't be as well prepared to lead as you could have been—even if we only mean leading yourself. What happens in Vegas never stays in Vegas. It always stays with you and changes you.

The more consistently you do the right thing at all times in all aspects of your life, the better prepared you will be to do the right thing when times are really tough and challenging. You will have very strong integrity. It will make you a better leader and a good person. You will be well-prepared for the test.

The good news is that if you really commit to the leadership challenge, you will become a highly-skilled and wise person of honor and integrity, who is well down the path of goodness and fulfillment. You will become a very successful leader. The challenge is that becoming a good leader is something that requires total commitment 24-7-365.

The Leadership Components provide us the specific areas that we need to address as we develop the next generation of leaders. The more people trust your skills, character, bearing and vision, the more they will follow you even in very difficult, life and death situations.

The Leadership Components also give us the ingredients we need for a recipe to form the next generation of leaders in a systematic, deliberate manner. We need to make sure that the development process for the next generation of leaders fully addresses each of these areas to maximize the leadership potential of each young person. If we are going to inspire the next generation, our children, to become the best leaders possible, we need to make sure that we do the best we can to improve our own skills, character, bearing, vision and wisdom. That will maximize our own leadership effectiveness, put us in the best position to help the next generation of leaders, and provide the best example of leadership that we can for that next generation.

The Power of Love

The desire for fulfillment is a very powerful motivation in the Wisdom Paradigm. If you can make the activity or work that you are leading fulfilling, you will have plenty of people willing to join you, and they will be committed and work hard. You will get very good performance.

But there is one motivation still more powerful. One thing that will get even deeper commitment. The deepest commitment.

Love.

When the people on your team know that you love them, that you really do care about what is good for them, they will give you the deepest commitment and highest performance possible.

We're used to talking about love in our personal lives but we're not used to talking about it in our work lives.

Like leadership, love runs completely through our lives. Our lives are filled with relationships all of which have the potential for love. The loving relationship of the family. The love of friends. Romantic love. The love that binds those who have faced tough challenges together. Love for others as simple human beings.

We need love. From the very beginning. In the womb, babies respond to their mother's voice and touch. They can distinguish between her voice and others.

As infants and young children, we seek love and affection. Children who receive affection from and bond with their parents have the best chance to have healthy and happy relationships in life. They are much healthier physically and mentally. Babies who don't receive love can wither and die.

We grow up playing and bonding with our friends. One of the worst things that can happen to a child is being excluded. Not being invited. Not picked for a team. It can be devastating psychologically.

The Greeks used several different words to describe different aspects of what we would understand as loving relationships.

Storge is the Greek word for the fundamental affection that we feel for family members, friends and colleagues. It is an instinctual empathy.

Philia is the brotherly love we feel for friends who are equals. It is the joy we get when we are with our friends, and flows from being virtuous.

Eros is often known as erotic love. It may involve, but does not require, sexual attraction.

Agape is the word for the unconditional love that God has for his children.

Agape also describes the totally self-giving love that can exist between people. That self-giving love is completely focused on what is good for the other person. It flows from the highest character and the most virtuous life.

Good leaders make work fulfilling, and help their team and teammates become good so they can find fulfillment and achieve Happiness. The focus is on developing good character, deep trust and honor.

We can take it to yet another level.

The best leaders love their people (agape) and engender the love of their people.

When people know that you love them, they will do almost anything for you. Because your love (agape) for them means that you will do anything you can to help them become good.

People often join the Marine Corps for the fulfillment, for the kind of person the experience will make them, for the honor of serving their nation. Those are all great reasons.

But the reason they are willing to die for each other is because they, through shared hardship, have developed deep *agape* relationships with each other.

Love will always get the deepest commitment and highest performance from your team—whether at work or in your personal life.

Culture and Tradition of Excellence

The Wisdom Paradigm has given us a consistent way of understanding life, human nature, relationships, purpose and goals.

From the Wisdom Paradigm, we have derived an understanding of leadership that includes a proper understanding of purpose, covenant teams and the components of leadership. We have the knowledge and ingredients we need to make the next generation of leaders we can trust to wield our enormous power and lead us through the difficult challenges of the future. We have the knowledge and ingredients we need to put together the most powerful people and teams possible— people and teams with the trust, commitment and motivation needed to beat the competition.

These things become far more powerful if we can surround them with a culture and tradition of excellence that sustains them and provides an environment for growth.

If we develop the next generation of leaders within a culture and tradition of excellence, it will provide them with the narrative and framework to most deeply understand the Wisdom Paradigm, covenant relationship and leadership components in the widest variety of environments.

As the current generation of leaders, we need to establish a culture and tradition of excellence so that our leadership—both in our work, everyday life and in forming the next generation—will be most effective.

We need to ensure that a sense of excellence, that the expectation of excellence, and that a tradition of excellence permeate every organization we can. Everyone within our organization should have a sense that what they are doing is important, carries real meaning and is done very well. Everyone should work with the expectation that other team members and our organization as strive for excellence in everything we do. Finally, everyone in our organization should know the story of our organization and their role within that story, understanding that they are extending a long tradition of excellence into the future.

None of this can be phony. We can't simply pretend that everything is excellent when it is not. If things are being done poorly, they must be identified and fixed. The sense and expectation must be that problems are never papered over, ignored or swept aside, but aggressively and honestly identified, examined and corrected.

We don't necessarily need a long organizational history to establish a tradition of excellence. If our organization is young, perhaps a new startup, we can emphasize that this team has the privileged role of starting our story with high performance, expectations and dreams. They are establishing the tradition rather than continuing it.

We want an organizational culture that is a breeding ground for great leaders and high-performance teams. We want an organizational culture that sets and sustains the highest expectations generation after generation. We want a tradition of excellence that provides a strong sense of story and uses the high performance of previous generations to inspire even higher performance in following generations.

THE POWER OF TRADITION, CEREMONY, RITUAL AND CUSTOM

We all know that our police, fire and military people risk their lives for our safety. Sometimes we lose one of them in the line of duty. It is one thing to read about the loss in a newspaper article and think about their sacrifice.

It is a completely different experience, much more powerful and meaningful, to be at the burial, see the spouse receive the flag, and hear the sound of shots and the playing of Taps against the silence. The tradition of honoring our lost through the ritual of the burial, and the custom of presenting the flag and playing Taps is incredibly powerful. The tradition, ritual and custom transform an ordinary experience into a transcendent experience. It gives the event the depth that it deserves.

The US Marine Corps has a long history of success in combat and leadership development. The Marine Corps excels because they have a very strong story that inspires Marines to organizational, professional and personal excellence.

The Marine Corps takes average Americans and convinces them that they are writing the next chapter in the 230+ year story of our nation and Corps, and the story of their own life. Marines have heard story after story about Marine units achieving great things against overwhelming odds. They have heard story after story about average Marines just like them demonstrating incredible courage, discipline, tenacity and toughness even in the most dire, hopeless conditions.

It never occurs to the Marines of today that they will do or be anything less. The expectations are set and reinforced every day in Marine Corps culture. Those cultural expectations of excellence provide the impetus for Marines to push themselves harder in training, to be tough and persist despite bleak odds, and to hold their personal, professional and organizational honor high. They become part of the history of the Corps.

Their own lives become their personal story of discipline, sacrifice, integrity and honor.

The story of the Marine Corps is told not just in books and classrooms, but with much more impact in the traditions, rituals and customs of the Corps.

The Marine Corps traditions, customs and rituals are extremely powerful ways to connect the Marines of today with those of the past.

The red "blood" stripe on the dress uniform trousers worn by Marine non-commissioned officers hearkens to the bloody Battle of Chapultepec in 1847 during the Mexican-American War.

The curved Mameluke sword carried by all Marine officers goes back to Marine expeditions against the Barbary pirates in the early 1800's.

"From the halls of Montezuma, [Chapultepec]

To the shores of Tripoli, [Mameluke sword]

We will fight our country's battles…"[11]

Marines today remember and hail the epic accomplishments of their predecessors not just in uniform and sword, but in their very *hymn*—a special kind of song that honors.

During formal dinners called "Mess Night", Marines will often set an extra place setting for fallen Marines. The stories told are not just those from older times, but include Vietnam, Kuwait, Iraq and Afghanistan.

One of the most powerful Marine Corps traditions is the celebration of the Marine Corps Birthday every year on Nov 10th. Marines around the world commemorate their birthday with formal celebrations when possible, or informally when deployed in combat areas. It is quite common for retired and former Marines to celebrate the birthday though it has been decades since their active service.

Formal or informal, the celebration always includes a message from the Commandant of the Marine Corps and a ceremonial cutting of a birthday cake. The first piece of cake always goes to the oldest Marine present, calling to mind the sacrifice of and debt to previous generations of Marines. The second piece of cake goes to the youngest Marine present, pointing to the future of the Corps. Formal celebrations include a birthday ball with a parade of Marines wearing uniforms from the past.

There are no "ex-Marines". There are no "former Marines". Though they may be in different stages of life, there are only *Marines*. The present does not just connect with the past; the past connects powerfully with the present.

When referring to a United States Marine, the word "Marine" should be capitalized because "Marine" is understood to be a title earned through graduation of Boot Camp or Officer Candidates School.

These ceremonies, rituals and customs are all very powerful ways that the Corps connects Marines through time, ensuring that every aspect of Marine Corps culture is permeated with expectations of

[11] The Marine Corps Hymn

excellence. It dramatically increases the performance level of the Corps.

In a similar way, our organizations can establish a culture and tradition of excellence that ensures that the people and teams of the future continue to perform at the same levels that we have established today.

Start by understanding the story of your organization:

- Who are you?
- What are you about?
- How did you start?
- What where the dreams of the creators?
- What challenges have you overcome?
- Who in the past set high standards of excellence?
- What characteristics or qualities distinguish your organization from others?
- What are the hopes and expectations for the future?

Every organization has a story to tell. If your organization is new, then start articulating the story yourself.

What are you doing to celebrate the past and make it tangible in the present? Do you have any organizational customs, ceremonies, traditions or rituals? Perhaps it is how you recognize and celebrate success in awards presentations. Perhaps it is what you wear (or wore), how you serve clients or customers, or products that defined your origins.

One of the most successful businesses in Southern California, Ganahl Lumber, keeps a gigantic band saw with a 56 foot blade at the front of the headquarters store, and similar band saws at their other locations. It reminds the Ganahl workers, clients and owners of today that they are part of a story that started in 1884 when an Austrian immigrant named Christian Ganahl arrived in Southern California. While the products and services have changed over the centuries, the band saws remind everyone that the commitment to excellence upon which the business was founded has not changed.

If you ask Peter Ganahl, the CEO of the company, how Ganahl can be successful selling lumber—a commodity—in competition with places like Home Depot and Lowe's, Peter will tell you that their success is all about the high-trust, covenant relationships they have built with clients, not the price of the wood.

I work at a Catholic high school in Anaheim, California. The religious order of brothers and priests that founded and own the school, the Servites, originated in Florence, Italy, in the early 1200's.

We use a variety of means to help connect our high school students today with the order throughout the world and back through history. Throughout the year we celebrate Masses remembering the seven businessmen who started the Servite order in 1233. These very successful merchants met each other while doing community service, serving the poor and sick in a hospital in Florence. Working together over time, they eventually made the decision to give up their belongings and live together in community and follow Christ by serving the poor and sick.

We remember an early Servite, Peregrine, who became the patron saint of those suffering from cancer and AIDs.

We conclude each of our school Masses the same way Servites around the world have concluded liturgies for almost eight centuries— by singing the *Salve Regina* in Latin.

Servites throughout the world and throughout history are united by their *charism* which emphasizes serving Christ by:

1. Living in community
2. Service to others wherever needed
3. Service in the humble example of a poor young woman from Palestine

Across languages, across cultures and across history, the young men of Servite feel part of a much larger story that goes back almost 800 years. They are connected to holy men and women from the past and today. They feel part of a group of people who serve Christ by serving others throughout the world. And as part of that Servite history, they too understand that they have a responsibility to write the next chapter of Servites working to serve the poor and suffering of the world.

STARTING YOUR OWN TRADITION

You may not have many of these ceremonies, rituals, traditions or customs from the past in your organization. You may have to start them today as a gift to the future. Make a list of what you have and what you can start. Ask colleagues for their ideas. Even better, ask those from the past for their ideas as well. Organizational birthdays, original products, success stories, and ways of recognizing and honoring those who have performed well are good places to start.

The next step is to ensure that these expectations of excellence, and the ceremonies, rituals, traditions and customs that support those expectations, permeate your organization and shape your organizational culture.

THREE-DIMENSIONAL BONDING

A very effective way to ensure that these permeate your organizational culture is to engage what we call *Three-Dimensional Bonding*. By developing deep bonds across your organization in the *vertical*, *horizontal* and *historical* dimensions, you maximize the likelihood that the power of your covenant teams, your culture and your traditions will continue after you leave.

Historical Bonding

Historical bonding means ensuring that today's team members understand and feel like they are an important part of a larger story. Make them feel like they must not just meet the standards of the best performers of the past, but that they must write their own story and hand down even higher standards to challenge those who follow in the future.

We have already discussed how you can start your own tradition and establish ceremonies, customs and rituals that tie the present to the past and the future. Find out how other organizations have established traditions. What ceremonies or rituals have they established?

Do you have the history of your organization displayed in text, pictures and objects somewhere in your organization?

One effective way to connect team members of today with those from the past is to invite past team members to events to share their experiences and stories. They can be invited to formal events, celebrations and ceremonies. They can be honored at those formal events. They can be invited to informal events or even to spend time around the current team members. Do you have a mentoring program that pairs those from the past with current team members?

Properly done, historical bonding uses tradition, ceremonies, rituals and customs to improve current performance and ensure that expectations of high performance are transmitted from the past through current team members to the future.

Vertical Bonding

Vertical bonding uses the chain of command to improve performance, communicate high expectations and transmit a culture of excellence throughout your organization. It follows from successful implementation of our understanding of leadership.

We know from our understanding of leadership that the more people trust your skills, character, bearing and vision, the more they will follow you. The more your subordinates trust you as their leader, the more they will listen to and internalize what you communicate to them about tradition, performance expectations and excellence.

If you are a well-respected, good leader, you will create and communicate organizational culture just by doing your work. Colleagues and subordinates who respect you will embrace your way of doing things and, by repeating it themselves and teaching others, will make it the organizational culture. Take care of your people in the right ways for the right reasons.

As a leader, maximize trust up and down your chain of command to tighten vertical bonding, communicate high expectations and establish a culture of excellence.

Horizontal Bonding

Horizontal bonding runs perpendicular to the chain of command, bringing peers in the organization together to develop a broad sense of responsibility for the organization.

Imagine that you are the CEO of an organization that includes a level of vice presidents on the organizational chart, with a level of directors junior to them, and then a level of supervisors followed by team members.

Obviously, the most effective, efficient and important way to operate your organization is through the chain of command. Primary responsibility for operating the organization must always flow through the vertical chain of command.

That said, you can organize your team members horizontally to play a very important and powerful role in the success of the organization. By organizing a director's group and/or a supervisor's group and giving them (as a group) some secondary responsibilities, you can:

1. Develop within them a deeper sense of ownership in your organization

2. Communicate and reinforce the culture and tradition of excellence throughout your organization

3. Develop an informal reporting system that can uncover problems that might otherwise be missed.

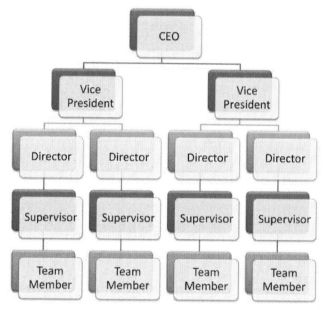

For instance, you might get the directors together as a group and reinforce (with your vice presidents) the importance of the role they play in the success of the organization. To give them an even deeper sense of ownership in your organization, you can invite them, as a group, to become a task force that tackles a long-standing problem within the organization or takes on a community service project. They can be the group that works on establishing the culture and tradition of excellence. It really doesn't matter what issue they tackle if the issue is outside the regular, vertical chain of command and they tackle it as a group of peers.

As they tackle the project, they will learn much about each other and bond more tightly as a group. They will take a deeper sense of ownership in the organization as it becomes "theirs" in a way outside of their normal work assignments.

If you assign one or more of them as the task force leaders, it can be an outstanding opportunity for them to develop and practice their own leadership. It will give you and the vice presidents an opportunity to observe their leadership potential outside of the usual chain of command.

The tighter their informal organization and the more secondary projects they tackle, the more they will develop that sense of ownership and responsibility in your organization.

Because they are being more highly valued as a director or supervisor, they will take more pride in their role. They will begin to develop high expectations of each other's conduct and performance.

If one of the directors behaves or performs poorly, the other directors are more likely to call out that misbehaving director. Perhaps they will call him out informally "among directors" at first and then, if it is not resolved, to more senior staff. They will do this because the director's misbehavior may be seen by the other directors as making them all look bad.

The increased sense of ownership, responsibility and pride will make them much more likely to support and reinforce the organization's culture and tradition of excellence because it has become *their* culture and tradition of excellence. Properly done, stronger relationships between directors or between supervisors should reduce unhealthy competition or infighting among people of the same position.

Finally, the horizontal bonding can provide an informal but powerful and important way for your organization to identify and solve problems that might otherwise go unnoticed. With Sarbanes-Oxley and other laws holding organizations responsible for the unethical or illegal behavior of employees, it is increasingly important that organizations have as many avenues as possible to identify unethical or illegal behavior early so they can correct it immediately.

Imagine that one of your directors is involved in unethical, immoral or illegal actions. You, your vice presidents and perhaps all the other directors may be unaware because the bad director has intimated or threatened those who know about the bad behavior—his subordinate supervisors and team members—to prevent them from revealing the misbehavior.

If this kind of situation goes on for long, it can be catastrophic for your organization. Bad behavior is always destructive to organizational performance. In addition, if the director's behavior is illegal or unethical, your organization could be legally liable.

If the director is creating a hostile work environment by threatening or intimidating subordinates or peers, the liability increases even more.

Finally, subordinates are likely to be disheartened by the misbehavior and intimidation, giving them a very sour experience of and causing them to lose faith in your organization. That will negatively impact their performance as well. If the misbehavior is obvious to them they will often assume that it is obvious to you and more senior staff as well. You may well appear hypocritical. How long will they stay part of your organization?

Good horizontal bonding provides an environment, a sort of informal support group, which makes it much more likely that someone will report the misbehavior to senior staff. With a greater sense of ownership, peer directors will be more likely to be offended by misbehavior because it reflects poorly on all of them. The offended director can, with the total group of directors, approach the misbehaving director early and informally to force a change in his behavior. If that doesn't work, it is much more likely that the group of directors will report the misbehavior to senior staff.

Even if we imagine that none of the other directors know about the misbehavior, if the supervisors have strong horizontal bonding, it is much more likely that an intimidated or threatened supervisor will go to his peer supervisors and their seniors to report the problem.

With strong horizontal bonding, a supervisor with a deeper sense of ownership of and commitment to the organization is more likely to be offended by the director's misbehavior and act. With strong horizontal bonding, the intimidated supervisor has a safe environment in which he can go to his peers with the problem, and through them to other directors and vice presidents.

Horizontal bonding can be a very powerful way to strengthen your organization, but there are some important things to remember.

- Horizontal bonding is always secondary to and never takes precedence over the primary chain of command
- Don't give tasks to horizontal groups that are properly handled by the chain of command
- Don't permit horizontal groups to organize formally with enough power or influence that they can interfere with decisions that are properly made through the chain of command.

After you get your high-performance covenant teams established and beating the competition, you need to ensure that the great team performance and leadership development is locked into your organization so that it continues even if something happens to you.

You need to establish a culture and tradition of excellence to ensure that a sense of excellence, an expectation of excellence and a tradition of excellence permeate your organization. You can accomplish this through *Three-Dimensional Bonding*.

Use *historic bonding* to ensure that your team members understand and feel like they are an important and meaningful part of a larger story. By using traditions, customs, rituals and ceremonies, you can help team members today understand that they have an obligation to not only meet the standards of the past, but to set even higher standards for future generations.

Maximize *vertical bonding* by maximizing trust up and down your chain of command. That is part of your duty as a leader anyway. Use the high trust to communicate high expectations and the culture of excellence to others in your organization.

Done correctly, *horizontal bonding* is a very powerful way to:

1. Develop a secondary sense of ownership among peers
2. Communicate and reinforce the tradition and culture of excellence
3. Serve as an informal but powerful and important way for the organization to identify and solve problems that might otherwise go unnoticed

Putting It All Together

Let's review what we have discussed so far.

Our nation and world are facing unprecedented challenges. We've lost trust in the leadership of many of the most important institutions in our society. Our nation is dividing and fragmenting along moral, social and political lines. We are losing the common ground and shared foundation that are critical to the unity and future success of our nation.

To be successful—perhaps just to survive—we need to develop the next generation of leaders who we can trust to make good decisions in fast-paced, complex, globally diverse situations. We cannot develop real solutions for the tremendous challenges we face until we first address the problem of leadership.

Unfortunately, we haven't had the ability to develop a generation of good leaders in any systematic or reliable way. Despite the hundreds of billions of dollars spent, leadership studies are stuck in a quagmire of competing, irreconcilable and mutually exclusive paradigms of life. Not only is the clock ticking on our national and global challenges while we founder, things are getting worse. We are getting further from a solution because the Postmodern Paradigm is becoming increasingly influential, and dividing and fragmenting our nation.

We know that the Wisdom Paradigm is right because it is philosophically and logically consistent, and its understanding of human nature and human relationships provides the foundation for developing the highest performance people, teams and leaders for our future.

We all seek fulfillment and Happiness in life, and that can only be achieved as we develop the virtues within ourselves and become good. Just like one can only get in good physical shape through exercise, so we can only get in good character shape by using activities to develop virtues like honesty, justice, love, courage, integrity and wisdom.

We find the opportunity to practice the virtues and become good by being part of covenant teams: groups of people committed to each other and pursuing some good goal. The more we commit ourselves to the team, the more deeply and quickly we will develop our teamwork, skills, character and leadership. The more I give to the team, the more I grow in every dimension.

The more the team invests in me, the better I become and the more the team benefits from my improvement. The good of the team and my good are linked at all levels: my personal development; the mission success of the team; and achieving both the team's and my purpose of becoming good and achieving fulfillment.

Because the good of the individual and the good of the team are the same, the covenant team is high-trust, highly stable and draws deeper commitment from team members. The deeper commitment and trust maximize individual and team performance, giving the covenant team a large performance advantage over other teams grounded in modern contractual or postmodern power relationships.

The covenant team leader gets deeper commitment, trust and motivation than other leaders because he offers team members the opportunity to develop skills, teamwork, leadership and the virtues, and to become good, and pursue fulfillment and Happiness.

Covenant teams are the most powerful, highest-performance teams possible.

With the paradigm for maximum performance teams clearly identified, we can fully understand leadership and identify the components of a leader. The more that people trust their leader's skills, character, bearing, vision and commitment to continuous improvement, the more they will follow their leader. Becoming a better leader means maximizing the development of skills, character, bearing and vision.

Being a good leader demands attention 24—7—365 days a year. Everything you do can either contribute to or undermine your leadership development. Everything you do either helps you become good and achieve fulfillment, or takes you another direction.

As a leader you can use *Three Dimensional Bonding* to create and perpetuate a culture and tradition of excellence throughout your organization that remains strong even after you leave. This culture and tradition of excellence will not only support leadership and teams within your organization, but will intensify their performance and impact.

All of this leads to several other important realizations:

1. **Leadership and life are the same**. The path to becoming a good leader and the path to becoming a good person are the same.

2. **Everyone is a leader**. Leadership is not an activity reserved for a separate or elite class. Every person is called to be a leader in several dimensions. At a minimum, each person must lead himself to goodness, and lead others around him to goodness by the example he displays. Most people also lead their family, their children and people with whom they work.

3. **Leadership from below**. You can lead others from a subordinate position, inspiring them to higher performance by the example you set and high standards you achieve

GOOD LEADERS, LEADERSHIP AND MANAGEMENT

Once we fully embrace the Wisdom Paradigm, we can definitively answer several age-old questions:

1. What are the differences between a *good leader*, *bad leader* and an *effective leader?*
2. Are good leaders born or made?
3. What is the difference between leadership and management?

You have probably already figured the answers out for yourself.

Good, Bad and Effective Leaders

An "effective" leader is one who achieves the goal within the parameters given to achieve the goal. As long as it is within the parameters, it doesn't matter how he achieved that goal. Effectiveness is nothing more than an evaluation of whether the goal was accomplished or to what extent a goal was accomplished.

A "good" leader achieves goals and has well-developed leadership components:

1. **Is effective**. The leader is effective in accomplishing the team's mission and purpose
2. **Has good leadership skills (Skills)**. The leader inspires and motivates subordinates, has good people skills, and is skilled at organization and project management
3. **Is a good person (Character)**. The leader is a person of honor and demonstrates good character and the virtues—especially integrity—in all activities. He is worthy of trust.
4. Can make tough decisions under pressure (**Bearing**). This contributes directly to #1
5. Has vision linking activity and work with mission and our purpose of becoming good (Vision). This also contributes directly to #1.
6. **Has high trust relationships with and develops subordinates**. The leader develops the skills, teamwork, character, bearing and leadership of all those on the team, helping them become good, and pursue fulfillment and Happiness.

A "bad" leader is a person who falls significantly short in any of the qualities of a good leader above.

Are good leaders born or made?

Some people are naturally good at things while others struggle.

Some people have an incredible, natural swing with the golf club. Others have natural charisma and are great people-persons. Still others can pick up a musical instrument and start to play it with little or no training. Some people are good at taking apart things and putting them back together. Some people have a knack for software coding. They just seem to have a natural talent for that activity.

In the same way, some people seem to be born with the great people skills, a sense of vision and the ability to give people direction. They know what needs to get done and how to do it. They are at their best when they are called to perform under pressure. They have natural charisma. They seem to be born with these abilities and possess them at higher levels than their peers. They are natural leaders. Some people seem to be born leaders.

Other people aren't born with all these attributes in a mature state. We must work our tails off, with greater and lesser success, to develop each of these leadership components within ourselves. We aren't born leaders. We must make ourselves into leaders.

We see this in other areas of life too. Some people seem to be born as incredible football quarterbacks who can run and pass well with little instruction, and can lead a team down the field to score. Others must practice and work extensively to achieve similar results. Some are natural, born quarterbacks. Some must make themselves into good quarterbacks.

So, can anyone become a leader?

Yes, given hard work, almost anyone can become a leader at some level or another.

Some people are born leaders. With the Wisdom Paradigm and our understanding of leadership, we can now also systematically develop people into leaders.

Leadership vs. Management

There has been a long-running debate over the difference between leadership and management.

The simple and true answer is that you *lead people* and *manage things*. Let's dig deeper.

When the industrial revolution was at the forefront of our economy, *management* got all the attention. While there might have been a big difference between skilled and unskilled labor, or between various skill sets required to run the factories and make the economy move forward, within those skill sets people were pretty much interchangeable. One pipe-fitter was as good as any other. One machine operator was as good as any other. The workers weren't treated as individual people bringing unique qualities to their work, but treated as functional, interchangeable parts.

The industrial revolution treated people as just another resource, input or cog in the massive industrial machine. You *managed people* just as you would manage any other resource or thing.

The problem is that when you treat people like things, they tend to act like things. Treating people as things devalues and de-humanizes them, and your team's trust and commitment levels will be very low. When you manage people as things, team performance will be poor.

In contrast, when we talk about *leading*, we are always referring to guiding *people*. We never talk about leading things. Good leadership is dignifying and humanizing because it means seeing and treating each worker as an individual *person*. Good leadership means seeing each person as a unique individual with strengths and challenges, who is on his or her own life journey to become good.

Your responsibility as a good leader is to ensure that as long as that person spends time with you, you help them grow in every area—skills, character, teamwork, bearing, vision and leadership among them. Remember, the more you treat them as a real person and invest in their growth, the more you will develop trust and commitment, and the more they can contribute back to the team.

You help them grow not just professionally, but also personally. That does not mean that you must dig deep into their private life, but it does mean that you develop their people skills and virtues, and encourage them to be healthy physically, mentally, emotionally and spiritually. All of this helps them become a better person and helps your team become a better team.

Management is important to a leader as a skill. A good leader will be very competent at managing the things in the organization: resources, tasks, timelines, assignments, etc. Management is an important part of the skills that a good leader must develop, but it's not the fundamental thing a leader does.

As we move forward into 21st century situations that are chaotic, ambiguous, high-stress, diverse, fast-paced and global, America's future—America's ability to prevail in global competition of all kinds—depends on our ability to form the highest-performance people, teams and leaders who are creative, innovative and flexible.

That demands leadership of creative, innovative and inspired people and teams, not management of things.

Love your people enough to lead them, and you will make them better team members and people, enhance trust and commitment, and develop higher performance people and teams.

And by the way, when you practice leading people instead of managing them as things, you practice important virtues like empathy, patience and love that help you become good.

The Recipe for Leaders

One of the biggest problems with leadership studies is that we have dozens of descriptions of good leaders, but we don't have any recipes for making good leaders. We can't reliably produce a generation of good leaders if we don't have a systematic, deliberate process for doing so. Even when a systematic process might exist—like the leadership development programs in the US military—they are often seen as developing leadership that is relatively limited in its application (i.e. military service).

Once we make the commitment to the Wisdom Paradigm, coming up with a recipe for developing the next generation of leaders is straightforward. The recipe develops leaders no matter what the application—military, business, non-profit, public service, profession, family, etc. The recipe is much easier to develop because we have removed all the confusion caused by competing paradigms, and because purpose, motivation, covenant relationships and life itself all line up in a very powerful, but also simple and elegant way.

What follows is a recipe that provides general guidance on how to develop leaders. We've kept it general so that you can modify it to fit a variety of leadership development situations: work, youth athletic teams, family, etc.

The first section deals with the context and knowledge necessary to develop leaders. The second section deals with developing the Leadership Components that provide the foundation of trust so important in covenant leadership. And the last section tackles learning by practicing leadership.

CONTEXT

1. **IMMERSION**. From the earliest age, everyone should be raised in the Wisdom Paradigm and understand that their purpose in life is to become good and achieve fulfillment. The more deeply they are immersed in the wisdom understanding

of life, Covenant Leadership, covenant relationships and knowledge of their purpose in life, the more they will internalize this knowledge and the better prepared they will be for life and leadership. This cannot start too early.

2. **UNDERSTANDING.** The Wisdom Paradigm should be taught and constantly reinforced as the way to understand all aspects of life, especially their purpose of life, the nature of human relationships, and how they become what they practice. This should be done in an age-appropriate manner with increasing depth and complexity as people get older and take on positions of greater responsibility. They must seamlessly and intuitively understand every aspect of life in terms of the Wisdom Paradigm. As they get older, they should be taught the other paradigms so they can recognize their influence.

3. **PRACTICE.** Make them a part of covenant teams as much and as early as possible so they can learn to become a good team member. This should be done within the family, in activities, in sports and play, at school and work, and in any way possible. Emphasize the importance of the covenant relationship and developing skills, character, bearing and vision by giving maximum effort.

4. **SIGNS OF GROWTH.** Continue the process until they are ready for more. You will know they are ready when they:
    a. Can articulate their activities in terms of the Wisdom Paradigm, especially how their work and activities contribute to their own development as a good person
    b. Push themselves to continually improve their skills, teamwork and character
    c. Understand and demonstrate through their actions that they will become good people faster and more

deeply by committing themselves to others and the team

DEVELOPING THE LEADERSHIP COMPONENTS

5. When ready, put in place a training plan that develops each of the leadership components—skills, character, bearing and vision—in a systematic, deliberate manner

    a. **Assess their level of competence** in each Leadership Component (skills, character, bearing, vision)

    b. **Set goals in each component**. The goals for skill development are well-developed in many areas. In athletics, it may be a goal to achieve a certain time, lift a certain weight or perform a certain skill. At work, it may be achieving qualifications required for that work. The goals for character development might include being on time, being dependable or demonstrating courage in tough situations. Bearing is developed by practicing decision-making in increasingly stressful situations.

    c. **Implement a training plan** that helps them achieve their goals in each area. You should provide them with opportunities—as part of covenant teams—to develop their skills, character, bearing and vision towards those goals. Just as someone who is new to running should begin running short distances on flat ground at a slow pace, so the leadership apprentice should begin in simple situations, under supervision and active coaching, with minimal complexity and pressure. The training program should progress to increasingly complex situations with increasing risk and pressure, and less coaching.

    d. **Provide continuous performance feedback** so the apprentice understands what he is doing well and what he needs to do to continue to improve. Create a context where the feedback is felt as coaching towards excellence rather than criticism for poor performance.

PRACTICING LEADERSHIP

6. **LEADING.** The training plan should have the apprentice lead teams of others to accomplish goals. This gives the apprentice the opportunity to practice and develop each of his leadership components.

   a. **Skills**. The apprentice should be able to articulate in a compelling way the purpose and meaning of the team and activity to the team members. He should demonstrate competence in the skills associated with the activity. For instance, the leader of a team tasked with painting should be a competent painter himself. Moving from simple, low pressure and heavily supervised leadership experiences to complex, high pressure and less supervised leadership experiences, the apprentices should demonstrate good people and project management skills at each level.

   b. **Character**. The apprentice should demonstrate virtues like honesty, wisdom, love, justice, courage, perseverance, tenacity, etc. in every aspect of life, 24 hours a day and 365 days a year.

   c. **Bearing**. The apprentice should be able to make good decisions while under pressure in increasingly complex situations. The apprentice must demonstrate composure that instills confidence in and develops trust with others.

   d. **Vision**. Given different situations, how far down the road can the apprentice see? Does she see and avoid problems early? How early does she recognize and act on opportunities?

7. **INCREASED RESPONSIBILITY**: Promote the apprentice leader to positions with more authority and responsibility when she demonstrates appropriate levels of mastery in each area of the leadership components.

The key difference between this recipe/leadership development program and any other development program is the total focus on becoming good and achieving fulfillment. Once we have made the commitment to the Wisdom Paradigm, purpose and covenant relationships, the recipe becomes easy.

The big key in being able to systematically form the next generation of leaders is understanding that we need to select one paradigm, derive the leadership recipe and stick with it. Once we understand that the Wisdom Paradigm gives us the best leaders and highest performance people and teams, the leadership development recipe is relatively straightforward.

A Good Understanding?

The next part of our story addresses how we can take all this leadership and paradigm knowledge and apply it in our lives, community and society to develop the next generation of leaders that we so deeply need.

But first, let's find out if our Covenant Leadership model is the best among all the leadership theories out there and addresses the issues that have made leadership studies a mess for years. If we can answer these issues, we can be confident that we have found the best road to travel out of the leadership quagmire and that we are headed in the right direction for real progress in leadership studies.

LEADERSHIP THEORIES

We can categorize the potential leadership theories in three ways:

1. Theories that come from a commitment to the Wisdom Paradigm
2. Theories that come from a commitment to either the Modern or Postmodern Paradigms
3. Theories that come from combining concepts from two or more of the paradigms.

The reason that we have so much confusion in our leadership studies and theories today is that they take conflicting concepts from irreconcilable paradigms and attempt to assemble them into a single theory. It's like taking parts from a gas engine, a jet engine and a steam engine and trying to assemble them into an engine that works even better. It doesn't work. The pieces don't fit together. Even a poor gas engine, jet engine or steam engine will perform better than an engine assembled from parts from all three.

Leadership theories in Category #3, those that come from combining concepts from two or more paradigms, suffer from fundamental flaws and inconsistencies that always make them worse than those theories that come from a single paradigm.

So what about Category #2—leadership theories that come from either the Modern or Postmodern Paradigms?

If we were to make a commitment to the Modern or Postmodern Paradigms, it would certainly be possible to derive a leadership theory from within those paradigms much like we developed Covenant Leadership from within the Wisdom Paradigm. Because the Modern and Postmodern Paradigms understand relationships and motivation very differently than the Wisdom Paradigm, leadership theories from those paradigms will look very different as well.

We can use our knowledge of these paradigms to describe some general features that leadership theories from each of these paradigms would possess.

We know that leadership theories from the Modern Paradigm are going to:

- Keep life and leadership divided into the public/work and private/personal
- Try to motivate people to work within low-trust, contractual relationships primarily through compensation
- Describe very different types of leadership depending on the purpose of the organization (i.e. profit vs. non-profit vs. public service, etc.)

A postmodern leadership theory substitutes postmodern power relationships for the Wisdom Paradigm's covenant relationship and teams. Postmodern leadership emphasizes manipulation as a motivation rather than an appeal to goodness and fulfillment. That manipulation might be through an appeal to a person's base desires. It might be through addiction, compensation or fear. The manipulation could occur by inspiring people to dedicate themselves to some manufactured "higher cause" or meaning. The key is to remember that, no matter what the appearance, postmodern leadership is always based in the exercise of power by one over another.

One of the more obvious contrasts between wisdom and postmodern leadership development programs is in the Leadership Components. Under the *skills* component, the Postmodern Paradigm would add a need for *manipulative skills*. Effective postmodern leaders need to be skillful in using whatever means are most effective—even if they are deceptive, involuntary or violent—to get followers to do the will of the leader.

A postmodern leadership development program would probably replace the wisdom *character* leadership component with *ruthlessness*. The Wisdom Paradigm has *character* as a leadership component because the Wisdom Paradigm emphasizes high performance teams based on high-trust relationships. High-trust relationships require character and seeing other humans as *ends in themselves* who are to be loved, supported and developed for their own good.

In contrast, the Postmodern Paradigm's emphasis on *power relationships* always understands other people as a means to your own goals and desires. For the postmodern leader, genuine care for others is useless, even dangerous. The postmodern leader must be willing to do whatever it takes—*ruthlessness*—to accomplish his goal.

In the Postmodern Paradigm, compassion is a weakness that makes the leader vulnerable to manipulation by other postmodern leaders who are more ruthless. Are you the postmodern leader willing to do whatever it takes to achieve your desires? Or are you the postmodern leader who will eventually submit to those who are more ruthless?

In the final analysis, well-designed theories originating wholly within the Wisdom Paradigm are always going to outperform similar theories from the Modern or Postmodern Paradigms because:

- The covenant relationships and teams within the Wisdom Paradigm are higher trust and more stable than the Modern Paradigm's contractual relationship or the Postmodern Paradigm's power relationship
- The focus on purpose, fulfillment and Happiness will get deeper commitment and motivation than the motivators available in the Modern or Postmodern Paradigms

The Covenant Leadership theory that comes from a commitment to the Wisdom Paradigm is the best because it structurally outperforms leadership theories from the Modern or Postmodern Paradigms. Now we need to ask whether Covenant Leadership addresses the issues we brought up in the chapter *Defining Success*.

Effectiveness

Covenant Leadership provides the most effective understanding of leadership because it:

- ✓ **Provides us with the highest performance people and teams**. Covenant Leadership provides higher-trust and more stable covenant relationships than the Modern Paradigm's contractual relationships or the Postmodern Paradigm's power relationships. Covenant Leadership inspires the deepest trust, motivation and commitment, and therefore maximizes the performance of people, teams and leaders. By establishing a culture and tradition of excellence, Covenant Leadership increases the likelihood that leadership and high-performance teams are sustained within an organization.

- ✓ **Understands how leadership is developed and cultivated over time**. When we fully embrace the Wisdom Paradigm, our understanding of leadership becomes clear and uncluttered with aspects of other paradigms. We can understand the interrelationships and dynamics between leadership, relationships, goals and human nature, and develop an understanding of how leadership is developed and cultivated over time.

- ✓ **Identifies and understands fundamental components of leadership**. Covenant Leadership clearly identifies and fully explains each of the leadership components—skills, character, bearing and vision—talking in depth about where they come from, why they are important, and how to develop them.

✓ **Enables us to identify leadership gifts and potential in young people**. With knowledge of the leadership components, we know what qualities and characteristics to look for in young people. By watching young people participate in a variety of team-based activities from family life through academics, performing arts and athletics, we can evaluate and measure their current skills, character, teamwork, bearing and vision. We can quantitatively and qualitatively assess where they are at today, and what their potential is for the future.

✓ **Supports a step-by-step program (recipe) to develop good leaders and top teams**. With a clear and better understanding of leadership and how it is cultivated, we have developed a step-by-step process—a recipe—for forming good leaders and high performance teams. With knowledge of the leadership components and the leadership recipe, we can fine tune and quality control the leadership development process to maximize the formation of each individual leader.

✓ **Enables leadership studies to make deliberate, systematic progress**. The Wisdom Paradigm and Covenant Leadership put leadership studies on a firm and common foundation. We know what the *leadership components* are. We know what the elements of the *team dynamic* are. We understand the relationship between activity, mission and purpose. We know that team performance depends on trust, commitment and motivation. We have a systematic process for forming the next generation of leaders. While we have a basic understanding of purpose, covenant teams and the relationship between trust, commitment and team performance, there is an enormous amount of further work to be done in each of these areas, and how they relate to each other, to people, and to application in life. We can establish leadership knowledge baselines, and then make, identify and assess systematic progress in leadership studies against those baselines.

✓ **Allows us to evaluate leadership and distinguish between effective, good and bad leadership.** Once we embrace the Wisdom Paradigm, we have the means to evaluate leadership, and distinguish between effective, good and bad leadership.

Comprehensive, handling all types of leadership

Covenant Leadership is comprehensive because it shows that leadership is essentially the same across all types of human relationships, organizations and activities whether it is business, military, public service, non-profit, church, community, athletics, family, etc. Leadership is the same across the board because the Wisdom Paradigm understands that the purpose of all people and teams is the same across the board: to become good and achieve fulfillment.

Accounts for other paradigms and leadership theories

The Wisdom Paradigm provides a framework that fully accounts for the Modern and Postmodern Paradigms, and their understandings of leadership. The Wisdom Paradigm understands that the Modern and Postmodern Paradigms have flawed understandings of human nature, purpose and the nature of human relationships, and therefore have flawed and less effective understandings of leadership. The Wisdom Paradigm also provides a narrative that accounts for how these opposing paradigms developed, why they view reality the way they do, and why they are ultimately in error. The different leadership theories that have been popular through the 20th century—like Great Man Theory, Group Theory, Trait Theory, Behavior Theory, Contingency-Situation Theory and Excellence Theory[12]—can be accounted for within the Wisdom Paradigm.

---

[12] See Rost for an accounting of these theories and their development.

Common leadership concepts that sound good in leadership training or seminars but never seem to fully work in the real world like *communication with subordinates*, *aligning goals or interests*, *making ethical decisions* and *taking care of subordinates* work well in the real world when applied within the Wisdom Paradigm's understanding of leadership and relationships. That is an independent indication that the Wisdom Paradigm is right. The fact that these concepts don't seem to work in the Modern Paradigm's understanding is evidence that the Modern Paradigm has serious shortcomings.

Seamlessly integrates leadership, ethics/morality and your understanding of life

One of the best parts of the Wisdom Paradigm and Covenant Leadership is that it naturally integrates your private/personal life with your public/work life. *Leading yourself*, *leading at work* and *leading your family* are all united and focused on developing the virtues, becoming good and seeking meaning and fulfillment in life. Leadership, character and fulfillment in life are all aligned. Unlike the Modern Paradigm, in the Wisdom Paradigm and Covenant Leadership there is no split between public and private life, nor the idea that some areas of public life like business and science lie outside morality.

The Wisdom Paradigm provides an understanding of human nature, purpose and human relationships that gives Covenant Leadership a high-trust, high-stability foundation that is always stronger and better than the foundation of any theories from the Modern or Postmodern paradigms. That stronger foundation means that Covenant Leadership will get higher trust and deeper commitment, and always outperform leadership theories from the Modern or Postmodern paradigms.

Covenant Leadership also addresses the issues we brought up in the chapter on *Defining Success*:

- It is the most effective understanding, provides us the highest performance people and teams, and gives us a step-by-step recipe to form leaders
- It is comprehensive and able to address leadership no matter what type of organization
- It flows from the Wisdom Paradigm which provides a narrative that accounts for all other life-paradigms and leadership theories, showing how they fit within a historical framework and broader understanding of life
- It seamlessly integrates leadership, morality and life into a unified, consistent and focused whole

PART IV
THE NEXT GENERATION OF LEADERS

We have lost trust in major institutions in our society including government and big business. We are foundering in a culture war largely between Wisdom and Postmodern understandings of life. We have lost the common, shared morality that used to bind our society together and are left with fragmented, individual opinions about why something is right or wrong. We have lost the shared understanding of life that bound us together as Americans, and our society is becoming increasingly divided, fragmented and polarized. With no common ground, we have gone from disagreeing with the opposition to demonizing and de-humanizing them. This terrible polarization, fragmentation and loss of trust threatens to undo the very things that have made America great.

If these issues weren't enough, we're also facing challenges like unemployment, education, a huge national debt, immigration, terrorism, genetic engineering, pandemics, drug abuse, global warming, nuclear proliferation, environmental issues, infrastructure collapse and [insert your challenge here].

More than ever, we need great leadership in our nation. Forming the next generation of leaders that we can trust is the central, defining and most important challenge of our generation and time, for the solutions to all our other challenges can only be created and implemented if we have good leadership first.

Good leadership gives us:

- The best chance to successfully tackle the tough challenges we face
- The wisdom we need to use our enormous power without destroying ourselves
- The foundation to prevail in global competition

We've spent a long time understanding the nature of our leadership crisis, the paradigm/culture conflict that underlies our crisis, and the Covenant Leadership model that provides us leaders we can trust, and the highest-performance people and teams.

So what is next? What do we need to do to get our community and nation back on the right path? How do we take the knowledge and wisdom we have and put it into action?

We need to refocus and align our society with the Wisdom Paradigm because it is true, provides the best understanding of human nature and life, provides the highest performance people and teams, and brings hope and promise. As our society becomes aligned with the Wisdom Paradigm, we can implement our Covenant Leadership recipe to systematically form the next generation of leaders. If we don't align our society with the Wisdom Paradigm, we'll keep heading down the same dark road we are on.

But we will never get our society aligned with the Wisdom Paradigm unless we—as individuals—make a full personal commitment to the Wisdom Paradigm ourselves. We must embrace and fully live the Wisdom Paradigm in all aspects of our lives. Indeed, it is only by each of us living out the Wisdom Paradigm that our society will change course. The Wisdom Paradigm is not just an intellectual choice; more important, it is a lifestyle choice.

Know that this personal commitment will be a big challenge. There are many who are addicted to the pleasures of a postmodern way of life who will be loath to abandon those pleasures. There are many others who are so deeply invested in the Postmodern Paradigm—either professionally or in their understanding of life—that they are almost incapable of really considering the Wisdom Paradigm.

All these people will fight tenaciously to hold on to the Postmodern Paradigm. They will oppose you. They may hate you. They may accuse you and vilify you because you will threaten their fundamental understanding of life. Some may resort to violence.

If the history of the world can be understood as a history of the rise and fall of great civilizations, how will our society write our chapter in history? Are we going to be the generation that failed to step up, and let our children and world slide into increasing darkness? Are we going to write the history of how humanity moved forward and prospered by forming great leaders?

Your life is the story of how you use your unique talents to pursue meaning, fulfillment and Happiness. How will the story of your life read? Are you going to drift through life like so many do, barely conscious, living with regret, avoiding pain and grasping for fleeting pleasures? Or do you have what it takes to be a leader and make the commitment? Are you going to respond to the call to greatness, seeking goodness by maximizing your talents, overcoming challenges and serving others?

Your Individual Commitment

If you want to embrace the Wisdom Paradigm and create the leaders we need for our future, you must make a personal, life commitment to the paradigm for at least three reasons.

First, at its core, the Wisdom Paradigm is about finding fulfillment and Happiness in life. That includes your life. You should make a commitment to the Wisdom Paradigm because it will help you become a good person and find fulfillment. It will help you become a much better leader and therefore more successful at work. It will help you lead your family and give your children the best chance to find fulfillment and Happiness in their lives.

Second, you are a leader in your community. You lead your family. You lead others in your work. You likely lead even more people in activities like coaching, community service or your church. In each of these areas, people watch you and seek guidance. The more you provide good guidance and develop trust; the more you display virtues like honesty, justice, love and integrity; and the more you show that these qualities lead to success, the more people will respect you and follow your example. That helps others become good people and leaders themselves. That helps them find fulfillment and Happiness. Your commitment to the Wisdom Paradigm changes the lives of those around you.

Finally, as a citizen and consumer you are a leader in our community and nation. You shape the future with your choices at the ballot box, at the store, and by what you read and say. While your individual immediate impact may not be particularly evident, when you set the example with others and inspire them to choose wisely, the collective impact of your example can be immense.

THE NEXT GENERATION IS ALREADY BEING SHAPED

We are already shaping the next generation of leaders of our nation and world in every dimension. We have been shaping them, for better or worse, since they were born. For the next generation of politicians, business people, military leaders, scientists, educators, accountants, lawyers, mechanics, doctors and, perhaps most important—parents— is being shaped every minute by a multitude of factors including our media, education, parents, religion, the economy and so much more.

Our choice is not whether the next generation will be shaped or not; they are already well on the way. Our choice is whether we will use all these factors and more to proactively and deliberately form a generation of great leaders—or let them be shaped by accident.

To get the best results, we must ensure that these cultural factors are aligned synergistically to produce the best leaders possible. Every day that we fail to align these factors to form our future leaders in a deliberate manner is another day that we roll the dice with the future of our nation.

OUR RESPONSIBILITY

It is important to remember that in America, *we, the people*, are the real leaders of our nation.

We, the people, have the responsibility for electing our political leaders.

We, the people, are responsible for what our elected leaders do.

We, the people, are responsible for our culture and what is acceptable in business, science, technology, media, education and all else.

With our wallets, our votes and our commitments, we, the people, exercise the real power in and have the real responsibility for what happens in our nation.

That means that it is our responsibility, as *we the people*, to form the next generation of leaders. It is our responsibility to make sure they are good leaders.

Forming the next generation of leaders certainly means developing, listening to and following leaders adept in a variety of fields to help guide us through difficult challenges. We must have good leaders upon whom we can depend to use our power wisely. That's part of forming a generation of leaders we can all trust to help lead us.

But we must also be aware that with that there lies a constant temptation and danger.

When we form leaders whom we truly and deeply trust, it becomes easy for us to become complacent. It becomes tempting to turn final responsibility over to the "experts". It becomes especially tempting to turn responsibility for forming the next generation of leaders over to our government—for who has more resources or power to do something so important?

We must avoid the temptation to become complacent and abdicate our final responsibility to the government or the experts. We, the people, must remain actively involved in our own leadership and forming the next generation of leaders for several very important reasons:

- **It is our opportunity to become good**. Actively leading our nation and taking responsibility for forming the next generation of leaders is an excellent opportunity for us— as individuals and as a community—to become good. Actively leading our nation forces us to practice the virtues and be responsible to each other within our community and nation.

- **We, the people, possess the real power**. The real power in our nation lies with the people, not with the government or experts. The government only has the power that *we the people* give them. Acting together, we the people possess the economic, cultural and political power to move our nation forward. Our government can only crudely influence the flow of that power.

- **It prevents corruption**. Knowledge is power and power can corrupt. It is not uncommon for the experts or those who wield power—whether it be in the government or other powerful institutions—to begin thinking that they are better than *we the people*. It is easy for them to begin thinking that the power they wield is theirs by right instead of being temporarily delegated to them by us. The more active *we the people* are in our own leadership, the less likely those in leadership positions will be corrupted by the power with which they are entrusted.

- **It prevents fragmentation and polarization**. The more actively we are involved in our own leadership, the more we work with and are responsible to each other, the less likely we are to become fragmented and polarized politically, culturally, morally or economically. We come together best by working together.

- **Leaders are best formed by We, The People**. *We the people*—parents, peers and immediate community— have by far the biggest impact on the formation of our future leaders. We shape the culture in which our leaders develop. We shape how our leaders understand life. We shape the habits they possess and the very foundation upon which leadership starts and grows.

- **We are ultimately responsible**. In the end, whether we think so or not, *we the people* are ultimately responsible for what happens in our own lives, our community and our nation. It may appear that power and responsibility lie elsewhere, but ultimately, we wield the power, we benefit or pay the price, and the fault or praise that follows lies with us.

We should develop, use and depend on experts in a variety of fields to help us through difficult challenges, but we must never forget that *we the people* are ultimately responsible.

While we can exercise power through our government, we exercise ten-thousand times more power through the way we raise our children, spend our money, engage our work and focus our lives on goodness.

It is our responsibility to ensure that following generations of leaders are good. To turn leadership formation over to the experts or to our government is to abdicate our primary responsibility as Americans and as humans.

Remember always that our government is, at best, a reflection of us, not a replacement for us.

THE NEXT GENERATION OF LEADERS

This makes us—as a generation and as individuals—the leaders of the next generation of leaders.

If we are going to be effective in forming the next generation of leaders, then our generation must establish a high-trust relationship with their generation. As individuals, we must develop high-trust relationships with individuals of their generation. The more the next generation trusts us on all levels, the more they will listen to us and follow us, and the more effectively we can form them.

If we are going to form the next generation of leaders that we can trust, we must first be worthy of their trust and commitment. That will only happen if we are a generation and individuals of good character ourselves. That means that our effectiveness forming the next generation of leaders depends directly on the formation and goodness of our own character.

If we want the next generation of leaders to be great, we need to step up with great character ourselves—as a generation and as individuals.

And so we come to realize that **forming the next generation of leaders is not something to be delegated to others—to some set of leadership experts somewhere else—but a task that is yours right now whether you want it or not**.

Your interactions with the next generation—in your family, in the teams you coach and activities you lead, at church, at the store and in your community—are already shaping the next generation. They are already making judgments about you. They judge you some by what you say, but mostly by what you do and who you are.

When they see a gap between what you say and what you do, or a gap between what you do in one part of your life and what you do in another, they lose trust in you. If they see a pattern of this in their encounters with our generation, they become cynical and lose trust in our generation. We will be in a very poor spot.

If they judge you a person of right knowledge and right action (good character)—that is to say a *wise person*—then they will respect, honor, trust and listen to you. They will follow you because it is the smart thing for them to do. If they see a pattern of this in their encounters with our generation, they will respect us, call us a great generation, and listen and follow with open minds.

If they know that we are not just wise, but love them too, they will readily commit to the wisdom we share and example we set.

Right now, you are forming the next generation of leaders by the person you are, and the character and wisdom you demonstrate. The better person that you are, the better you form the next generation.

Forming the next generation of leaders isn't much about putting some magical leadership development process in place. It is about how you impact and shape the lives of those around as a parent, a friend, a worker and a neighbor.

Remember the people who really changed your life for the better and why. Was it the coach or teacher that had confidence in you when you or others didn't? Was it the neighbor that helped you with something important? Be that person for others.

When a ship drops anchor for the night, the more comfortable the people on the ship are that the anchor is set well and that the ship will not drift, the better they will sleep. The more firmly they feel anchored, the more confident the people are and the more they trust.

The better anchored you are in your own character and life, the more people around you will trust and follow you. Being well anchored in life means that you've put a lot of time and energy into important questions about life:

- What is the meaning of life?
- What is my purpose and direction my life?
- What am I doing to travel that direction and achieve my purpose?

More literally, how are you *leading your own life?* Developing the next generation of leaders is directly tied to your own leadership development. If you lead your own life well, you will be able to guide the next generation well because you have already walked the path they are walking now.

As a nation, do we have what it takes to shape a great generation of leaders? And since our nation is really the product of our individual efforts, do you have what it takes to earn the respect, trust and commitment of those in the next generation that follow? If not, what are you doing to change that?

If you want a better world, are you doing everything you can to become a better person?

In the end, the next generation is our legacy, our chapter and our responsibility. They are our children, and a reflection of how good we are—or not.

LIVING THE WISDOM PARADIGM

We know that to form the next generation of leaders we must align our society with the Wisdom Paradigm. We know that it is our responsibility to form the next generation of leaders, and that our success depends on our personal character.

The key to both these is relatively simple: fully embrace and live the Wisdom Paradigm.

When you make the commitment to live the Wisdom Paradigm, you develop the knowledge and character—the wisdom—that earns the respect and trust of those in the next generation. They will follow your example and embrace the Wisdom Paradigm themselves.

The personal benefits are enormous. When you make the commitment, you will become a better leader and more successful at work. You will become a better leader at home. Your work will stop being a job and become a vocation, providing fulfillment in addition a paycheck. Your life will be focused on becoming good and achieving Happiness.

When people see that you are fulfilled and Happy, they will want to be fulfilled and Happy too.

What does it mean to make a full commitment to the Wisdom Paradigm?

> **Focus everything in life on becoming good.** Everything you do, say and even think can help you move closer to or further from your purpose of becoming good and achieving fulfillment. Live deliberately, trying to build good habit patterns—virtues—in everything you think and do.

> **Engage team-based activities that provide opportunities to practice the virtues.** You become a good person by practicing the virtues until they become habits, and then seamless qualities of your character. Seek team-based activities to practice the virtues because the team will help you develop those virtues faster and more effectively than you can on your own. The more you put into the team, the more you will grow in teamwork, skills and (most important) character. The more you grow, the more you will become a leader and influence others to become good. Team-based activities include your family, friends, church, neighborhood, school, charities, athletic teams, clubs—any group of people committed to each other and some noble goal.

> **Study life and pursue wisdom.** The more you understand life, the more you will understand Truth and the Good, and the better you will be able to write the story of your life. Your life-experiences will help you better understand life. Your understanding of life will provide context for your life experiences. *Study and live your faith tradition.* To be worthy of the trust of others, you must dive deep into yourself to understand who you are, what life is about, and the nature of your talents or gifts. What makes you *you*—unique—

different from all others? You must ask the hard questions about life and death. You must become well-grounded in who you are without pride or arrogance. Pride and arrogance are huge obstacles to becoming good because they close us to listening to and learning from others. Pursue wisdom by maximizing both your knowledge (Truth) and character (goodness).

> **Learn the differences between the paradigms**. As you study life and develop wisdom, you will learn the differences between the paradigms. As you recognize the often-subtle influences of the Modern and Postmodern Paradigms, you can identify and eliminate them in your life and your community. You will also be in a position to counsel others seeking to align with the Wisdom Paradigm.

> **Write the story of your life**. This is your life. There is only one of you. Uncover and develop your gifts, and see where they take you. Don't drift through life; actively pursue life. Write the best story of your life that you can. As you become good, you achieve success and help others write their best story.

> **As a citizen and consumer, lead society and others**. You shape others, your community and society by your choices as a citizen and your choices as a consumer. The fastest, most effective way to impact our government leaders is to become a good person and good leader yourself, so you can best recognize and vote for good political leaders. The fastest, most effective way to impact the media, entertainment, business and every other aspect of our society is to support those things that reinforce the Wisdom Paradigm and refuse those things that reinforce the Modern or Postmodern Paradigms. When you are a good person that others trust, you become a leader around whom others will gather. They too

will reinforce support of wisdom and refuse to support the modern or postmodern.

The fastest and most effective way for you to help develop the leaders we need for our future, to increase our economy and society, and to enable America to prevail in global competition is to become a good person and leader yourself.

It is extremely important that you become *good* before you become *vocal*.

If you become vocal before you become good, you can be easily manipulated by those who sound like they speak truth, but have ulterior motives. You will be vulnerable to postmodern people who use the right words that are attractive to you, but mean something very different by those words. You will not be prepared to identify the wolf in sheep's clothing. You will not be prepared for the difficult tests of your character that will inevitably come.

If you become good before you become vocal, you will possess the wisdom necessary to see through evil and choose the good. You will be able to identify and choose good political leaders, business leaders, scientists, etc. You will be able to recognize the wolf in sheep's clothing. You will be best prepared to handle the difficult tests of your character and your understanding of life that inevitably come.

FOCUS ON YOUR FAMILY

Our family is our most basic community and has a tremendous impact on the life and development of those within it.

Our family fundamentally shapes the way we understand and approach life.

Our family teaches us how to think about relationships and gives us the habit patterns we keep for the rest of our lives. It is in our families that we learn about love, discipline, and relationships. For better or worse, our family sets the foundation for what we become the rest of our lives.

Parents are the natural leaders of the family. They bring the family into existence. From the earliest stages of childhood, parents have the greatest and most immediate impact on shaping their children's understanding of life. Parents direct, support and nurture their children from infancy through adulthood.

Raising your children is the most direct and highest impact way you help form the next generation of leaders. Whether they lead big organizations, small groups, families or just themselves, your children are the next generation of leaders. No one shapes your children, their leadership and their future as much as you do.

When our society moved away from the Wisdom Paradigm and the focus on *purpose*, on becoming *good*, parents and families gradually lost their sense of purpose as well.

Today, there is a lot of confusion around what it means to be a parent and what parents owe their children.

Are parents supposed to immerse their children in a religion or let their children choose a religion for themselves?

What does it mean to be a *good parent* or *bad parent*?

Should parents be tough on their children, emphasizing discipline and performance, or easy on their children with an emphasis on letting children "discover" things for themselves?

We often hear that there is no parent manual issued when parents have their first child. How is a parent supposed to know what to do?

As a parent, what if you make a mistake with your child?

Do you feel guilty about how you raise(d) your children?

Making a commitment to the Wisdom Paradigm quickly eliminates most of the confusion surrounding parenting and brings clarity.

Here is the very short summary of the Wisdom *Parent Manual*: In the Wisdom Paradigm, the purpose of the family is clear: *Prepare your children to become good people.* Everything you do as a parent should be focused on your purpose of helping your children become good.

There is one overriding principle that your children must internalize: *Everything I do and think in life should help me become good.*

If you come from a religious tradition, that principle should be something like: *Everything I do and think in life should help me develop a closer relationship with God.*

Love your children because it helps them become good and because practicing love helps you become good. There is no deeper way to love your children than to ensure that your children are on track towards goodness. There is no way to help your children become good that does not come from love.

Each of your children is a unique human being unlike any other who has ever existed or will ever exist. Each of your children has a unique set of gifts that makes her who she is. Your child exists to discover herself, to understand her unique gifts, and to go through her journey of life becoming good and achieving Happiness by using her gifts in the world.

To help your children become good, you must help them become the person they are meant to be. That means that you must love your children for who they are, not what you want them to be.

Your children are your gift and responsibility, not your possession. Your child is not your ticket to Hollywood or wealth. Your child does not exist to become the big-league athlete that you couldn't be. Your child does not exist to be like you in terms of where she goes to college and the profession that she selects.

Your role as a parent is not to be your child's friend.

Your role is not to ensure that your child goes through life in a protective cocoon, avoiding all pain and suffering.

Your role is to love your child by putting her on the path to wisdom and goodness.

Your role is to help her discover, understand, cultivate and use her gifts.

Your role is to help your child understand that her life is her journey to goodness and Happiness, and that life, relationships, work, actions and thoughts are all opportunities to become good.

Your role is to help your child understand that the difficult challenges that she encounters in life—chronic illness, early deaths of loved ones, addiction, misfortune, suffering and pain—are both difficult experiences and opportunities to learn, lead and become good.

When your child succeeds, you love and praise her, and help her keep her success in proper perspective.

When your child fails, you help her recognize her responsibilities, and you help her get back up and move forward.

Your role is to remind her when she strays from the path of goodness. And your role is to love her unconditionally no matter how far she strays. For when all seems lost, your unconditional love may be the only thing remaining that points her back to goodness and life.

In the Wisdom Paradigm, leadership necessarily depends on relationships. There is no tighter relationship or deeper motivation than love. As we form the next generation of leaders—especially our children—we must teach them the commitment, beauty, strength and performance that flow from love.

If you accomplish this, you will be a great parent and your children will be good leaders that we can trust.

Strive for goodness yourself

The best way to help your children become good is to strive for goodness yourself.

Your children naturally love and idolize you. They see you and your family as the model for how they should live. They naturally regard whatever you do as right. If you model a full commitment to goodness in everything that you do, they will seek goodness as well. If you model something less, then they will naturally seek less.

The best way to guide your children on that journey to goodness is to make the journey ahead of them.

When you are ahead of your children, you will be able to anticipate and help them through the various challenges they will face in their lives. You will show them shortcuts. You will help them uncover and avoid hidden dangers. You will help them find the hidden treasures that life can offer. If you live your life well always seeking goodness, then you will always be ahead of them on that journey and always be ready to guide them from love.

Your children will encounter addiction, illness, the loss of loved ones, suffering, disappointment and the temptations of easy pleasures.

If you can't show them—in some compelling way—why it is worthwhile for them to pursue goodness despite these challenges, they will quit. They will not achieve fulfillment or Happiness.

You need to prove to them that the pursuit of goodness is worthwhile by showing them, every day, how committed you are to goodness in your own life. They will know how important it is to pursue goodness when they see how hard you pursue goodness.

Find opportunities for your children to become good

We all know that getting into great physical shape requires commitment, and involves real pain and suffering.

If someone insisted that they should be able to get into great physical shape without going through that pain and suffering, we would conclude that they just don't understand the nature of fitness.

Building bigger and better muscle requires the tearing of earlier muscle. If you are in the weight room or on the field and you haven't felt the burn, then it is a sign that you haven't pushed yourself to maximum physical performance and development.

The same is true with the development of your child's character. Goodness does not just happen in a child's life. The hard truth is that goodness is the result of a lot of hard work that is often grueling and tough, and often involves pain and suffering.[13]

As a parent, it is your responsibility to give your children the best life foundation you can for their life journey toward goodness. From love, your responsibility is to do all you can to prepare your children in all dimensions—character, spiritual, physical, mental and emotional—to become good.

From the very beginning, find activities that help your children practice and habituate virtues like self-discipline, honesty, sharing, love and faith.

---

[13] There is pain and suffering that builds muscle and character, and pain and suffering that causes injury. Just as it is important for a coach and athlete to recognize which physical pain and suffering leads to development and which leads to injury, so it is important for all to recognize which pain and suffering builds character and which can cause injury. A wise life-coach or spiritual advisor understands these distinctions.

As infants, children should feel deeply loved and come to understand that there are limits—things that they can touch and things they cannot touch. Before they can even understand what you are saying, they should be hearing that their life is their journey to goodness. They should hear about their relationships to others in terms of covenant relationships. Every aspect of their lives and every experience should be explained in terms of the Wisdom Paradigm.

From the very beginning of our children's lives, my wife and I told our kids that their purpose in life was to get closer to God. When they were very young and we talked with them about their behavior, we asked them whether what they did grew flowers in their heart or weeds. Later, we asked them whether their behavior got them closer to or further from God. Our children have been taught from the very beginning to think of everything they do in terms of their relationship with God—in terms of whether they are becoming good or not.

As your children get older, help them find activities that require and build perseverance, endurance and determination. Athletics and the arts teach them that practice builds skill and character. Team-based activities teach them how to work with and be responsible to others. They should become increasingly aware of who they are, from where they come spiritually and culturally, and discover the gifts and talents that make them one-of-a-kind.

Everything they do should be explained and understood as contributing to their journey to goodness—including their covenant relationships with others. They have an obligation to help others become good as they have an obligation to become good themselves. They must become increasingly aware of the temptations and traps that can take them in very dangerous and wrong directions away from goodness. Everything understood in terms of the Wisdom Paradigm.

As they become more mature, help them into activities that will deepen love and justice, and develop wisdom, integrity and honor.

As they demonstrate real responsibility they should receive increasing authority in their own lives, so that the transition from childhood to adulthood—when they become completely responsible for their own lives—is as smooth as possible.

Every step of the way, they should constantly frame their experiences, activities, challenges, victories and defeats in terms of their journey towards goodness. This is something you and other family members should be discussing with them all the time. Encourage them to discuss, reflect and journal their thoughts on this. As they actively reflect on life, they will gain wisdom.

As they get older, their earlier, simpler understanding of life will be challenged by events, experiences and encounters with postmodern influences that will threaten their journey to goodness. This happens in college and now, increasingly in high school and middle school.

Rather than reject the Wisdom Paradigm, your children must be prepared to move from earlier, simpler understandings of life in terms of the Wisdom Paradigm to more complex, nuanced understandings of life in terms of the Wisdom Paradigm. They should be able to understand, recognize and reject postmodern influences in their lives from culture and media.

The more that you explain all aspects of life in terms of the Wisdom Paradigm to your children, the more that you provide them activities and experiences that ground the wisdom understanding in their minds, the more that they practice the virtues, the better your children will be prepared for that journey to goodness that is their life. The better prepared they will be for leadership.

It Takes Communities

Next to your role as parent, the most influential factors in the development of your children are the communities in which you participate and the schools that your children attend.

In older days, a child was not just raised by the parents, but by other family members and local neighbors. A neighbor adult wouldn't think twice about telling your child to stop doing something wrong, and would let you know about it too. There was a sense of shared responsibility for developing each other's children.

Today, with the breakdown in shared, community morality, we are much more reluctant to say something to each other's children and much less likely to correct them if they do something wrong. You can't be confident that your neighbor shares the same outlook on life and morality that you do. That leaves many parents feeling isolated while raising their children.

We spend time on social media seeing all the posts by other families whose children and lives and situations appear perfect, and then feel like bad parents when we think about the challenges our own children and families face. That leaves us feeling isolated.

Today, as a private school educator, I talk to dozens of families every year that are embarrassed by something that their child did or ashamed of a situation their family is in. They feel like they are the only family in which something bad has happened in a sea of perfect families.

It has gotten to the point where, when I welcome incoming families to our school, I tell them that no matter how good their child is, there is an 85% chance that he is going to do something so incredibly dumb that it will completely embarrass and humiliate their family. And when that happens, they should remember that it happens to the very best parents in the very best families and they are not alone.

They are not an isolated family outside of a perfect community of perfect families with perfect parents and perfect kids. Instead, they are an imperfect family with imperfect parents working hard with other imperfect families—as a community—to raise all these children to be good and wise men and women.

And that is the point: You need to find communities of like-minded parents seeking wisdom and goodness in the Wisdom Paradigm as you all raise your children together.

You need to find these like-minded communities in your churches, local athletic teams, hobbies, youth activities and neighborhood groups. The more your children spend time with other adults and families pursuing life in terms of the Wisdom Paradigm, the better they will be formed into good men and women.

School

School is a very influential factor in your children's development and the formation of the next generation of leaders.

In a following section, we will discuss why our society and culture must move from a concept of *education focused on academics* that is prevalent in most all our schools to a concept of *formation focused on wisdom* that is necessary to create the next generation of good leaders.

Do everything you can to get your children into a school that emphasizes proper *formation* rather than simply education.

LEADERSHIP AT WORK

It makes sense to make a full commitment to the Wisdom Paradigm at work. The benefits are enormous:

- Increased personal performance
- Better leadership performance
- More powerful and higher performance people and teams that win
- Deeper personal fulfillment as you integrate your public/work life with your personal/private life
- It forms the next generation of leaders

The key is consistency. Ensure that you are the same person at work and home: a person who seeks excellence and goodness in all your actions.

When you strive to maximize your skills, your character and your teamwork, you can't help but become a good person who is worthy of respect and trust. People will trust your skills, they will trust your character and they will trust your teamwork.

That respect and trustworthiness you earn becomes the foundation for all that follows.

You will increase your personal performance because you will have improved your skills, character and teamwork.

Your leadership performance will increase because people will see that you are successful, respected and trustworthy—so they are much more likely to follow you.

As you weave a deeper sense of purpose into your work and teams, the teams around you will respond and slowly shift from *contractual relationships* focused on money to *covenant relationships* focused on becoming good. They will follow you because they respect and believe in you; not because you're paying them. With the stronger motivation that comes with covenant relationships, your teams will be more deeply committed and begin to maximize their individual and team performance.

Finally, and perhaps most important, as you become good personally and professionally, those in the next generation will develop respect for and trust in you. It won't matter if they are co-workers, subordinates, supervisors, clients, competitors or anyone else with whom you happen to spend time. They will see that your life is integrated and that your work is more than a job—it is fulfilling. They will see your higher performance and professional success. They will recognize that you are respected and trustworthy, and that other people follow you. They will want whatever it is that you have. They will follow you because they too admire, respect and trust you. They won't follow you because you tell them to. They will follow you because they want to be like you. They will follow you because it is the smart thing to do.

You are already forming the next generation of leaders by the kind of person that you are. Your children, family, community members, church members, fellow workers, clients, etc., are all continuously shaped by their encounters with you.

In the most important, powerful and effective way, by making a deep and intentional commitment to the Wisdom Paradigm, you will ensure that we form the best generation of leaders possible. You will achieve this by the example you set and the life you lead. If you engender admiration, respect and trust, the next generation of leaders will strive to be like you. You will forever shape your family, your community, the people with whom you work and the people you encounter in every aspect of your life. As you become a better person you will move closer to fulfillment and Happiness, become more successful professionally, and happier as a better leader at home.

In a confused and increasingly postmodern world, your example will be a light shining in the darkness showing others the way to meaning, fulfillment and a better future.

Become the change we need in the world.

Society: Forming Great Leaders

We started with the individual commitment because no matter how good a societal structure we establish, without the personal commitment to give it life, we won't get far. Success starts with your individual commitment.

Nevertheless, to produce the great leaders we need for our future, we must create the right culture and environment that continually shape and form our future leaders in a systematic, deliberate way.

The more every aspect of our society and community is aligned with the Wisdom Paradigm, the more they can come together in a single, integrated, seamless and synergistic approach to form our leaders. We will be forming good leaders we can trust with great effectiveness and efficiency, and minimal risk of failure.

What are the most important and effective ways we can create the best cultural environment for the formation of good leaders?

- As community and society, commit to and align with the Wisdom Paradigm
- Move from education focused on knowledge to formation focused on wisdom and leadership
- Teach and implement Covenant Leadership
- Focus our cultural power to align media, technology and science, and solve social problems

SOCIETAL AND COMMUNITY COMMITMENT TO THE WISDOM PARADIGM

The more the Wisdom Paradigm pervades our society and communities explicitly and implicitly, the more successful we will be forming good leaders. We need to make it clear as a society and community that we are fully embracing the wisdom approach to life:

- That human nature is timeless and that it is our nature to pursue goodness, fulfillment and Happiness
- That each of our lives is the story of how we achieve Happiness through the pursuit of goodness
- That all aspects of our lives—including our public/work life and private/personal life—should be seamlessly integrated in the pursuit of goodness
- That we are fundamentally social beings who can only be fully understood in the context of the communities in which we live and grow
- That individuals become good by practicing the virtues as part of covenant teams
- That our communities pursue goodness by helping each member become good
- That the good of the individual and community are the same
- That there are moral facts—*virtues*—that we should habituate to become good
- That *vices* should be avoided because they lead us away from goodness and can become addictive
- That we embrace the Wisdom Paradigm and Covenant Leadership because they are the best account of the reality of human nature, human performance and life

We need to be unafraid, unhesitating and unapologetic in our embrace of the Wisdom Paradigm.

FROM EDUCATION TO FORMATION: FOCUS ON WISDOM AND GOODNESS

The key to our future: Trust and wisdom

As we have seen, the future of our nation, community and children depends on our ability to form a generation of leaders that we can trust to wield the enormous power that we possess.

If we form that next generation of leaders that we can trust, we'll build the high-performance leaders and teams we need to prevail in global competition—whether it is economic, social, cultural, political or military. Our nation, communities, families and individual people will be united in a journey together towards goodness and Happiness. We'll have the best opportunity to achieve Happiness in our own lives.

A generation of leaders formed in the Wisdom Paradigm is by far our best chance for a bright future.

More than anything, the key component to our bright future is *trust*. The more we can trust our leaders, the brighter our future is. The less we can trust our leaders, the darker our future.

And remember, by *leaders* we're not just talking about our national or big business leaders, but all those people—all of us—who provide guidance to others. Our days are filled with leadership interactions.

We certainly need to trust that our leaders have *right knowledge*. If we're not sure whether our doctors, attorneys, business leaders, national and community leaders, or mechanics know the best practices in their areas of expertise, then we won't trust them to lead us through those issues. You simply won't trust the leadership of a mechanic who doesn't know how to fix your car.

Trust that our leaders are skilled in their work is important, but only a small part of the picture. We must also trust their character; that they will not just *know* the right thing but *do* the right thing.

Our future depends on a generation of leaders who are not just knowledgeable, but *wise*; leaders who possess *right knowledge* (truth) and *right action* (character). *Wisdom* is the key to maximizing the performance of our leaders, our people and our teams. Wisdom is the key to our personal success, professional success and the success of our families. Wisdom is the key to our nation maximizing performance in every area and prevailing in global competition.

Our modern education system can't develop wisdom

As Americans, we spend a tremendous amount of time, energy and money on our schools—and rightfully so. Our schools are our single biggest commitment to the development of our children and our future. Throughout our society and media, we hear constant talk about our need to invest in our future by investing in our children. Given the resources we expend on our schools and the time our children spend in our schools, any serious attempt to form the next generation of leaders must address what our schools are doing.

Unfortunately, our school system is immersed in a Modern Paradigm concept of *education for knowledge* that emphasizes gathering information and critical thinking skills, not on developing wisdom and leadership. Consider the dictionary definition of the term *education*:

1. The act or process of imparting or acquiring general knowledge, developing the powers of reasoning and judgment, and generally of preparing oneself or others intellectually for mature life

2. The act or process of imparting or acquiring particular knowledge or skills, as for a profession

3. A degree, level, or kind of schooling

4. The result produced by instruction, training or study

5. The science or art of teaching; pedagogics (Houghton Mifflin 2000)

Education is about developing the mind, the intellect. We see this tremendous emphasis on *education for knowledge* in how we run our schools today. Deep down, our schools are all about academics. We obsess over test scores. We pit academics against athletics and the arts. When money is tight, arts and athletics programs are the first to be cut because academics is considered more important. We hear people say that education is "All about the classroom." We tend to justify music and drawing programs insofar as they contribute to better academic results.

In many American school districts, vocational programs like metal shop and auto shop have disappeared because many administrators have embraced an elitist notion that all kids should be headed to college.

Instead of a school system that helps our young people find and develop their gifts and passions—and then direct those gifts into work in which they will find maximum performance and fulfillment—we have created an education system that demeans the non-academic and looks down on those with gifts elsewhere.

We tell our kids that if they don't study they'll end up like the school custodian. Then we wonder why many of our young people are alienated by their high school experience and drop out of school. Some of the most honorable people I have met have served the community as a custodian.

Worse, when we assume that all kids are supposed to be academically focused and we fail to help them identify, develop and celebrate their real gifts and passions, we leave them feeling discouraged, unmotivated and outside the community. Then we wonder why they turn to activities less beneficial to society.

Our nation has a deep need for good leadership based in wisdom and high-trust relationships, but we have an education system focused on individual academic performance.

Our school system isn't helping us solve our leadership crisis. It may well be making it worse. When our school system graduates really smart people (right knowledge) but fails to shape their character (right action), we produce leaders with great power, but little character or wisdom to keep that power focused on good things.

Remember what we said at the beginning of this book: The most dangerous result from a school system is not a high school dropout with a gun, but the highly-educated graduate who lacks a well-formed character and conscience. The graduate of a top university who is motivated by money and leading a Wall Street firm can do tens of billions of dollars of damage and ruin lives in ways that a high school dropout could never approach.

Not only does our school system fail to produce the wise leaders we need, but so long as it embraces the Modern Paradigm and education, it will continue to fail. Our schools will fail because:

1. By its very nature, modern education can never produce the leaders, people or covenant teams from the Wisdom Paradigm that we need

2. Modern education overemphasizes individual intellectual development, and neglects proper development of the will (character) and team-based performance
3. Public schools embracing modern education are in a very poor position to develop character

Why is that?

First, so long as our schools embrace modern education, they will be teaching our children how to understand reality, human nature, relationships, motivation, leadership and human life according to the Modern Paradigm. It is impossible to form the next generation of leaders in the Wisdom Paradigm and Covenant Leadership when teaching from the Modern Paradigm. You can't teach someone golf while teaching them football.

Second, modern education overemphasizes development of the intellect at the expense of the proper development of the will or character. As long as our schools embrace modern education, we will be developing leaders who have the very dangerous combination of great knowledge (great power) and poorly formed character. They will have a poor understanding of relationships and leadership. Our schools will fail to help us form the next generation of leaders because we won't be able to trust that our leaders will have the character to use their power wisely. So long as our schools embrace modern education, they will produce knowledgeable graduates, but not the wise leaders we need.

Finally, even if our public schools wanted to try to develop character and wisdom, so long as they embrace a modern approach to education, they will fail. Remember that the Modern Paradigm rejects purpose and splits life into public and private spheres. When the Modern Paradigm rejects purpose, it removes the justification for saying that it is a fact that some actions are right and other actions are wrong. When subsequent Modern attempts to provide a justification for morality fail, morality moves from the public side of life to the personal/private side of life.

MORAL FRAGMENTATION

Remember the moral fragmentation we discussed earlier. Just because we all might agree that *cheating is wrong* doesn't mean that we all mean the same thing. When morality is on the public side of life, the meaning of *cheating* and the meaning of *wrong* and the *reason why cheating is wrong* are shared and constantly discussed and affirmed. We all agree on what those things mean because we continuously publicly discuss and affirm them.

But when we reject purpose and morality moves to the personal side of life, those shared meanings are lost because they are no longer publicly discussed and affirmed. Over time we lose the shared meanings and the shared reason why cheating is wrong, and replace those with our own personal reasons.

We go from a public, shared understanding that *it is a fact that cheating is wrong* with a public, shared reasoning for *why cheating is wrong*, to *it is my opinion that cheating is wrong* and *I have my own personal opinion why cheating is wrong*.

Because we use the same words, there is the false appearance that we mean the same thing by *cheating is wrong*, when in reality we likely have very different and perhaps even conflicting definitions and reasons.

We're back to showing up at the *ball* game where we are going to carry, kick, fumble and pitch a *ball*, but some are thinking foot*ball* while others are thinking base*ball*, basket*ball*, golf *ball* and cannon*ball*.

That move of morality from the public side of life to the private side poses an enormous problem for any public schools that wish to develop character or teach morality. For if we no longer have a public, shared understanding of *what is right and wrong and why*, then whose personal morality are the public schools supposed to enforce and why?

Consider something as simple as a teacher or coach telling a student that *cheating* is wrong.

- What does *wrong* mean? When the teacher or coach says that something is *wrong*, is he stating that it is a *fact* that cheating is wrong or expressing his *opinion* that he does not like cheating?
- Is it wrong because if you get caught you'll get punished?

- Is it wrong because if everyone cheated the world wouldn't be a nice place?
- Is it wrong because God says so? Whose God? What if you don't believe in God?
- Is it wrong only insofar as it hurts other people? (And whose definition of *hurts other people* are we using?)
- Is it wrong for some other reason?

In a society where 100 people might have 100 different reasons why they believe cheating is wrong, whose reason is going to be imposed on the student and family?

As soon as the public-school teacher or coach makes a commitment to a reason why cheating is wrong, isn't that teacher or coach imposing his personal morality on the student—especially if the student is punished?

If the answer is that by participating in a public-school community you agree to live by certain values (i.e. not cheating), then isn't the state school really using its power to impose its morality on the student and family through those values?

In a postmodern world of values, *honesty* and *high test scores (cheating)* are equivalent. It is impossible to judge one value to be more true than the other, so who is the state to force their value of honesty on a student and judge him?

Who is the state to judge one value, one moral or ethical approach, better than another?

Isn't this just another example of those with power oppressing people with alternative moral beliefs, different values, not because it is factually right or wrong, but because they can?

Bottom line: As long as our public school system is tied to the Modern Paradigm with a focus on *education for knowledge*, we cannot form the next generation of leaders with the wisdom we need for our future.

If we want a bright future for our children, we must create a school structure and experience that is optimized to systematically and deliberately produce good leaders. We must move:

> From an ***education system*** that focuses on ***knowledge*** and critical thinking skills to create smart people

> To a ***formation system*** that focuses on ***wisdom***—*right knowledge* and *right action*—to create smart, wise and good leaders.

The wisdom approach to formation and wisdom is inclusive of the modern approach to education[14]. Both give prominence to *right knowledge*. But where *modern education* stops at knowledge, *wisdom formation* augments knowledge with *right action*, character, conscience and morals. It augments individual academic achievement with leadership, teamwork and accountability.

For example, both modern education and wisdom formation know that smoking is harmful to your health. But knowing that smoking is harmful and quitting smoking are two different things. Many of us have friends who know that it is harmful to smoke but aren't able to take the right action to quit smoking. To quit smoking, one must match the *knowledge* about the harm of smoking with the *right action* and *will*power to stop.

Modern education puts intellectual development at the center of the student experience asking *how much can this student learn?* In contrast, wisdom formation puts the student herself at the center of the experience asking *how can we align the totality of her experiences to help her become wise and good?*

---

[14] Wisdom formation recognizes that critical thinking skills are very important and should be developed to the greatest extent possible, but also must be balanced by good character to achieve wisdom.

Formation flows from the Wisdom Paradigm

Formation and the Wisdom Paradigm go together. Formation flows from and only makes sense within the Wisdom Paradigm's view of human nature. It is the idea that we should actively shape a person through a systematic, deliberate process so they can become wise and good, and fulfill their human nature and achieve Happiness.

Development of the person in the other paradigms is not formation because their views of human nature—and therefore how they develop human nature—are different.

The Modern Paradigm rejects (at least publicly) the idea that humans by their nature have a *purpose*. So, the Modern Paradigm calls human development *education* and focuses on the intellect and knowledge.

In the Postmodern Paradigm, human development is *indoctrination* because it is focused on instilling the desired understandings (constructs) of life into the person.

Forming the next generation of leaders to be wise and worthy of our trust is possible only within the framework of the Wisdom Paradigm.

Formation aligns all aspects of life

Formation is a systematic and deliberate process that aligns everything in the student's life, all the student's experiences 24 hours a day, 7 days a week, 365 days a year, to help her become wise and good.

Some education programs claim to be holistic and focus on the development of the whole student, but these programs are almost always focused primarily on academics and then add other areas, like ad hoc accessories, to that academic focus.

It's the idea that we can use schools to do a lot of things like help get kids more physically fit or feed them a healthy breakfast, but in the end, we all know that school is really all about the classroom and academics.

A true formation program is different in that it puts the student, not academics, at the focal point and uses all the student's experiences, including academics, to shape that student.

> Formation is the deliberate, systematic process of shaping a person to help her become wise and good, and fulfill her human nature and achieve Happiness

Academics are very important, but they are only one element in the total formation of a person. The formation program must also seamlessly weave character development, leadership, teamwork, accountability and bearing into the experience. At a minimum, the most effective formation program will integrate and align:

- Parents and family
- Academics
- Leadership
- Arts
- Athletics
- Activities, clubs and organizations
- Church
- Friends
- Community (including service)

A good formation program will connect experiences in each of these areas in powerful ways so that they impact the student synergistically, reinforcing each other. A student should be able to connect her experiences with friends, the arts, academics and character development together so that her experiences in the arts inform and add to her experiences in church, athletics and leadership, and so on.

A key aspect of a good formation program is that there is constant reference to and reinforcement of the *why*, the purpose of life and formation: to become wise and good, and achieve fulfillment.

In the formation program, character development goes way beyond the intellectual study of right and wrong, and how to identify right action in a case study. Much more important, the formation program will drive actual development of the student's character by providing opportunities for the student to practice the virtues in the real world with real consequences.

Formation focuses on instilling good habits into a young person. It is one thing to *talk* about being honest in a classroom. It is something else to *become* honest by putting the student in situations where the student practices honesty until it becomes a habit and, eventually, a seamless part of his character. The best places to practice virtues like honesty are sometimes outside of the classroom, in team-based activities like athletics, the arts, activities, at church and within the community.

You get good at something through practice. You become what you practice. Formation properly shapes not just the intellect, but the will, the body and the spirit—through practice.

In formation, team-based activities are just as important as what happens in the classroom. To learn about themselves, become accountable and develop the leadership components, all young people should participate in team-based activities where they must learn to achieve some task as part of a team performing under pressure.

It doesn't matter what the team-based activity is—dance, music, theater, athletics, speech and debate, robotics competitions—so long as the student learns to perform under pressure and be accountable to others on the team.

These team-based activities will not only optimize a student's musical skills, for example, but give him a real-world opportunity to practice the virtues, teamwork, bearing and leadership. The team-based experience provides the student with a vital opportunity to become good, develop wisdom and pursue fulfillment.

The formation program must make the young person dig deep into herself to think about life, her gifts and how she will write the story of her life. This means going way beyond the standardized career aptitude test that measures how a young person is like those in certain professions, to helping a young person understand how she is unique, one-of-a-kind, unlike any other who has ever been or ever will be.

The formation program must help each student uncover and develop her gifts into work and a vocation about which she can be passionate, and in which she finds meaning and fulfillment. It helps her put her gifts and challenges, her personality, character and relationships into the context of her life so that she can write the best story of her life. Not only will this process help her become fulfilled in life, but also inspire her to her maximum performance and contribution to our community.

Many of our best teachers, coaches and administrators have been doing their own version of formation for decades. These are those special teachers and coaches who have always taken a real interest in their students as *persons*.

The teachers and coaches that care less about your grades or your performance on the field than they did about you becoming a good person.

The teachers and coaches we remember the most are often the ones that shaped us the most.

It is time that we take what they did as individuals and make it part of a system so that their gifts can be shared with everyone in a much more powerful way.

How do we transform our schools from education to formation?

So how do we transform these noble sounding ideas into real application in our schools?

We start by making it clear that our schools are shifting from a modern education system focused on knowledge to a wisdom formation system focused on knowledge, character and wisdom. We must make it clear that this change is being made so that parents, schools and communities can work together to form the next generation of leaders we can trust with our future. The change is being made so that our children and nation have the brightest possible future possible. We are making the change so our children can pursue goodness, fulfillment and Happiness.

In modern education, the English teacher is there to teach English. The history teacher is there to teach history. A coach is there to win ball games.

In wisdom formation, an English teacher helps a student become good through English. A history teacher helps the student become good through understanding history and developing skills associated with the subject. A coach, choir director, music director or theater director helps a student become good by practicing the virtues, leadership and teamwork through participation on a team. The subject matter is important, but the primary focus is on forming a good person. The subject how the teacher forms the student.

Embracing formation means that administrators and teachers must abandon the idea that their primary task is to fill student's heads with information and improve test scores.

It means embracing the idea that their primary task is to form a good person using their area of expertise: teaching a subject, coaching a sport, leading an activity, directing in the arts.

Moving from education to formation will be a big challenge. We have spent hundreds of billions of dollars devising an enormous structure to support this modern idea of education for knowledge. We have millions of teachers and administrators that have invested themselves in this educational structure, and are very familiar with and comfortable in it. Moving from education to formation will demand an enormous culture change in our schools. It will demand a culture change in our parents, school boards and educational bureaucracy.

Given the right emphasis and process, that change will happen. I have met too many teachers and coaches who, deep down inside, want to form kids, to change lives, but are handcuffed by requirements to drive test scores.

With a formation program, teachers will feel more fulfilled as they can help students become good, not just smart. Because formation focuses on the students as unique individuals with unique talents, not just as academicians, we are more likely to keep students engaged in school and lower dropout rates. Formation also aligns our school system with the actual needs of our nation: developing the next generation of leaders we can trust, and improving our people and high-performance teams. Formation will develop more successful young people.

The biggest reason, by far, that we will move from education to formation is that parents, businesses and other communities in our society will demand it.

They will demand young people they can trust to hire into their businesses.

They will demand young people they can trust as lawyers, accountants, doctors and politicians.

They will demand young people they can trust to lead their teams, their communities and their nation to greater success at every level.

They will demand formation because it produces higher trust, better prepared and higher performance leaders.

They will demand wisdom formation because it outperforms modern education in every phase.

PURPOSE THAT INTEGRATES LIFE

When a student understands that his purpose in life is to become good and achieve fulfillment, and that everything in life is directed to that goal, he has a framework within which he can understand why all other things in his life are relevant and important.

Academics becomes more important and relevant because it provides knowledge and critical thinking skills, and becomes a way to develop important virtues like perseverance, determination, and attention to detail.

Physical fitness becomes more important and relevant because he understands that mental, physical and other types of performance in life are impacted by his physical fitness.

Character development becomes more relevant and important because it is necessary to develop wisdom, and to pursue fulfillment and Happiness.

Practicing respect for the dignity and worth of all people helps us become compassionate and good. These same patterns apply to all other areas of a student's life.

When students understand purpose in life, they come to understand that life in general and their individual lives have real meaning, importance and value. It makes their self-worth real and tangible. It helps them understand that the story that is their life is unique and wonderful.

As their understanding of life and themselves deepens, their confidence, motivation and performance will deepen and improve as well. Wisdom formation outperforms modern education because it provides young people with meaning and purpose that unify and make sense of their lives.

MORAL – ETHICAL - CHARACTER DEVELOPMENT

As we saw earlier, the moral fragmentation of our society that results from the Modern and Postmodern Paradigms has made public schools incapable of addressing the crucial need to develop character and right action in our youth.

Embracing the Wisdom Paradigm and formation can bring our parents, community and schools together to develop young people with the good character required for the high-trust, high-performance people and teams we need for our future. It provides young people with common, clear and compelling reasons why they should strive to develop and habituate the virtues. It will dramatically enhance the moral development of our young people because they will be hearing a consistent, reinforcing message everywhere they go and from all they encounter.

This wisdom approach is consistent with the basic approach to morality of the world's great religions, so it gives us a shared, public foundation for understanding and discussing basic morality across religions and communities. That shared wisdom moral foundation can unite our nation and repair the deep damage done to our society by postmodern moral fragmentation.

Character development will result in fewer disciplinary problems at home, higher trust relationships at school, home and in our community, and higher performance people and teams. As young people develop, practice and habituate the virtues, the virtues they internalize will improve their personal performance.

As character development leads to higher trust relationships, team performance will improve.

Most important, character development will put young people in the best position for fulfillment and Happiness in life.

By providing a shared moral foundation for our society and improving character development, wisdom formation dramatically outperforms modern education in the development of future leaders and high-performance teams.

SENSE OF COMMUNITY

By embracing the Wisdom Paradigm, we—as local community and larger society—can embrace a common, society-shared approach to American life that crosses religious, political and regional boundaries.

For the most part, the Wisdom Paradigm is not replacing age-old understandings of the *American way of life*, but putting the *American way of life* on a solid foundation so it can be consistent, fully understood and shared by all. By sharing a common understanding of life and what it means to be an American, we can greatly reduce the polarization and fragmentation that has occurred in our nation over the last few decades. We give ourselves the shared understanding we need to come together as a community and nation, and achieve great things.

Wisdom formation outperforms modern education because formation provides the shared understanding of life we need to unite as community and nation.

HIGH PERFORMANCE TEAMWORK.

Embracing the Wisdom Paradigm means teaching our children about high-trust, high-performance covenant relationships where the good of the individual and the good of the team are the same. This accomplishes some very good things:

- It moves our schools from an overwhelming focus on individual academic performance to much more team-based and project-based learning, which is how the real-world functions after graduation.
- When students spend much of their time as part of a covenant team, they learn that they are not only responsible to themselves, but to others as well. To avoid failing their teammates, they must maximize development of their skills, character, teamwork and leadership.
- Finally, as part of a covenant team, they will learn in a very tangible way that the more they put into the team, the more they will develop their skills, character, teamwork and leadership. It is a life-lesson that will give them great benefit as they move into the future.

The more our young people experience and learn from high-performance teamwork in school, the better they will perform in work and life. Wisdom formation outperforms modern education because it better teaches teamwork, accountability, character and leadership, and gives young people direct experience with high performance covenant teams.

LEADERSHIP.

Daily life is full of leadership relationships. If our children, communities and our nation are going to be successful, our children must become trustworthy leaders.

Moving to wisdom formation in our schools will emphasize skill, character, teamwork and leadership development in each of our children. It will move away from dozens of individual students sitting in classrooms passively receiving lecture information to a much more dynamic environment of team and project-based experiences in a much wider variety of environments including activities, the arts, family, sports, church and work in the community. School will go beyond preparing kids for standardized testing to better preparing them to lead others in life.

When all is said and done, our school system will move away from modern education to wisdom formation because formation will be much more successful developing the next generation of leaders our nation so deeply needs.

Formation will be embraced because it outperforms education.

Wisdom formation aligns all aspects of a student's life to shape a generation of students with better academic performance, better character, and higher performance leadership and teamwork.

They will have a much better sense of who they are as individuals, as a community and as a nation.

They will have a much better sense of life, and its meaning and purpose.

They will work together much more efficiently and effectively because they will be working from a shared understanding of life and what it means to be an American.

They will be in the best position possible to guide our generation and our nation through the many challenges that we will all face in our future.

Formation in practice: Servite High School

Formation and leadership development are not just theoretical concepts, but are being developed, applied and tested at Servite High School in Southern California.

Servite High School is an all-male, Catholic, college-preparatory school with 850 to 900 students in Anaheim, California. The student body is diverse ethnically, socially and economically. Some students live in high income housing while others have been effectively homeless. About 40% of students receive financial aid and the school is more than 50% minority.

Servite is known for its rigorous academics, its competition in one of the top athletic conferences in the nation, robotics, and its arts programs—especially classical guitar and theater.

At Servite, the goal is producing the next generation of leaders. Formation is the process by which we produce leaders. While informal formation had been taking place at Servite since its opening in 1958, in 2005 Servite introduced a formal program for formation and leadership development.

The program began with formation of the faculty and staff so that they understood their new role was not just to present curriculum in the classroom or coach on the field, but to form students into leaders using their curriculum, coaching and any other means at their disposal.

To provide unity across the Servite experience, Servite published the four *Formation Themes*. Faculty, staff and coaches are expected to frame their teaching and coaching using the formation themes so that students come to understand how experiences on the athletic field or stage are directly related to what is taught in the classroom, or experienced in church liturgy and community service.

Students are evaluated not just on their academics, but also in terms of their leadership-teamwork development and character-spiritual development. There are progressive objectives associated with each of these three evaluations axis and students who fall behind in any of them receive help from their class formation team.

At the same time, Servite started *Freshman Formation Weekend* which is an intense, three-day formation, leadership and teamwork exercise for all incoming freshmen. The purpose of Freshmen Formation Weekend is to provide students a foundation for their four year Servite experience by grounding them in who they are, what Servite is about and what it means to live *The Servite Way*. We begin the weekend by getting incoming freshmen to start understanding the world in terms of the Wisdom Paradigm and to begin eliminating influences of the Postmodern Paradigm. All aspects of the three-day exercise are run by student leadership under the close supervision of faculty and staff.

Usually held the last weekend of July before freshmen year, all freshmen are divided into 16 small communities called *priories* of about 15 students each. They are divided so that academic, athletic and artistic talent are evenly spread across the priories, and so they don't know many in their priory.

The students and priories are then challenged, as teams, in a variety of artistic, academic and athletic competitions that compel the students to become part of a team, recognize that they are unique and have something special to contribute, and to fight through pressure. There are instructional times where students listen to a presentation then discuss it, reflect on it and journal about it. Later, the students will go through a physical experience of the issue designed to make them practice working as a team, develop virtues and overcome fear.

For example, students will listen to a talk on faith, and then will discuss, reflect on and journal about faith in their lives. Later, students will undergo a rappelling exercise in which they must demonstrate and practice faith in themselves and others. Later in life, when they are confronted by a serious situation that demands faith, they can refer back to the faith they practiced in the rappelling exercise to help them through that situation.

Over the next four years, Servite teachers, coaches, families and alumni try to provide students with a consistent, integrated and seamless formation experience that will enable Servite young men to become wise and good. Parents go through formation programs themselves so that the message to our young men—whether at home, at school, or visiting others—is consistent, synergistic and reinforcing.

Each class year, freshman through senior, has a designated *formation director* who leads a *formation team* of the grade-level teachers and coaches. They are responsible for tracking each student in that class in terms of academics, leadership-teamwork and character-spiritual development. Each class formation team also has an assistant principal, counselor, campus minister and clergy assigned. If a problem develops or a student falls behind in any area (i.e. academics, leadership, character development, etc.) the formation director gathers the formation team and works with the parents to help get the student where he needs to be.

Servite offers multiple real-world leadership opportunities to students. The Servite ASB student government program was closed and transitioned to the *Servite Priory Leadership Council*. The school is divided into eight *priories* (communities) of about 110 students each, and further sub-divided into 40+ *homerooms* (six per priory) of about 20 students each.

Each priory is led by a student *prior*. Each homeroom is made up of freshmen through seniors, and is led by an *assistant prior*. The entire priory system is led by a student Prior General with a staff of three other students.

The school is largely run by the students through the priory system. Each week, the student leadership must create, plan and execute two 45-minute leadership labs. Student leaders evaluate the leadership and teamwork of subordinates, and all students receive a quarter and semester leadership grade. Student leaders are expected to know their men, and help them in formation, leadership, academics and socialization.

Trinity Corporation is a second major student leadership opportunity with a student CEO, three student vice presidents, 10-12 student managers, and 300+ employee interns. Trinity Corp earns about $1,000,000 in revenues each year as the students directly run Servite retail sales, online sales, cafeteria, catering, snack bar and other revenue areas. Trinity Corporation net revenues support the Servite financial aid program.

The third major leadership opportunity, *Her Servants Kitchen*, supports the homeless and poor in Anaheim and north Orange County. Students beg for food for the homeless and each Thursday, whether school is in session or not, prepare and serve 80-100 meals to the homeless of north Orange County. Students in *Her Servants Kitchen* also support several families who have undergone physical or spousal abuse, and have become leaders in the effort to help the homeless and poor of Orange County by engaging local cities, private donations and community support.

At Servite High School, *everything* is focused on forming the next generation of leaders. We strive to form young men who can lead good lives, lead a good family, lead in their profession and lead people to Christ by their example.

Leadership is the goal. Formation is the process.

Servite has rigorous academics to form leaders. Athletics to form leaders. Activities and the arts to form leaders. Church, community service and spiritual retreats to form leaders.

Teachers and coaches fully align their classes, activities and sports with the formation program. Coaches must allow student-athletes to participate in multiple sports or activities if they wish to do so. Coaches, not the student, are responsible for working with other coaches and faculty to set the student's schedule so there isn't pressure put on the student to be loyal to one sport or activity over another.

That is because activities and athletics are practiced at Servite to provide the best formation opportunity for the student, not for the coach to win ball games. Everything is focused on helping young men become good and wise, and forming them to be the next generation of leaders for our community and nation.

The results?

Students have become much more responsible. Positive discipline is high and disciplinary problems have been greatly reduced. In the 2016-2017 academic year, Servite had two student disciplinary boards. Academic, artistic and athletic performance has improved. Students have moved from an "us against them" mentality with faculty and administration to much more of a mentoring and coaching relationship.

Servite students are sought by colleges, businesses and other organizations for admissions, internships and jobs because of their demonstrated character and leadership abilities. Servite has won the California Interscholastic Federation (CIF) award for good sportsmanship in athletic events, and Servite coaches and athletes have won numerous local, state and even national awards for their leadership, character and performance.

Most important, after graduation, Servite men take care of each other. Servite men are the best men at each other's weddings and the godparents of each other's children. When Servite students or alumni are injured or become ill, their brothers rally around to support and ensure that they and their families are well-taken care of.

When they pass away, Servite brothers bear each other's coffins. Servite men have become founders and leaders of well-known businesses and non-profits, leaders in the Church, medicine, law and the arts, and leaders of families.

A lot more than education for knowledge. Formation for goodness, wisdom and leadership.

Transforming our universities

Our colleges and universities have an enormous impact on our society through the students they graduate, the research and studies they conduct, and the intellectual authority they carry within our society. Our colleges and universities play a critical role in developing the next generation of leaders that we need.

Our colleges and universities can play a very positive role if they help the next generation pursue Truth, wisdom and goodness.

They can challenge the next generation to understand more deeply what they know about life and why.

They can challenge the next generation to push themselves academically, socially and spiritually.

They can challenge the next generation to best understand their role in our community, society and world.

They can challenge our next generation to become the wise and great leaders we need to wield the tremendous power we possess and to navigate the tough challenges our world will face.

Our colleges and universities can play a very positive role so long as they do all of this in the pursuit of Truth, wisdom and goodness.

Unfortunately, our colleges and universities are one of the deepest bastions of postmodern thinking and teaching in our society.

Rather than helping students pursue Truth, wisdom and goodness, many professors seek research knowledge for its own sake or seek to undermine the poorly framed understandings of life of incoming college students. Many of these professors have integrated postmodern thinking so deeply into their life's work that their life and postmodernism cannot be separated.

They believe that they are doing college students a service by freeing students from the *wisdom construct* imposed upon them by their parents, churches and society. They free students from the chains of *wisdom constructs* by cynically undermining concepts like Truth, wisdom, goodness, and morality, and offering in their stead ideas like subjectivism and values.

Because these professors have tenure, they cannot be easily removed. From their safe and untouchable positions, they often find great pleasure taking a stand against society not to help society find Truth or become good, but for their own sake.

Our challenge is to form a generation of good leaders in college despite these professors. It will be very difficult to get any of these postmodern academicians to embrace the Wisdom Paradigm because they are so heavily invested in the postmodern in their work and careers. As tenured teachers, they are largely invulnerable to direct pressure to reform.

Our best course is to heavily encourage our college-aged children to attend universities and colleges that fully embrace the Wisdom Paradigm. These are the universities and colleges that emphasize core curriculum that teaches students the timeless concepts that bring us together as humanity and a nation. These are the universities and colleges that use that foundation of shared, timeless concepts to help our students best understand who they are, and what life, wisdom and leadership are all about.

We should insist that our government and businesses provide grant funding only to those researchers and institutions that are fully committed to the pursuit of Truth, wisdom and goodness.

Remember, *academic freedom* in the Wisdom Paradigm is valuable because it gives us freedom to pursue Truth.

But for those who advocate the Postmodern Paradigm, *academic freedom* means something very different. It is a rhetorical device that enables the postmodern professor to do whatever he wants for whatever reasons he wants while eliminating accountability to anyone. As we actively embrace formation over time, hopefully those professors committed to the Postmodern Paradigm will lose relevance, retire or move on.

Forming the next generation of leaders

By having our families and schools integrate intellectual, character and leadership development in a coordinated and focused experience of life, we can develop a generation of leaders that not only possess outstanding professional and technical skills, but has the wisdom and character that we can trust to make good decisions for our future.

This new generation will be able to create and lead high-performance people and teams that will maximize our economy and help us prevail in global competition.

With wisdom formation, we improve performance through efficiency because we align all aspects of our child's experience to form them into the best person possible.

We improve performance because we draw out and maximize the talents of our children, and teach them how to perform together as part of a high-performance team pursuing a goal.

We substantially reduce our future risk of leadership failure— whether its national or local, political, business, educational, professional or public service—because we'll know how our leaders were formed, how they think, and we'll have an objective means for evaluating their leadership performance. We can adjust the formation program to maximize the potential and meet the needs of each student.

Finally, the formation program helps *all* young people, not just those who are academically inclined. It prepares all young people for life, not just for more intense academic studies.

Formation makes our community and nation better because it calls forth and develops the deepest passions, greatest talents and a sense of calling from our young people—increasing performance and raising results—rather than try to force them into an academic box whether it is a good place for them or not.

Most important, formation prepares our young people to become good leaders because we are all called to be leaders as citizens with the vote, workers, family, and members of a variety of communities.

When we embrace the Wisdom Paradigm, we move from a modern education system that limits itself to the intellect, knowledge and academics, and introduce a formation program that shapes a generation of leaders who are not just smart and knowledgeable, but also possess character and wisdom.

TEACH AND IMPLEMENT COVENANT LEADERSHIP

It may sound obvious, but as we embrace the Wisdom Paradigm, we must actively teach Covenant Leadership to those throughout society.

When we teach Covenant Leadership to the young, we introduce them to a powerful way to understand who they are, how they relate to others, and how their actions impact their relationships with others. We teach them how to achieve the right goals the right ways for the right reasons. And we teach them how to do it with maximum effectiveness and efficiency.

As part of a family, class or athletic team, they can begin to understand that when they do good things it helps them become good, provides an example for others to become good, and helps build respect between them and others.

They learn that teamwork, leadership and trust depend on the actions and habit patterns they practice.

Most important, they can learn that the primary reason we have family, class and sports teams is to help us practice the things that make us good.

As children get older, they can be taught and they can experience the connections between the four Leadership Components—*skills*, *character*, *bearing* and *vision*.

As they come to a much deeper understanding of the Leadership Components through their real-world relationships, they will realize that they can become better leaders, better teammates and better people by using that knowledge to develop their skills, character, bearing and vision. When they fully understand that the purpose of all team based activities—especially sports—is to become good, then the question of why cheating is wrong will solve itself.

Perhaps most important, they can learn the relationship between activity, mission and purpose, and use trust and commitment to build their own high-performance teams.

Young leaders in high school, college and business will have a foundation for fully understanding and investigating leadership. They will have a model in which they can study both contemporary and historical leadership.

Given Covenant Leadership, what did historical leaders do that was successful or unsuccessful and why?

Looking at more contemporary leaders, from what understandings of life—from what paradigms—were people like Stalin, Gandhi, Mao-Tse-Tung, Reagan, Martin Luther King or Saddam Hussein leading?

I know many successful leaders today who are already practicing aspects of Covenant Leadership though they may not be conscious of it.

In these cases, the Covenant Leadership model does not teach them something new so much as it gives them a more powerful way to understand and apply what they already know and do well. They can use Covenant Leadership to fine tune and maximize the power of their leadership techniques, and to systematically teach the next generation to become good leaders themselves.

The more we integrate Covenant Leadership into how we teach, understand and practice leadership, the more we all get on the same sheet of music, the more we will increase the performance of our people and teams, the better we will become as people and communities, and the stronger our communities and nation will become. Teaching Covenant Leadership and experiencing the success it brings will help our communities and society understand why fully embracing the Wisdom Paradigm is right and good.

Teaching Covenant Leadership is not about forcing an unwanted leadership approach on the leaders in our society, but about turbocharging our economy and nation by giving our leaders an understanding that will dramatically increase their professional and team performance.

The proof is in the performance. Those who do not want to embrace Covenant Leadership will find their competitors using Covenant Leadership to beat them in the marketplace, on the sports field and in life. Repeatedly losing is a strong motivation to embrace something new and more powerful.

FOCUS OUR CULTURAL POWER TO ALIGN ALL AREAS OF OUR SOCIETY

Finally, to create the generation of good leaders that we so deeply need, we must ensure that the Wisdom Paradigm permeates all aspects of our society, culture and nation. We must embrace the ideas and practices that help us become a healthy, free and good community and nation, and reject and eliminate those things that degrade and harm us. The more that each area of our society and culture embodies, restates and reinforces the Wisdom Paradigm, the more quickly, effectively and surely we will improve our culture, economy and nation.

Media, entertainment and the arts

Media, entertainment and the arts have an enormous impact on our society, shaping our understanding of life in powerful ways through news, stories, art and shows.

Whether broadcast, online or print, the way that news media choose stories, frame issues, ask questions, select information and present stories has a big influence on our community and nation. It impacts how we understand history, problems and conflicts within our communities and between nations, and the ongoing trends in our society.

The entertainment and art sectors give us diversion and fun, and the opportunity for self-reflection. We are a hard-working people who need the opportunity to rest and relax.

We need a creative entertainment industry that brings us together—in community—to laugh, to sing, to share and even cry. Entertainment is powerful because it provides the community with shared stories, a shared mythology and shared experiences.

Entertainment is a gift that unites us and provides that sense of awe as we watch others do amazing things. Just as important, entertainment gives us diversion, rest and rejuvenation so that we can continue the hard work of life.

Whether literary like novels or poetry, or visual like paintings or photography, or performance-based like theater, symphony and dance, the arts provide us with very powerful and multi-dimensional ways to celebrate, reflect upon and more deeply understand Beauty, Truth, reality and life.

Media, entertainment and the arts are extremely important influences in our society.

Unfortunately, many in media, entertainment and the arts believe that these areas exist for their own sake, or exist to make money.

Many believe that media, entertainment and the arts should operate independent of the good of our communities, society and nation.

Some claim to "serve" society by exposing us to provocative things to cause us to think and reflect, when they are really attempting make money by appealing to the base and prurient aspects of human nature.

Some use "art" as a license to violate societal norms and demonstrate, postmodern style, that they are not bound by society, but free to define themselves as they desire.

Some examine difficult and legitimate issues with audiences— perhaps children—who are not prepared to handle them.

Others simply use media, entertainment and the arts to attack a wisdom way of life that they believe is narrow, ignorant and contrived. They hope to advance a postmodern way of life that they believe is progressive and liberating.

Media, entertainment and the arts must come to realize that they do not exist for their own sake, or to maximize profits, or to provide a means for some postmodern temper tantrum against the Wisdom Paradigm. Instead, they are called to fulfill a very important and powerful role to help us as individuals, community and nation become good.

This does not mean that every story or production must be as innocent as the *Brady Bunch*.

The media, entertainment and the arts should challenge us if the challenge is intended to help us become good.

They may provoke us so long as the provocation isn't for its own sake or to undermine what is good, but to provoke us towards what is good.

They may certainly make a profit so long as profit-making is the mission and not the purpose of the endeavor.

They should examine difficult issues in human life so long as the intent is to help us become good and not appeal to the obscene.

Older and more sophisticated people need to be challenged by our media, entertainment and the arts to think more deeply about life, relationships and rules. The media, entertainment and the arts should force us to contemplate what we understand about life and why. There is tremendous value in using media, entertainment and the arts to make us feel uncomfortable and to challenge our current understanding of truth, so that they more deeply reflect on and make progress toward what is True and good.

There are several ways that we can encourage the media, entertainment and the arts to help our people, communities and society become good.

First, we need to understand that *artistic license, artistic freedom* and *freedom of speech* are not justified in themselves, but are justified when they are used to help the artist, people and society become good. Freedom of speech only makes sense if it is a means for people, communities and society to bring up ideas in the pursuit of what is good. We don't justify freedom of speech to help us become bad or evil. We must have the freedom to put most everything on the table for well-intentioned and honest consideration, but we must also be vigilant against those who would abuse free speech to advocate the postmodern.

Communities should have the right to determine community standards, to determine what kinds of artistic expression help the community become good, and what kinds of artistic expression lead the community away from goodness.

From the Wisdom Paradigm's sense of tolerance, a good, healthy and mature community might give artists wider discretion to pursue Truth, Beauty and goodness as they best understand it.

But that tolerance is not free license to pursue or express whatever an artist wants simply because it is an expression. Free expression is properly understood in terms of and guided by a drive for Truth, Beauty, goodness and wisdom. A community should have the right to protect itself from those who intentionally lead people and the community away from what is good and healthy.

Finally, the most powerful way to encourage the media, entertainment and the arts to embrace the Wisdom Paradigm is to watch, support and purchase media, entertainment and art pieces from those who pursue Truth, Beauty and goodness. Ignore those who lead people in other directions. Poor media, entertainment and art can only exist if people in the community buy it. Let's stop pretending that pornography is "art" and harmless. Let's stop pretending that "art" designed to do little more than shock or arouse the viewer has any redeeming value.

Let's use the power of our purchase to make a better community, society and nation by encouraging our media, entertainment and arts to embrace the Wisdom Paradigm and help form the next generation of leaders that we so deeply need in our nation and world.

PART V
WHAT STORY WILL YOU WRITE?

It can be very easy to feel swept up and powerless in the midst of all the dynamics of our society, the world and life.

It is easy and tempting to feel like there is little that we can do even when it comes to things close to home like our work, our families and our community.

We face big issues in our world from climate change to a failing economy, overwhelming government debt, nuclear proliferation, terrorism, and generation of kids who don't listen because they don't think we have anything worth listening to.

We have people who think that business, science and technology exist for their own sake and that humanity is just along for the ride.

We have a rising generation who believe that there are no moral facts, and that the words *right* and *wrong* are the moral equivalent of *I like this* and *I don't like that*.

We have lost our ability to make a compelling argument why there is objective Truth, Beauty, morality and honor.

We have constructed an idea of life where we spend most of our lives working at a job that we don't find fulfilling so that, hopefully, we can retire old and spend a few years pursuing what we find fulfilling.

We took all that gave us direction, purpose and meaning in life, and tossed it aside. We took the map to fulfillment and Happiness and put it up in the attic to gather dust. Then we promptly forgot where we are and where we are supposed to go, and began wondering why life seems overwhelming, meaningless and increasingly dark.

But there is hope. You are the hope. It begins with you.

It begins with us. We are the leaders.

We must remember that of all the things we can do to make our lives, our futures, and our nation better, developing good leaders must be at the top of the list, *for all other things that we can do to make our world better depend first on good leadership.* We must form the next generation of leaders that we can all trust to use our power wisely and navigate the tough issues we face.

We must possess the knowledge, character and wisdom to be worthy of their trust so they will listen to us. We must be good leaders if we hope to form them into even better leaders.

The next generation of leaders must possess more than just knowledge. They must possess *wisdom—right knowledge + right action.* They must possess skills, character, teamwork, bearing and vision.

We must teach them that their purpose in life is to become good, wise, happy and fulfilled. They must understand that their life is best understood and lived as a unified whole—public, private, family, work, community—all bound into one seamless pursuit of the good, Truth, Beauty, wisdom, fulfillment and Happiness. They must understand that to achieve Happiness, they must fully embrace the Wisdom Paradigm.

We must teach them to become good by practicing, habituating and making the virtues a seamless part of their own character. It must be obvious to them that the best way to practice the virtues is by making a commitment to a covenant team focused on a good activity, mission and purpose.

We must teach them that Covenant Leadership is a way of understanding life, relationships and goals that will both move them most quickly towards goodness and fulfillment, and give them the highest performance people and teams.

They must understand that our best chance to prevail in global competition is to embrace the innovation, creativity, teamwork and high-performance levels that only come with Covenant Leadership and the Wisdom Paradigm.

They must learn about the Wisdom, Modern and Postmodern Paradigms so that they can fully embrace the Wisdom Paradigm and eliminate the postmodern.

To form the next generation of leaders is to transform the world. It is a huge task for us. It is a life-task.

Many of us have grown up familiar with compelling epic adventure hero stories like *Lord of the Rings, Star Wars* and *The Chronicles of Narnia.*

The stories usually begin with a reluctant, unassuming person who encounters evil but is unwilling to leave the comfort of his present situation to do anything about it. Inevitably, despite his reluctance, the person finds himself on a quest for something important and transcendent; something that changes everything. He must become part of a team. He must break through his limitations. He must dig deep inside himself to find strength, courage, faith and endurance that he didn't know that he possessed.

The odds are stacked heavily against success, but he marches on because that is what Honor, Friendship, Duty and Love call him to do as he pursues what is right and good. He is transformed by the experience from a person into a hero.

As we read or watch, sometimes we imagine ourselves the hero and wonder how we would do on the quest.

Would we show courage when required or flee in fear?

Would we remain loyal to our team or abandon them?

Could we resist our deepest temptation?

Would we find the strength to take one more step towards the goal even when the chance of success appears impossible?

Would we risk our lives for what is just, good and True?

The culture war we face is a conflict far more real, important and decisive as any of those in *Lord of the Rings, Star Wars* or the *Chronicles of Narnia.*

You, like the reluctant hero, are every bit as involved in the conflict whether you like it or not.

So how will you write your hero story?

When your children tell your story to your descendants, what will they say?

WORKS CITED

Alexander, Delroy, Greg Burns, Robert Manor, Flynn McRoberts, and EA Torriero. "Repeat Offender Gets Swift Justice." *Chicago Tribune*. September 4, 2002. http://www.chicagotribune.com/news/chi-0209040368sep04,0,3317970,full.story (accessed September 23, 2011).

Altman, Roger C. "The Great Crash 2008." *Foreign Affairs*, 2009.

—. "Ex-Congressman Begins Prison Sentence." *MSNBC.com*. March 4, 2006. http://www.msnbc.msn.com/id/11655893/ns/us_news-crime_and_courts/t/ex-congressman-begins-prison-sentence/ (accessed September 23, 2011).

Bajaj, Vikas. "Household Wealth Falls By Trillions." *New York Times*. March 12, 2009. http://www.nytimes.com/2009/03/13/business/economy/13wealth.html (accessed April 24, 2011).

Brooks, David. "If It Feels Right." *NY Times Opinion Pages*. September 12, 2011. http://www.nytimes.com/2011/09/13/opinion/if-it-feels-right.html (accessed September 23, 2011).

CNN Wire Staff. "Retracted Autism Study an Elaborate Fraud British Journal Finds." *CNN.com*. January 5, 2011. http://www.cnn.com/2011/HEALTH/01/05/autism.vaccines/index.html (accessed April 24, 2011).

—. "Merrill Lynch's $50 Billion Feud." *CNN Money*. April 15, 2010. http://money.cnn.com/2010/04/15/news/companies/merrill_lynch.fortune/ (accessed September 23, 2011).

Confucius. "Analects, Confucius." *eBooks@Adelaide (University of Adelaide)*. 2011. http://ebooks.adelaide.edu.au/c/confucius/c748a/book2.html (accessed April 12, 2011).

Continental Congress. "Declaration of Independence." *USHistory.org*. July 4, 1776. http://www.ushistory.org/declaration/document/ (accessed October 4, 2011).

Enron. *Enron Annual Report*. Houston: Enron, 2000.

Gallup Poll. "Honesty/Ethics in Professions." *Gallup*. November 19-21, 2010. http://www.gallup.com/poll/1654/Honesty-Ethics-Professions.aspx (accessed April 24, 2011).

Hobbes, Thomas. *Leviathan*. London, 1651.

Holmes, Steven. "Fannie Mae Eases Credit to Aid Mortgage Lending." *New York Times*. September 30, 1999. http://www.nytimes.com/1999/09/30/business/fannie-mae-eases-credit-to-aid-mortgage-lending.html (accessed September 23, 2011).

Houghton Mifflin. "Dictionary.com." *Yahoo Education--American Heritage Dictionary of the English Langauge, 4th Edition*. 2000. http://education.yahoo.com/reference/dictionary/entry/paradigm (accessed October 2, 2011).

Isidore, Chris. "7.9 Million Jobs Lost--Many Forever." *CNN Money.com*. July 2, 2010. http://money.cnn.com/2010/07/02/news/economy/jobs_gone_forever/index.htm (accessed April 24, 2011).

Kedia, Simi and Philippon, Thomas. "Enron's Final Accounting." *Stern Business (NYU)*. Spring 2006. http://w4.stern.nyu.edu/sternbusiness/spring_2006/enron.html (accessed April 25, 2011).

Kuhn, Thomas. *The Structure of Scientific Revolutions*. Chicago, IL: The University of Chicago Press, 1996.

Locke, John. *Two Treatises of Government*. London, 1689.

MacIntyre, Alasdair. *After Virtue 3rd Ed*. Notre Dame, IN: University of Notre Dame Press, 1981.

MacIntyre, Alasdair. *Three Rival Versions of Moral Enquiry*. Notre Dame, IN: University of Notre Dame Press, 1991

MacIntyre, Alasdair. *Whose Justice? Which Rationality?* Notre Dame, IN: University of Notre Dame Press, 1989

Martin, Daniel. "150 Human Animal Hybrids Grown in UK Labs: Embryos Have Been Produced Secretively For Past Three Years." *Daily Mail (UK)*. July 25, 2011. http://www.dailymail.co.uk/sciencetech/article-2017818/Embryos-involving-genes-animals-mixed-humans-produced-secretively-past-years.html (accessed October 7, 2011).

McRowe, Arthur Watkins. "Stereochemistry of the Vicinal Hydride Shift." *Worldcat.org*. 1966. http://www.worldcat.org/title/stereochemistry-of-the-vicinal-hydride-shift/oclc/47973035 (accessed Oct 3, 2011).

National Council of State Legislatures. *Teen Suicide Prevention-State Health Lawmaker's Digest*. 2011. http://www.ncsl.org/default.aspx?tabid=14111 (accessed April 24, 2011).

Newport, Frank. "Conservative Democrats, Liberal Republicans Hard to Find." *Gallup*. September 9, 2009. http://www.gallup.com/poll/122672/Conservative-Democrats-Liberal-Republicans-Hard-to-Find.aspx (accessed April 24, 2011).

Online Etymology Dictionary. *Dictionary.com. Doublas Harper, Historian.* http://dictionary.reference.com/browse/incommensurable (accessed October 2, 2011).

Pink, Dan. "RSA Animate--Drive: The Surprising Truth About What Motivates Us." *Youtube.com*. April 1, 2010. http://www.youtube.com/watch?v=u6XAPnuFjJc (accessed May 1, 2011).

Random House . *Random House Dictionary*. 2010.

Rost, Joseph. *Leadership for the 21st Century*. Santa Barbara: Praeger Paperback, 1993.

Rousseau, Jean-Jacques. *The Social Contract*. Paris, 1762.

Saad, Lydia. "American's Confidence in Military Up, Banks Down." *Gallup*. June 24, 2009. http://www.gallup.com/poll/121214/Americans-Confidence-Military-Banks-Down.aspx (accessed April 24, 2011).

Smith, Christian, Kari Christoffersen, Hilary Davidson, and Patricia Herzog. *Lost in Transition: The Dark Side of Emerging Adulthood*. Oxford University Press, USA, 2011.

SPAN-USA. *American Federation for Suicide Prevention*. 2011. http://www.spanusa.org/index.cfm?fuseaction=home.viewPage&page_id=0D213 AD4-C50A-1085-4DD96CE0EEED52A0 (accessed April 24, 2011).

Teen Depression Statistics. 2011. http://www.teenhelp.com/teen-depression/depression-statistics.html (accessed April 24, 2011).

US Forest Service. "Forest Service Comments on Article "Lynx, Lies and Media Hype" Audobon Magazine May 2002." *US Forest Service*. July 2002. http://www.fs.fed.us/r1/wildlife/carnivore/Lynx/PointsResponse.pdf (accessed April 24, 2011).

Williams, Ted. "Lynx, Lies and Media Hype." *Audobon.org*. May/June 2002. http://www.scottchurchdirect.com/ted-williams.aspx/lynx-lies-media-hype (accessed April 24, 2011).

Made in the USA
Middletown, DE
01 June 2020